COOKING KOSHER: The Natural Way

COOKING KOSHER: The Natural Way

by
JANE KINDERLEHRER

jᴅ | **Jonathan David Publishers, Inc.**
Middle Village, NY 11379

Jonathan David Publishers, Inc.
63-22 Eliot Avenue
Middle Village, New York, 11379

Library of Congress Cataloging in Publication Data
Kinderlehrer, Jane.
    Cooking kosher: the natural way.

    Includes index, glossary
    1. Cookery, Jewish.   2. Cookery (Natural foods)
I. Title.
TX724.K56   641.5'676   79-27807
ISBN 0-8246-0240-4

Printed in the United States of America

Dedicated to the memory of my Mom and
Dad, Sophie and Samuel Sapadin, who im-
bued in me a deep love for my heritage and
who were looking over my shoulder as I wrote
this book.

Table of Contents

Foreword

Just because certain foods are kosher does not necessarily mean they are healthy to eat. The laws of kashrut—like those of Shabbat, circumcision and others—cannot always be justified on the grounds that they produce health. Observance of Jewish law, tradition and ethics may indeed lead to good health, but this is not the explicit, primary aim.

Indeed, everyone knows that kosher junk food is ubiquitous in modern Jewish society. Chemical compounds serve to blur the traditional milk-meat distinctions to such an extent that recently a non-Jewish guest at a major kosher Catskill resort ate for three days before she discovered, by accident, that the rich food on the overloaded tables was kosher.

Our modern authorities, physicians, have totally failed to lead us in the direction of good nutrition. Our traditional authorities, rabbis, have likewise failed to protect us from the "better living through chemistry" mentality of the American food industry. Occasional voices are heard in the wilderness, such as those of Toronto Rabbi Gedaliah Felder who, in a recent article (*Torah U'Madah*, 1975) dealing with chemical substances in food, stated that while these may not be *trafe* or unkosher per se, they may yet be dangerous to life and, for this reason, should be prohibited even though present in only tiny amounts. Rabbi Felder concluded that if the rabbis fail to disqualify these dangerous contaminated food substances, they are guilty of misleading the people.

Yet, the Jewish people indeed are being misled. Otherwise, how could Rabbinic sanction be given to infant formulas—grandaddy of all the junk food? How could generations of Jewish babies be deprived of human milk? How could antibiotic-contaminated meat and estrogen-saturated fowl, and poisonous additives and preservatives be allowed to endanger the health and lives of Torah-observant Jews?

The failure of modern Jewish law to cope with the abuses of modern American nutrition has produced attitudes of cynicism and contempt among many young Jews who see as their only alternative turning to other life styles that offer healthy discipline in food preparation, selection and ingestion.

Thus, Jane Kinderlehrer's book appears at a crucial time. While the Bible appropriately sits in the living room, *Cooking Kosher: The Natural Way* belongs in every Jewish kitchen. As a matter of fact, I would recommend *Cooking Kosher: The Natural Way* as a gift for every Bar Mitzvah boy, every Bas Mitzvah girl, and for every Jewish bride and groom. This book may well be an essential ingredient in our eternal quest for Jewish—and biological—survival.

Robert S. Mendelsohn, M.D.

Kosher Is Not Enough

Many of the special dishes from the wonderful world of kosher Jewish cookery have been handed down from mother to daughter for countless generations. In the process, they have picked up some ingredients which, in the light of the new knowledge of nutrition, are definite no-no's. They may be kosher, but they are neither wholesome nor nutritious. In fact, they have been shown to be harmful and have been implicated as contributing to such debilitating conditions as high blood pressure, diabetes, atherosclerosis, obesity, constipation, hyperactivity in children, pyorrhea, hemorrhoids, and other embarrassments one can live very nicely without.

Before going further, let's review what is meant by "kosher food." The word *kosher* literally means "fit or proper to be used." In Leviticus 11, the laws of *kashrut* (the kosher dietary laws) are set forth. Accordingly, those of us who observe the dietary laws are permitted to eat the following foods:

- all fruits and vegetables.
- the meat on all animals that have split hooves *and* that chew the cud—beef, lamb, etc. Thus, pork or pork products are not permissible.
- all seafood that has fins and scales. Thus, foods such as shrimp, lobster, clams, and oysters are not permissible.

- most domesticated fowl, including chicken, duck, goose, pigeon, and squab.

In addition to being limited to only these foods, later (rabbinic) law added further requirements and restrictions. According to these laws, in order for meat to be kosher it has to be slaughtered by a *schochet* (an individual trained to slaughter animals with a razor-sharp knife in keeping with a specified procedure). Kosher meat that has been slaughtered in this manner is readily available today, not only in kosher butcher shops but in major supermarkets as well.

Rabbinic law also states that all meat or fowl must be *koshered* before it may be used. This procedure involves the rinsing and salting of the meat or fowl in order to remove the blood. Most meat sold commercially as kosher has already undergone this procedure, although it is possible to do this yourself at home.

One more important point: kosher law dictates that meat and dairy products not be mixed during cooking and serving. Thus, for example, chicken would not be basted with butter (a dairy product) during cooking, nor would butter be served at the same meal with the prepared chicken, even if the butter were intended to be used as a spread for rolls or bread.

Generally, we refer to meat products as being *fleishig* (sometimes pronounced *fleishik*) or *fleishedig (fleishedik)* and dairy products as *milchig (milchik)* or *milchedig (milchedik)*. There are also foods that are neither fleishig nor milchig—including fruits and vegetables, grains, fish, eggs—and these are said to be *pareve*. Such foods are "neutral" and may be used in the preparation of a meat or dairy dish and may be served with a meat or dairy meal.

Centuries ago, the laws of kashrut protected those who observed them from many foods that proved to be troublemakers. Whether these laws were primarily designed for spiritual well-being and only incidentally proved to be beneficial to physical well-being is immaterial. The fact is that those laws have stood the test of time and, according to Dr. R. Schoental of the University of London, are still protecting us even though we now have advanced technology, refrigeration, and government inspection.

"Recent scientific evidence," says Dr. Schoental, "indicates that some of these [kosher] dietary traditions may have served to prevent health hazards particularly as regards to consumption of meat from 'unclean' animals frequently fed left-over human food, likely to be mouldy.

"It has now been recognized that under appropriate conditions some of the common moulds can produce toxic and/or carcinogenic secondary metabolites, such as the trichothecenes, ochratoxins, sterigmatocystins [implicated in fungal infection of the ear canal], and aflatoxins."*

These are all disease-causing molds which, says Dr. Schoental, may present health hazards not only to those who ingest them directly, but also to those who are exposed to them "by proxy" when consuming meat and other products derived from animals that have ingested toxic fungal metabolites in their feeds. Indeed, there have been instances reported of high concentration of aflatoxins in bacon and lard, and significant amounts have been found in the carcasses of pigs which, after slaughter, have passed inspection.

Other toxic substances only recently recognized as cancer-causing are the nitrosamines which are formed from food constituents and nitrites. "The preparation of kosher meat, which includes salting and soaking," observes Dr. Schoental, "is likely to diminish the risk of nitrosamine formation by removing the water-soluble products of protein autolysis and amines. It makes one wonder how people so many centuries ago could have acquired the insight into problems that only now receive scientific explanation."

So, the practice of eating kosher food has contributed much to the well-being of many people over the centuries. Of course, food is meant to be enjoyed, but its first function is to nourish and sustain the body, mind, and soul.

ADDING NUTRITION TO TRADITION

Chopped liver with grated black radish, moistened with ren-

---

*Reprinted with permission from *Food and Cosmetic Toxicology*, Vol. 14, No. 1, R. Schoental, "Dietary Traditions and Toxic Foods," copyright 1976, Pergamon Press, Ltd.

dered chicken fat and a whisper of chopped onion—pure ecstasy in the mouth. Fluffy knaidlach swimming in chicken soup flecked with gold; hot knishes, crisp and delicious with spicy potato, kasha or cheese fillings; hamantaschen bursting with poppy seeds or prunes; or honey-soaked teiglach or creamy kugels—pure bliss to bite into. Mushroom and barley soup to warm your bones; hearty kasha varnishkas with hot gravy; strudel with heavenly fruit and nut fillings. You don't need a fiddler on the roof to tell you that these foods spell tradition. Their very names evoke blissful memories of small kibitzers crowding around the big black stove, and a lovely warm feeling that Mama's in the kitchen and all's right with the world.

One generation passes, and another takes its place. Now, it's our turn. What kind of memories are we cooking up in our pots and pans? What kind of heavenly aromas say "welcome home" to our loved ones?

Can we, in this age of instant mashed potatoes, TV dinners, frozen blintzes, nondairy creamers, and "foam rubber" bread, provide not only the spirit and spice of Jewish hospitality, but also the nutrients our loved ones need for the lovely glow of health?

Yes, we can!

- We can make kugels that are kind to the arteries.
- We can put a little heart in all our chopped meat dishes.
- We can provide delicious *nosherai* we will be happy to see our families devour because every crumb contributes to health.
- We can make fabulous creamy, pareve desserts without resorting to that bag of chemicals called "nondairy creamer."
- We can avoid dangerous additives—and save money—by making homemade salad dressings, mayonnaise, yogurt, granolas, and convenience mixes.
- We can make delicious honey cakes, mandelbrodt, and strudel without sugar and hydrogenated fats.
- We can avoid the hormones and antibiotics in beef by occasionally serving delicious high-protein vegetarian meals.

By making some modifications in buying and preparing foods,

you will notice a remarkable improvement in both your own disposition and that of your family. If you have hyperactive youngsters, they will probably calm down, do better in school, and get along better with their peers.

Good health is not just the absence of disease. It is feeling truly alive with champagne bubbles in your veins, a song on your lips, shoulders thrown back ready for any challenge. That's what this book can do for you.

Cooking Kosher: The Natural Way can help you, the kosher cook, achieve good health and all that goes with it.

When the dietary laws were given to us, there was no refined sugar, no bleached white flour, no hydrogenated fats, no nondairy creamers—none of the thousands of chemicals of dubious safety which are causing many health problems today.

Although our food supply has changed drastically since the Mount Sinai encounter, the laws of kashrut have not. That's why I say, kosher is not enough.

How can we give our families nutrition and tradition—the taste of love and an enduring link to their culinary roots? How can we, in good conscience, enjoy Grandma's old favorites?

This grandma, after extensive experimentation, has come up with adaptations of the old recipes, eliminated the negative, added the positive, and multiplied our chances of enjoying them in good health. These are the recipes I shall hand down to my kitchen kibitzers and hopefully start a new tradition, while preserving the *tam* of the old Jewish dishes.

These revised recipes are much more in keeping with the spirit of the biblical injunction, "Take heed unto yourself and take care of your life." (Deuteronomy, 4:9.)

Do you realize how many times you transgress this directive? At practically every meal, every snack, and every raid on the refrigerator—unless . . .

Unless you are aware of what has been done to your food, what has been added in the way of chemicals that are destructive to the mind and body, what has been taken away in the refining process—food factors which your body must have in order to function in good health.

Introduction II
How to "Naturalize" Your Kitchen

If you were to ask me to teach you how to cook kosher, the natural way, I would say—*stay as close to Nature as possible*. Avoid the four whites: white sugar, white flour, refined white salt, and devitalized white rice. All the rest is commentary. Go thou and learn.

And there is much to learn. I was cooking kosher, the natural way, long before most people could spell granola, and I'm *still* learning.

Three questions will occur to you immediately: Where do I start? Will my family accept it? Is it expensive?

You start by discarding "negative" foods and stocking up on health-building foods. Caution: do it gradually.

In your good nutrition department, you should have:

1. WHEAT GERM, RAW OR TOASTED

Keep it refrigerated and buy from a dealer who keeps it under refrigeration. Raw wheat germ has more nutrients than the toasted because it has not been subjected to heat. The toasted has better keeping qualities and a flavor that is more acceptable to some palates. To give raw wheat germ a toasty flavor, toast about one-half cup in a 250-degree F. oven until light brown and add to the rest in the jar. The whole jar of wheat germ will taste toasted. Or roast some raw peanuts along with the wheat germ. You will improve the flavor of both.

If your family prefers the toasted to the raw, by all means cater to them in this respect. Better they should eat the toasted than none at all because wheat germ is a nutritional goldmine. Consider these health-building dividends: lots of protein that repairs and builds the cells, organs, and tissues of the body; large quantities of polyunsaturated oils for glowing complexions and efficient metabolism; generous amounts of vitamin E to protect the polyunsaturated oils from oxidation and thus retard the aging process and damage to the circulatory system; practically every vitamin in the B complex and in generous amounts. These vitamins are crucial to maintaining a healthy heart, the ability to cope, lovely complexions, good blood, a pleasant disposition, and a clear-thinking mind. Believe it or not, some of the B vitamins have been shown to improve the developing intelligence of children.

Wheat germ provides lots of iron, the organic kind that does not fight with Vitamin E. Inorganic iron cancels out vitamin E. If you are taking an inorganic iron supplement on a doctor's prescription, make sure you take vitamin E 12 hours later. Dr. Wilbur Shute, who treats heart patients with vitamin E, forbids his patients to use commercial bread that has been fortified with inorganic iron.

Nutrients per 100 grams (about 3½ ounces)

	"Enriched" White Flour	Whole Wheat Flour	Raw Wheat Germ
Protein (grams)	10.5	13.3	26.6
Fiber (grams)	.3	2.3	2.5
Calcium (mg.)	16	41	72
Iron (mg.)	2.9	3.3	9.4
Potassium (mg.)	95	370	827
Magnesium (mg.)	25	113	336
Thiamine (mg.)	.44	.55	2.01
Riboflavin (mg.)	.26	.12	.68
Niacin (mg.)	3.5	4.3	4.2
Vitamin B_3 (mg.)	.06	.34	1.15*
Pantothenic Acid (mg.)	.465	1.1	1.2*

*Toasted wheat germ

Compiled from data in the United States Department of Agriculture Handbook No. 8 and Home Economics Research Report No. 36.

Wheat germ also provides magnesium and potassium—so essential to every beat of the heart—and zinc—so important to one's sense of taste and smell, ability to heal, blemish-free complexions, and to one's sex life. Furthermore, wheat germ contains a lot of natural fiber, which has been shown to prevent constipation, varicose veins, diverticulosis, and cancer of the colon.

You will be making an important contribution to your family's health and happiness if you make it a practice to get more wheat germ into their foods. Present it to your high-chair thumpers. It has a nutlike flavor that little ones enjoy—if their taste buds have not been jaded by too much sugar, salt, and overprocessed foods.

Wheat germ is a food with life-nurturing properties. Therefore, life-seeking bacteria like to dine on it. To discourage this infiltration, always keep the wheat germ refrigerated once the jar has been opened. If you have an open jar languishing on a pantry shelf, discard it. If you have an open jar sitting in your refrigerator for more than a month, give it the nose-and-taste test. If it has the slightest off-smell or a slightly bitter after-taste, throw it out. Rancidity is not only harmful to your health, it can turn your family off and seriously impede all efforts to improve nutrition.

2. BRAN

Coarse miller's bran is available at health food stores and can be added, as a source of additional fiber, to cereals and baked goods. Be sure to increase your liquid intake when you eat bran. Like wheat germ, bran should be kept under refrigeration.

3. NUTRITIONAL OR BREWER'S YEAST

Excellent for boosting protein and other nutrient values of soups, stews, casseroles, baked goods, beverages, and for revving up your own motor when energy slumps. Mix a tablespoon with hot water, add a dash of Spike or other good vegetable seasoner, sit down, put your feet up, and enjoy a break.

4. HONEY

It should be raw, unprocessed, uncooked. Heating destroys important enzymes. Clover honey is the mildest in flavor and is recommended for baked goods while you are weaning the family away from sugar. Once they are accustomed to the taste of honey, experiment with other varieties. Buckwheat, my favorite, is great in honey cakes, where you especially want the taste of honey to come through.

5. WHOLE WHEAT FLOUR

Preferably stone ground. Keep it in the freezer or refrigerator and buy it from a source where it is kept refrigerated and preferably fresh ground. If no health food store or co-op in your area sells this top-quality flour, you can order it by mail from Walnut Acres, Penn's Creek, Pennsylvania. All of their grains are stored in special cold rooms, thus obviating the necessity for the frequent fumigation that commercial whole grain flours are subjected to. Better yet, buy your own grains and grind flour as you need it. Since you are keeping your flour refrigerated, always warm it before combining it with yeast. Put as much as you need in the oven for 15 minutes at 200 degrees F.

6. SOY FLOUR

A protein booster. Two tablespoons added to one cup of flour will greatly enhance the protein value of your baked goods.

7. CAROB POWDER

Use it as a substitute for cocoa and chocolate. It has no theobromine (a caffeinlike substance), no oxalic acid which ties up calcium, no fat, and very few calories. Another name for carob is boeksur (pronounced "boxer"); it grows abundantly in Israel. Until your family is accustomed to the slightly different taste and aroma of carob, add a tablespoon or two of cocoa to the carob container.

8. OILS—PRESSED

Use sunflower, sesame, safflower, corn, soy, or olive oil. Do not use cottonseed oil. Since cotton is not considered a food, its production is not governed by safety precautions on the use of pesticides which govern food crops. It is heavily sprayed, and who knows how much of this poisonous stuff gets into the oil? Do not use solvent-expressed oils. Some of the solvent, usually hexane, may get into the oil. Pressed oils are available at natural food stores. Keep them refrigerated.

9. SEEDS

Buy sesame, sunflower, pumpkin, and poppy seeds. Every seed

contains that mysterious vitality which can produce a new plant. Seeds are Nature's storehouse of enzymes, vitamins, minerals, protein, and unsaturated fatty acids so essential to every cell in our bodies. Buy them unsalted and unroasted. They are great in cakes, cookies, salads, or for noshing.

10. SEEDS FOR SPROUTING

Buy alfalfa, mung bean, lentil, wheat, rye, triticale, garbanzo. All these make delicious sprouts that give you fantastic nutrients and save you money. Get them from food stores, not from garden suppliers where seeds are frequently treated with fungicides.

11. SEA SALT OR MINERAL SALT

We're going to cut down considerably on salt, but there are times when you need a little, even if it's just to gargle. Commercial table salt is approximately 99.5 percent sodium chloride, plus iodine for prevention of goiter, dextrose as a stabilizer for the added iodine, sodium bicarbonate for whiteness, and an anticaking aluminum compound for free flowing. Sea salt (available at natural food stores) contains about 44 minerals, including chlorine, sodium, calcium, potassium, and phosphorus.

12. LECITHIN GRANULES AND SOY GRITS

Lecithin is a natural emulsifier which helps to keep cholesterol circulating happily. Recent research indicates that lecithin (soy grits is a good source) increases by a factor of three the amount of cholesterol that can be dissolved in bile salts. Bile salts are the vehicle by which the body rids itself of excess cholesterol. M.I.T. scientists have determined that lecithin in the diet improves memory and can actually make one "smarter." It helps manufacture acetylcholine, which helps the brain to transmit nerve signals. (*New York Times*, January 26, 1978.) Lecithin is high in phosphorus, so more calcium is needed to keep the proper balance. Sesame seeds, dry milk, green leafy vegetables, and raw bone meal powder are good sources of calcium.

13. BEANS, BEANS, BEANS

Buy all kinds, especially soy beans. Most beans require presoaking. Exceptions are lentils, split peas, and mung beans. If you keep a tray of soybeans in water in your freezer, you will always have presoaked beans ready to go into your soup, stew, casserole, or cholent. Soybeans are not starchy. Because of their high protein content, they may be served occasionally as a substitute for meat or eggs. Serve them with a grain, like brown rice or bulgur, and you will have a biologically complete protein pattern.

Here's a great tip from Ellen Sue Spivack, author of *Beginner's Guide for Meatless Casseroles* (Deep Roots, Lewisburg, Pennsylvania): Soak a cup of beans overnight. Next morning, pour off the water, spread beans on a cookie sheet, and freeze. When the beans are hard as marbles, transfer them to a container or plastic bag. Keep them in the freezer and use as few or as many as your dish requires. They will not stick together. I keep a variety of beans—navy, pinto, lima, kidney, soy—in separate containers in the freezer. Thus, my creative culinary urges are not stymied by a long soaking period.

14. GRAINS

Kasha or buckwheat; millet, a terrific grain said to be the manna from Heaven that sustained the Israelites on their trek through the desert; whole barley; brown rice; bulgur or cracked wheat; and oats are all good sources of nutrients and fiber.

15. UNSWEETENED COCONUT, DRIED FRUIT, RAW NUTS—SUNFLOWER SEEDS, SESAME SEEDS, PUMPKIN SEEDS

Mix nuts and seeds together with some raisins for a dish of *nosherai* that will keep your family and guests munching very happily and healthfully. This combination is high in potassium, low in sodium, and rich in zinc, a trace mineral very important to healing, to your sense of taste, and to your love life. Prostate problems and zinc deficiencies march in the same parade.

16. MOLASSES

Buy the unsulphured kind, preferably blackstrap. Use it as a sweetener occasionally instead of honey, or half and half with honey until your family gets accustomed to the taste. It's a terrific source of iron, a good source of calcium, phosphorus, potassium, and B vitamins. Put a teaspoon in a cup of hot water for a caffein and acid-free "coffee" that gives you a lift but no letdown.

17. ARROWROOT POWDER

This natural thickening agent, a source of protein and trace minerals, is derived from the roots of plants that pull minerals from the soil. It is a much more natural and nutritious food than cornstarch, which is highly processed.

18. BAKING POWDER

Buy the kind that is aluminum- and preferably sodium-free. This is available at natural food stores, or make your own. To make your own baking powder, combine ¼ teaspoon baking soda with ½ teaspoon cream of tartar. This is equal to one teaspoon baking powder.

I can almost hear you saying, "Where am I going to put all that stuff? My cupboards are already bulging." Do not despair; don't move to a larger apartment; don't preempt the children's playroom or your husband's closet! I'll show you how to make lots of space in your pantry. Take two large garbage bags, and now let's go over to your shelves. Into one garbage bag, put all opened containers or bags of—

1. REFINED SUGAR

What do you need it for, to hasten your trip to cavity corners, put fat on your hips, increase your level of triglycerides—now recognized as a far more dangerous culprit than cholesterol when it comes to clogging up arteries? Sugar contains no body-building protein, no minerals, no vitamins—only empty, negative calories. But, sugar needs vitamin B, especially B1 or thiamine, in order to be metabolized. Since it has none of its own, it borrows yours and never pays back. Naturally, if you consume much sugar, and most of us do, you're going to suffer a deficiency in thiamine, which can lead to fatigue, neuritis, and depression for which your doctor will probably prescribe tranquilizers, which further complicate the problem.

A British physician, Dr. John Yudkin, says in his book *Sweet and Dangerous*, "Avoid sugar and you will lessen your chances of getting diabetes, dental decay, atherosclerosis, some forms of cancer, obesity, and gout. You will increase your life span and your chances of enjoying a healthy old age."

Scorning the sugar bowl does not mean embracing saccharin. There are at least a dozen animal studies that show that saccharin causes cancer—not only in the bladder but at many sites.

It's interesting to note that in Israel the packets of sugar served at restaurants and sidewalk cafes are twice the size of the ones served here, and most Israelis use two packets to each cup of coffee or tea! When questioned about this overconsumption of sugar, they say, in wide-eyed innocence, "But, we need it for energy!" Baloney.

Sugar gives a rush of quick energy and then a slide into fatigue and despair. The sugar rushes into your bloodstream without even stopping to make a courtesy call on your liver, which would detain it and dole it out slowly. Once in the bloodstream, it raises your body's blood sugar levels, making you feel high, energetic. But this much sugar in your blood is dangerous, so the insulin comes running out of the Isles of Langerhans in your pancreas and takes that sugar out of your blood; it then deposits it in your cells, where it is stored as fat. But the insulin goes in for overkill. It takes practically *all* the sugar out of your blood, and there you are in a dark blue funk, feeling more tired and depressed than before, and what do you do? You go scrounging around for a candy bar, a cup of coffee, or a cigarette, all of which will start the whole cycle all over again.

So, if you want to live to be 120 in good health, throw away the sugar bowl and the saccharin. You can live the sweet life without either.

2. BLEACHED WHITE FLOUR

Into the garbage bag. What's wrong with white flour? A whole book could be written about the crimes of white flour against society. Here's only what you need to know to justify to your family a quick switch to fresh whole grains.

The bleaching chemicals destroy vitamin E and the enzyme phosphatase—an enzyme which acts like an ax. It splits the minerals in our food so we can assimilate and utilize them. The lack of vitamin E in our refined flour may be at the root of a great many problems which plague today's society. Just think. In the year 1900, before we reaped the consequences of the milling process which extracted the vitamin E from the flour, coronary thrombosis was rare. In his book on heart disease, Dr. Paul Dudley White says, "When I graduated from medical school in 1911, I had never heard of coronary thrombosis, which is one of the chief threats to life in the United States and Canada today—an astonishing development in one's own lifetime!" What a terrible price to pay for white flour, foam rubber bread, and emasculated cereals!

3. HYDROGENATED FATS

Maybe you can use them as furniture polish or to take the squeak out of a door. But, please don't eat them. Hydrogenation is an artificial process which destroys the original oil with all its vitamin and mineral compounds and regenerates a new one synthetically. The new one is purified, deodorized, bleached, and an insult to your body.

One very important component lost is lecithin, which is an antidote to cholesterol. And, according to Dr. Royal Lee, one of the pioneers in the study of nutrition, so are the other phospholipids that cooperate with vitamin E in preserving the chromosome factors, the blueprints of life.

It is believed that these fats pass into the bloodstream from the digestive tract but will not be taken out by the cells of the body, which recognize them as fake. They are probably the main factors creating sludge which may block the blood vessels, thus precipitating, as you know, tragic results.

Butter and eggs, which are perfectly good foods, have been made the fall guys while margarine has been touted as safe. The truth is that margarine may be the cause of hardening of the arteries, says Dr. Fred Kummerow of the University of Illinois. Manufacturers tout margarine in medical journals, in the lay press, and on the air as the great "heart-saving" polyunsaturated fat. What they don't tell you is that the process of hydrogenation changes the polyunsaturates to a form called trans-acids, which are more damaging to arteries than either saturated fats or cholesterol. (*Science News*, April 20, 1974.)

Manufacturers use hydrogenated fats in many processed foods, not only in margarine and in those solid white shortenings put out by the manufacturers of soap. They're used in peanut butter, mayonnaise, and in practically all prepared cake mixes. Why?

Because hydrogenated fats keep far better than natural oils and fats. *They do not spoil.*

One of the rules you must heed if you are to cook kosher the natural way and preserve your family's health is this: *Never buy anything that does not spoil.* But use it before it does. Anything that does not spoil has been embalmed!

4. MINUTE RICE

The next item to get rid of is that box of minute rice. If it is half used, throw it out and whisper an apology to your family for even having used it. In my opinion, anyone who uses minute rice is committing a big nutritional sin. It is nothing but empty calories without the nutrients so essential to health which you get in brown rice.

Brown rice is easy to prepare, it is available at all natural food stores and even in some supermarkets, and it costs less than that abomination that "cooks up in a minute." Sure it takes longer to cook. So you start it earlier. It cooks on its own time—not yours. You can make the salad, set the table, nurse the baby, or read a book while the rice cooks.

5. PACKAGED GOODS

Now take a good hard look at all the packaged goods on your pantry shelf. Read the list of ingredients. Does it say BHA or BHT? Into the garbage bag. If it is an unopened package, return it to the dealer.

These chemicals are so toxic that Britain does not permit them in any food intended for babies and children. American kids gobble them up every day in their Wheaties, Cheerios, and Sugar Smacks. Is it any wonder we have so many hyperactive kids?

6. CANNED FRUITS IN SUGAR SYRUP

Open the can and pour off the syrup. Serve a small quantity of the fruit in a dish of fresh fruit, until you have used up your supply. Look for fruits that are canned in their own juices. There are more and more of them coming on the market. Better yet, put the emphasis on *fresh* fruit. When berries are in season, buy or pick an extra quantity. Spread them out on a cookie sheet and freeze. When they are as hard as marbles, put them in plastic bags for more convenient storage. What a pleasure to have strawberries in the fruit salad when the family gets together, and a nice blueberry pie when friends drop in.

7. NON-DAIRY CREAMERS

You can live without them. They are loaded with additives. When you are dining, lunching, or brunching out, make sure you get milk or cream with your beverage. Ask for it. What about great desserts for meat meals? See the chapter on tofu—the nondairy alternative. You can make delicious cheesecakes, creamy pies, and salad dressings—pareve.

WILL MY FAMILY ACCEPT IT?

It is not always easy to make the changeover to natural foods. If your family is 100 percent with you, you can make a clean sweep. Do it together. Make it a shared adventure.

If your family thinks the natural foods thing is "square" or "for the birds," then you will have to sneak it to them and make changes slowly. Start by cutting down on sugar in all your baked goods. Gradually switch to honey. Add wheat germ to your baked goods, latkes, and kugels. Just a little. Add nutritional yeast to soups, casseroles, gedempte flaish, and chopped meat dishes. Start with a teaspoon and build up gradually to two tablespoons. Start taking wheat germ and yeast yourself. You'll have that much more strength with which to cope with their *mishigasim*.

One woman got her resistant husband to attend one of my lectures. Several weeks later he asked his wife why she wasn't using "all that stuff Jane Kinderlehrer talked about."

"Because you don't like it, you lug."

"But, you're supposed to sneak it to me," he protested.

Don't push, don't nag, don't force, and don't be grim. Sing as you sprinkle, and really work on naturalizing your own diet. You will look so good and have such a nice lilt in your step, everybody will want to know your secret.

What about eggs?

Many people are obsessed with a fear of cholesterol. They avoid eggs and are horrified when I suggest organ meats. Well, let me bring you up to date.

Your body may have the type of cholesterol that is helping you to avoid atherosclerosis and its complications. In a study involving 12 people with normal lipoprotein levels, the administration of lecithin reduced the level of low-density lipoprotein (LDL) cholesterol, the kind that increases the risk of artherosclerosis, and increased the level of high-density lipoprotein (HDL) cholesterol, the kind that protects. (*Clinical Research*, Vol. 25, No. 2, 1977.)

You could have a high level of cholesterol, the protective kind, but if your doctor is not ordering the specific evaluation described above—and at this point most doctors are not—he's going to regard your level with a raised eyebrow and caution you to cut down on eggs and organ meats, which are high in lecithin content, the factor that increases high-density cholesterol.

What happens? Your total cholesterol level may go down. But, at what a price! You now have more of the dangerous factor and less of the protective factor.

"People should discard their obsession with cholesterol as the primary cause for heart attacks and pay more attention to how much sugar they eat," says Dr. John Yudkin, emeritus professor of nutrition at the University of London. More than anything else, this determines the amount of triglycerides in the blood, and it is the level of triglycerides rather than cholesterol that is, he believes, a better index of susceptibility to a heart attack.

So far as diet is concerned, Dr. Yudkin says, forget about limiting the number of eggs. Choose the cheese soufflé for dessert instead of a sugary pie or cake. (*New York Times*, December 21, 1974.)

Dr. Mark D. Altschule of Harvard Medical School holds that widespread fear of the cholesterol in food is uncalled for, "especially regarding our much maligned old friend, your morning egg." (*Executive Health*, August 1974.)

For many years doctors have blacklisted eggs for cardiovascular patients. Now, many doctors are recommending eggs to heart patients. New research has shown eggs eaten regularly do not cause any significant increase in serum cholesterol.

If your arteries are so clogged that you can't handle cholesterol without it ganging up in clots, then try Dr. Jacobus Rinse's formula, which he devised to help him overcome a case of debilitating angina that had plagued him for ten years. Dr. Rinse's formula—or breakfast mash—calls for one tablespoon each of lecithin granules, wheat germ, and nutritional yeast, one teaspoon of bone meal powder, two tablespoons of coarsely chopped sunflower seeds, 500 milligrams vitamin C, 100 international units vitamin E, 40 milligrams vitamin B₆, 500 milligrams magnesium oxide, and 30 milligrams zinc oxide.

Now in his late seventies, Dr. Rinse has the energy of a teenager and no sign of angina. He has given his formula to Dutch and American cardiologists, who have recommended it to their patients with marvelous results. I know personally of several victims of heart attacks who are making spectacular recoveries on Dr. Rinse's mash—which can also be used as a preventative.

You can incorporate the mash recipe into carob confections, halvah, bran muffins, hamburger, kugels, honey cake, and bread. You will find modifications of Dr. Rinse's mash in many recipes in this book.

What About Chicken Fat?

Chicken fat, or schmaltz, has long been the traditional fat in the preparation of many *geshmache* dishes. In fact, the word "schmaltz," like kibitzer, chutzpah, and schlemiel, has become part of colloquial English.

"Schmaltz it up," a director will tell his cast.

"Give it some schmaltz," an editor will advise a reporter.

What they mean is, give it some pizzazz; give it some *tam*. And, that's exactly what chicken fat, used discreetly, does for many dishes—chopped liver, knishes, kasha varnishkas, fleishidige kugels; for mashed potatoes instead of butter; spread on rye bread for a nosh, or spread on bread instead of mayonnaise for a scrumptious chicken sandwich.

I can almost hear you exclaiming in horror, "What about the cholesterol?" Well, I have news for you. Chicken fat is not saturated like other animal fats. Poultry fats are composed of ¼ to ¾ *unsaturated* fatty acids. (*Poultry Science* 56:166-173, 1977.)

"Poultry fats," say the authors of this report, "possess some unique aspects which make them promising as food fats." Because of their high unsaturation, poultry fats are fluid at room temperature. "This," say the researchers, "places them closer to vegetable oils than to other animal fats. . . ." And, they say, "the natural flavor of poultry fats is pleasant and desirable."

What about turkey and duck? They are similar in composition and in levels of unsaturation, but differ in tocopherol (vitamin E) levels. Chicken fat contains about five times more vitamin E than turkey fat, with duck somewhere in the middle.

Since vitamin E is an antioxidant which prevents rancidity, turkey and duck fat have reduced stability or a shorter keeping period. With today's freezer facilities, this should present no problem. Besides, if you make it in smallish quantities, it disappears long before it has a chance to spoil.

One of the nice things about using chicken fat instead of commercial fat is the fact that you yourself have processed it. Therefore, you know exactly what is in it. You know it is free of chemical preservatives and colorings. You know it hasn't been bleached, deodorized, hydrogenated, or otherwise robbed of its natural vitamin content.

SCHMALTZ AND GRIEBEN

First the fat from the poultry must be rendered. Cut the fatty skin and yellow pieces of fat into small bits. Put them in a heavy pot and cover with cold water. Cook, uncovered, until almost all the water has evaporated. Lower the heat and add chopped onion—about one onion to one cup of fat.

My mother used to add a few slices of raw potato to help clarify the fat. The schmaltz (chicken fat) is done when the onions and potato are nice and brown and the grieben are crisp. Or as Violeta Autumn says in her enchanting book *A Russian Jew Cooks in Peru* (101 Productions, San Francisco, California, 1973), "Grieben are ready when they talk: take a fork and gently tap floating grieben with the back of the tongs. Bring your ear to about six inches from the grieben. If they sound ch-ch-ch, they are ready. If they emit a dull thud sound, they need more cooking."

So, after the grieben make ch-ch-ch, let the pot cool a little, then strain into a clean jar to separate the schmaltz from the grieben. If the grieben snitchers don't get them all, you can store them in the freezer and use them when you're making chopped liver or potato knishes or whatever. To do this, cover the grieben with a thin layer of schmaltz.

Remember that all fats have a high calorie count and should be used sparingly, even butter and oil. You will note that the fat content of the recipes in this book is less than in standard recipes.

What About Lox?

If you just can't live without lox, make sure you have orange juice or some form of vitamin C before eating your lox and bagel. Lox and other smoked fish (and meats) contain nitrites which get together with amines in your stomach. The resulting combination, nitrosamines, are carcinogenic. But, vitamin C tends to prevent the linkage of these two substances. So, if you must indulge in lox, smoked fish, or an occasional salami sandwich or hot dog, first take vitamin C.

Is It Expensive?

At today's prices, you can naturalize your kitchen for about $30.00—give or take a few. How much do you spend on junk food—on candy, cookies, cereals, potato chips, corn curls, soda, and such so-called convenience foods as cake mixes, hamburger helpers, bread mixes, process cheeses, etc.? Figure it out, because that's what you're going to save.

You're also going to save on the dentist, doctor, and drugstore expenses.

As far as food costs go, after the initial investment you will actually save money. A young Canadian woman told me that because her child was hyperactive, she put him and the whole family on the Feingold diet (no additives and no sugar). Not only did her child improve, but she now spends $15.00 a week less for food for a family of four.

Peter Donovan, when he was food service director at Purchase College, New York State, told me that after they added natural foods, vegetarian entrées, and lots of sprouts, they saved $700.00 a week on the food budget.

When Sara Bell ran the food program for the Day Care Center in our town, she converted to whole grain natural foods, eliminated the junk and the processed entrées, and saved $3,000.00 on the food budget in one year.

Of course, the real dividends you will realize are in other areas–areas on which one cannot place monetary value. Can you put a price on vitality, on lovely complexions, pleasant dispositions, good teeth, sparkling eyes, the ability to cope? These are some of the rewards my family reaped after a year of cooking naturally. The children started coming home from the dentist with big "no-cavity" grins; we saw our doctor only occasionally, at Bar Mitzvahs and other social functions. The children performed much better in school; there was less squabbling but a lot of good-humored horseplay.

Those, my friends, are dividends you cannot write a check for. Their value cannot be calculated in dollars and cents. It is engraved in your life line. It is a far more precious heritage than diamonds and silver spoons. This kind of wholesome food builds genes that are handed down from generation to generation. This is an important link in the chain of survival.

SOME HELPFUL HINTS

Sugar and Honey

Replace sugar with honey in your own favorite recipes.

Use ½ cup honey for every cup of sugar. As a rule, reduce the liquid in the recipe by ¼ cup for every cup of honey and bake at a temperature 25 degrees F. lower than instructions call for. These adjustments have been made in the recipes in this book.

Tamari Soy Sauce

Some recipes in this book call for Tamari, which is a superior soy sauce made from fermented beans and wheat. It contains no additives or coloring.

Oil vs. Butter

Oil is 100 percent fat. Butter is 80 percent fat and 20 percent water. When using oil in a recipe that calls for butter, use 20 percent less oil. If a recipe calls for 1 cup of butter, fill a cup with oil and take off 3 tablespoons. Add 3 tablespoons of liquid to the recipe.

Distilled Water

In order to avoid the toxic substances that pollute most of the water supplies, many people drink distilled water, which is free of pollutants but is also devoid of mineral substances important to health.

You can restore the minerals to the distilled water by doing the following:

Add 10 whole almonds, ⅛ cup raisins, ⅛ cup oat groats, and ⅛ cup whole barley to a gallon of distilled water. Let it stand for 24 hours in the refrigerator. Then use. The jar can be refilled three or four times. The distilled water will leach out the minerals from these mineral-rich foods so your body can use them.

What About Food Supplements?

I wish I could say that if you eat according to the recipes in this book, you will have no need of extra vitamins and minerals. But, I can't. Even when we avoid all processed, devitalized foods, it is doubtful that we can get adequate nutrition from our food unless we are fortunate enough to raise our own food organically and to live in an atmosphere that is clear and fresh as a mountain breeze, unpolluted by the fumes and lead of traffic and the toxic wastes of industry—a Garden of Eden.

Modern agricultural methods, which lean heavily on inorganic fertilizers and insecticides, deplete the nutrients in the soil and in the foods grown on them. We can no longer depend on them for the vital trace minerals and other nutrients vital to glowing health.

If you are using wheat germ and brewer's yeast daily, you are getting a good supply of the B vitamins.

I'm not going to tell you which vitamins to take or in what dosages. Each person has his own biological individuality which determines his needs. I can tell you what my family takes:

Vitamin A: 25,000 international units from fish liver oil.
Vitamin C: 2,000 milligrams daily, more when we feel a cold
coming on or are fighting an infection or are

taking an antibiotic. Vitamin C potentiates the effects of the antibiotic.

Vitamin E: 600 international units daily (mixed tocopherols). If you have high blood pressure or a history of rheumatic heart disease, consult a doctor who knows his nutrition before taking vitamin E.

Vitamins A, C, and E work together as detoxifiers of the poisons all around us. They give us a certain amount of protection from heavy metals, such as lead and cadmium and insecticide residues.

Vitamin E is a boon to the heart because it increases the amount of oxygen available to the muscles and cells. Both vitamins A and E help to remove dangerous disruptive free radicals in the body and are therefore enormously helpful for preventing, or at least delaying, the signs of old age. They also strengthen the ability of the tissues to absorb oxygen, restore impaired circulation in the small capillaries, as in claudication, and have a beneficial effect on the health and vitality of the sex glands.

Besides these three supplements, we take an all-purpose natural formula, B complex, alfalfa tablets (very good for the pain of arthritis), calcium, magnesium, and zinc. We also take glutamic hydrochloride for better absorption of proteins and minerals, since research has shown that practically everyone over the age of 40 is deficient in this digestive acid. We never take antacids. What we need for digestion is usually more acid, not less.

COOKING KOSHER: The Natural Way

1

Seeds, Sprouts & Other Raw Foods

To stay young and vital all the days of your life, a doctor once told me, each day you should eat some food which, if put into the ground, would grow.

Knishes, kugels, and blintzes are all a pleasure to eat and should be enjoyed. But, if you put them in the ground, would they grow? Hardly.

What then can you eat which, if put into the ground, would grow?

The answer is—seeds. Put a seed in the ground, and it will grow.

A seed is—when you stop to think about it—the very essence of life. All life starts from seed. It has been noted that Nature is careless of the individual, but careful of the species. Therefore, the seed, which is Nature's instrument of perpetuity, gets the best of everything. The seed will pull from the soil all the elements necessary to produce a new plant. It contains more vital nutrients than the plant on which it was grown.

But what kind of seeds can you eat? Sunflower, pumpkin, caraway, squash, watermelon, sesame seeds—all are popular and can be enjoyed every day. They can also be used in many delectable dishes. There are many other seeds that are probably finding their way into your trash can, when they could be adding vitality to your menus and to you.

The next time you cut a pepper, regard those seeds with new respect. They contain the vital factor capable of producing a new plant. Add them to your salad, your stew, your soup. Never discard cucumber, tomato, or eggplant seeds. And the pomegranate, so popular in Israel, is a great fruit. It is all seeds.

Seeds are great—but sprouts are better! All the good things that are in the seed are in the sprout, only more so. A sprout is a seed in the act of creation. In a seed, the life force is still dormant. But, give that seed the proper conditions—air and water—and it will wake up, stretch, and burst into life. It becomes a sprout, gloriously alive and still steeped in creativity.

A sprouting grain is unique. There is nothing like it under the sun. What else can you consume humanely while the life force is still vibrant within it? A sprouting seed has within its kernel the essence and the mystery of life. While it is exulting in self-creation, it produces in glorious profusion almost every single element essential to sustain and nurture life. Manufacturers of food have never been able to pack into one small package what Nature develops so magnanimously in the sprout. If they did, they would be touting it as the miracle of all time!

When the seed explodes to release its vital force, it multiplies its vitamin values and actually develops some vitamins that were not in the original seed. Grains, for instance, contain no vitamin C. Sprouted grains, however, do contain this important nutrient. In fact, sprouted soybeans were used during World War II to prevent scurvy because oranges, fresh fruits, and other sources of vitamin C were very scarce. Some sprouts develop all the amino acids, thus becoming complete-protein foods.

Natural whole grains and beans are good foods and have their place in your dietary plan. But, these foods reach their peak when they are sprouted.

Sprouts are your wisest investment, nutritionally and economically. One pound of mung beans costs about one dollar and will yield eight pounds of sprouts. Eight pounds of these lightweight dynamos would practically fill your bathtub.

When you plant seeds in your garden, you must wait up to three months to harvest your crop. You can raise a crop of sprouts in three days—you don't need a spade, rake, or sunshade. And you can grow them anywhere, even in the trunk of your car or in your knapsack if you go backpacking.

Here's how you do it.

Get some organically-raised grains, seeds, legumes—wheat, rye, alfalfa, mung beans, garbanzo, soybeans, radish, parsley, cress, and so forth. *Do not get them from a garden supply store.* These seeds are meant for planting in the ground and are usually treated with fungicides—sometimes with mercury. Get your seeds, grains, and beans from food stores, especially natural food stores which cater to the needs of the sprouter.

I like to keep three jars of sprouts going at the same time: a bean, a grain, and a small seed. Their protein patterns complement each other.

So let's start.

Put two tablespoons of alfalfa seed in a strainer, give it a quick rinse to remove surface dust, then place it in a quart jar. Half fill the jar with tepid water. Cover and let it stand overnight. Follow the same procedure using three tablespoons of wheat berries in one jar and three tablespoons of lentils or mung beans in another. Mung beans become what is commonly known as the "chop suey" sprout.

Next morning, cover each jar with a double layer of cheesecloth or nylon net secured with a rubber band, or make screened lids yourself from window screening cut to fit canning jar rings. Lids with mesh screening are also available in various sizes at health food stores.

Now, without removing this cover, simply drain off the soak water into a jar. *Do not discard it.* It is a rich source of nutrients. Use it to start potatoes or rice or to steam vegetables. Use it in soups. If you have more than you can use in a few days, freeze it in ice cube trays, then dump the cubes into a plastic bag. Label them "Dynamite" and enjoy visions of rosy good health every time you use them.

Next, rinse the seeds and grains with tepid water. Feed the rinse water to your plants: they like it better than sweet talk. After rinsing, let the jars rest, slightly tilted so that any moisture can escape but a source of oxygen will remain. Remember that sprouting seeds, grains, and beans like to be moist but not wet.

They should never sit in puddles.

Now, put them in a dark place. I put mine under the sink where the hot water pipe warms the atmosphere. If this is not practical for you, rest them on the sink in a tilted position (place a sponge or a folded dishcloth under the bottom edge of the jar), and cover the whole shebang with a towel. The idea is to keep out the light. All things germinate best in the dark.

Repeat the rinsing procedure two or three times each day. By the end of the second day your wheat and lentils will be just about ready. When the weather is cold, they require a little more time. Don't let the wheat sprouts get any longer than the grain. Not that they are bad when they get longer; they simply don't taste so good as the shorter sprouts. If the sprouts do get longer than you like, spread them on a cookie sheet, place in the oven heated only by pilot light, or just warm if electric, and let them dry out. Then grind them in the blender and use as flour.

Alfalfa seed takes a little longer. As soon as two tiny leaves appear, on about the third day, keep your alfalfa exposed to the light instead of under the sink. They will turn a lovely green. They are now overflowing with chlorophyll (a blood purifier) and are ready to be enjoyed.

Be sure to eat the whole thing: root, seed, and sprout—everything in the jar.

Sprouting the Larger Beans

When you are sprouting the larger beans—garbanzo, soy, kidney, blackeye peas, pinto—the thing to remember is that they need lots of room. You can't crowd them.

First, soak about half a cup of garbanzos or soy overnight in a bowl or jar. Use plenty of water because they will triple in volume. Next morning, pour off the liquid. Don't save the soy water: it may contain an enzyme inhibitor. Remove any broken beans: they won't sprout.

Rinse the beans and spread them out in a soup plate or colander. Now dampen a dishtowel and place it on top of the beans. Slip the whole thing into a plastic bag in order to retain some moisture, but leave it open at one end to insure a source of oxygen. You could cover it with plastic wrap and then punch air holes in the wrap with an ice pick. Remove the plastic bag and dishtowel, and rinse them, three to five times a day. Garbanzos are ready in two or three days. Soybeans take a little longer. Be sure to pick out those beans that are broken, shriveled, or discolored, and any which fail to sprout. If you have many of this kind, you made need a fresh supply of beans. Old beans are not good sprouters.

Store your sprouts in the refrigerator as you would any fresh vegetable and use within a few days. If you can't use them up while they're fresh, then dry them. I dry them in the oven by the heat of the pilot light. I grind them as needed and use this as the base for a superior breading mix. It sure beats Shake and Bake.

During the winter, when lettuce is limp and skyhigh in price, use alfalfa sprouts on the sandwiches you send to school or office. They remain fresh and vibrant for several hours and bring the lovely taste of "springtime in the garden" to your lunch hour.

SPROUTS FOR BETTER HEALTH

Increase your chances of avoiding cancer. Dr. Ernst Krebs of San Francisco has long advocated the use of all kinds of sprouts because they are an excellent source of nitrilosides, which it is believed can control cancer. Lentil, mung bean, and alfalfa contain nitrilosides, but when they are sprouted they provide 50 times more of this factor than does the mature plant.

Now we have new laboratory evidence to confirm Dr. Krebs' claims. Extracts of wheat sprouts, mung beans, and lentils reduced mutagen activity by up to 99 percent when applied to the potent chemical mutagen 2-acetyl-aminofluorene, according to researchers from the University of Texas System Cancer Center, Houston. (*Food Chemical News,* December 4, 1978.)

The extract was most effective against acetyl-aminofluorene, but also reduced the activity of benzopyrene and aflatoxin. The researchers noted that "The inhibition of activation of carcinogens is quite strong at a reasonably low level of extract, and the wheat sprout extract is nontoxic even at high levels. . . ." They also noted that effectiveness declined after heating for 15 minutes.

You would be wise indeed to apply these test-tube findings to your table. Benzopyrene is the toxic element associated with tobacco smoke. If you have a smoker in the family, who hasn't yet kicked the habit, get lots and lots of sprouts into your meal plan.

In China, children eat bean sprouts more willingly than cabbage, spinach, or string beans. The Chinese housewife usually sautées the sprouts very quickly in just a little vegetable oil and adds salt to taste. Sometimes she garnishes the sprouts with chopped green onions, which provide a nice contrast in color and flavor. When sautéeing, use only one tablespoon of oil to two cups of sprouts.

TIPS TO GRANDMOTHERS: Keep some mung bean sprouts handy for when the grandchildren barge in. They love them. A few sprouts on the high-chair tray will keep a toddler busy and happy for at least two minutes. All of our grandchildren love sprouts and, believe me, when you give them sprouts instead of the usual *nosherai,* you are expressing your love, with a capital H—for health.

USING SPROUTS

How do you eat them? Let me count the ways: on breakfast cereal; in fresh salads, of course; steamed; in stir-fry dishes; in scrambled eggs; sprinkled on soups; in meat loaf and hamburgers; in breads, biscuits, cupcakes, rugelah, muffins, honey cake, strudel; in kugels, blintzes, and knishes; blended into healthful beverages; as a sandwich filling; as a substitute for lettuce; as a snack. They have practically no calories—a great TV nosh for waist-watchers.

Sprouts are unequaled as a garnish or a topping. When you float them in a bowl of soup, they add a touch of freshness. Or sprinkle lentil sprouts on top of steamed vegetables, mung beans on potato salad, wheat sprouts on pea soup, rye sprouts on potato soup. Rye sprouts taste a little like wild rice. Mung bean sprouts combined with brown rice are fantastic and offer complementary protein values. Add rye sprouts to brown rice and you have "mock wild rice," which makes a wonderful stuffing for fowl.

Sprouts (wheat, rye, alfalfa, sunflower) can be added to any bread dough to make a superior, moist, delicious loaf. You can chop them, blend them, or use them whole. Work the sprouts into the dough during the last kneading. Use up to one cup of sprouts for every liquid called for in the recipe.

Lentils have a pleasant peppery taste and can be used instead of celery and green pepper in your stews, soups, and casseroles. What a saving that is, especially in the winter.

Alfalfa and wheat sprouts, when dried, are sweet and crunchy and can be used to replace nuts in your baked goods. Ground wheat sprouts will make a superior flour for your baked goods.

Combine sprouts with fruits for superior gelatin salads.

Steep some sprouts in hot water for a zippy sprout tea.

There are innumerable ways to use sprouts, so get into the habit of sprouting and you will be taking a giant step toward improving your nutritional intake. Many recipes in this book call for seeds and sprouts of various kinds. Here are a few to get you started.

Papaya Pepper

The seeds of papaya have a pungent peppery flavor and are rich in enzymes and other valuable nutrients.

To make papaya pepper, remove the seeds from the papaya, place them with the filaments attached in a very low oven—just the pilot light of a gas oven will suffice. Leave the seeds in the oven until they are dry and crisp. Discard the fibrous material and put the seeds in your pepper mill. Add a few grinds to those foods which you like to pepper.

Pumpkin Seeds

Pumpkin seeds are a very good source of zinc—an essential mineral associated with the sense of taste and smell, the ability to heal, the control of acne, fertility, the health of the prostate gland, and one's sex life.

To make your own edible pumpkin seeds, remove the seeds and

fibrous material from the cavity of the pumpkin. Slowly dry them in the oven. Discard the fibrous material, reserving the seeds to munch on. This is a *kai and shpai* deal, like with unshelled sunflower seeds.

Sprout Soup

To make soup from sprouts, blend the sprouts of your choice with an equal amount of warm water seasoned with herbs. Garnish with watercress for a delicious body-warming soup that is chock full of vitality. Lentil sprouts are particularly tasty this way.

Sprout Milk

To make milk from sprouts, blend 1 cup of slightly sprouted wheat or another grain with 1 cup of water. Strain it or eat as is. Add a little bit of honey, pure maple syrup, or unsulphured molasses. Enjoy it with wheat germ or granola for a breakfast that will give you energy and keep you in high gear all day.

Wheat Berry Coffee

When coffee and sugar were scarce during World War II, the people of Austria would sprout wheat grains, roast them, grind them, then steep them in hot water—this was their ersatz coffee. The wheat starch converts to sugar in the sprouting, so it is sweet enough without sugar. And while it may not taste exactly like the ground brown berry we are accustomed to, it certainly can give you a lift and is a great improvement healthwise over the other "cup that cheers." This kind of beverage sipped at bedtime will encourage restful sleep instead of counting sheep.

APPLE-SESAME-NUT SALAD

A Waldorf salad with an extra dimension.

4 *tablespoons sesame seeds*

4 *unpeeled (if unsprayed) apples, washed and diced*

4 *stalks celery, diced*

½ *cup chopped walnuts*

1 *cup mayonnaise (preferably homemade—see Index for recipe)*

Toast the sesame seeds by placing them in a cast-iron skillet and setting the skillet over medium heat until the seeds pop—about 1 minute. In a bowl, combine the other ingredients. Mix with the toasted seeds and serve on a bed of greens. Serves 4 to 6.

PEACHES-AND-CHEESE
ALFALFA SANDWICHES

For your bridge party, try these Peaches-and-Cheese Alfalfa Sandwiches. They're light, satisfying, and absolutely delicious.

Peaches are not only beautiful to look at and heavenly to eat, they provide a veritable goldmine of vitamin A in every bite—1,330 international units in each yellow-fleshed peach; 50 international units for white-fleshed varieties. Both varieties provide some vitamin C, a sampler of B vitamins, lots of potassium (202 milligrams in a peach 2½ inches in diameter), and are a nutritional bargain when it comes to calories—only 40 calories for all that goodness.

Cream cheese brings a smooth, rich, satisfying quality to these sandwiches, plus some vitamin A, protein, and fat, and 100 calories in each ounce.

The alfalfa sprouts are a marvelous source of vitamin K, the blood-clotting vitamin, the valuable nutrient chlorophyll, and many valuable and rare trace minerals. Alfalfa has very long roots that reach deep into the subsoil and pick up minerals that shallow-growing plants can't reach. Alfalfa is one of the rare plant sources for vitamin B12, also called cobalamin, the only vitamin containing the essential trace mineral cobalt. B12 is necessary for the formation of red blood cells.

4 or 5 fresh peaches, pitted
3 ounces cream cheese, softened
1 cup cottage cheese
½ cup chopped walnuts
½ teaspoon grated lemon rind
1 unpeeled (if unsprayed) apple, diced
8 slices whole grain bread
3 cups alfalfa sprouts

Cut 1 peach into 8 slices. Chop 2 of the peaches into small pieces; slice the others. In a large bowl, combine the cream cheese, cottage cheese, walnuts, and lemon rind. Fold in the chopped peaches and diced apple. Spread this mixture on the bread slices. Sprinkle generously with alfalfa sprouts and top with a peach slice. Serves 8.

To delight the small fry, cut up another peach into 8 slices and make a mouth and two eyebrows with the slices. Use a walnut or a piece of carrot for the nose. The alfalfa provides a healthy set of hair and whiskers. This is a great dish for children's parties.

WHEAT OR TRITICALE SPROUT CONFECTIONS

Triticale is a grain, the "child" of a wheat "mother" and a rye "father." It excels both "parents" in protein content and has a marvelously nutty flavor. Both wheat and triticale sprouts are an excellent source of vitamin E, which among its many benefits has recently been found to retard the growth of mammary tumors in laboratory animals.

1 cup wheat or triticale sprouts
1 cup pecan meats, walnut meats, or sunflower seeds
1 cup raisins
1 tablespoon honey
Unsweetened coconut flakes

Chop the sprouts, nuts or seeds, and raisins (use a food chopper, food processor, or wooden chopping bowl). Add the honey and mix well. Form into 1-inch balls and roll them in the coconut flakes. Get the children in on the rolling. A few will roll right into their eager mouths, and that's fine. A nutritious dessert, too! Makes 32 Sprout Confections.

FESTIVE FIGS

The exceptional nutritional value of figs has been known since antiquity. The Talmud mentions the fig as good for the eyes, and it is recorded in the Book of Lamentations (Rabbah 1:2) that dried figs were distributed to the poor at the time of a famine.

No wonder. Figs are easy to digest and provide protein, essential fiber to stimulate the digestive process, some vitamin A, the B vitamins, and some bioflavonoids.

The fig is one of the few fruits that is more alkaline than acid, due to its large content of minerals—iron; blood-building copper; tissue-strengthening manganese; iodine; and fluorine, which is useful in the composition of tooth enamel and stimulates the metabolism of phosphorous.

12 *dried whole figs*
¼ *cup chopped almonds*
½ *cup wheat sprouts*
¼ *cup unsweetened coconut flakes*

½ *cup dry sherry*
Sesame seeds or unsweetened coconut flakes

Make a slit in 1 side of each fig. Combine the almonds, sprouts, and coconut. Stuff each fig with this mixture. Place the stuffed figs in a bowl and cover with the dry sherry. Let stand for 24 hours or more. Turn occasionally so all figs get well soaked. Drain. Roll lightly in sesame seeds or coconut flakes. As a substitute for sherry, try something more tame, such as cranberry, apple, or pineapple juice, or apricot nectar. Makes 12 Festive Figs.

Wheat Sprout Date-and-Nut Bread

Bake it in a can and cut this loaf into lovely round slices. Dates, which contain the highest natural sugar content of all dried fruit, contribute a lovely natural sweetness that does not cloy. Dates are an excellent source of potassium and have goodly amounts of calcium, iron, phosphorous, vitamin A, and niacin.

¼ cup honey
1 tablespoon butter, softened
16 dates, pitted
½ cup raisins
1 cup boiling water
1 teaspoon baking soda
2 eggs
1 teaspoon vanilla extract
½ teaspoon grated orange peel
1¾ cups whole wheat pastry flour
¼ cup soy flour
½ cup wheat sprouts
½ cup chopped walnuts, pecans, or sunflower seeds

Cream the honey with the butter in a large bowl and let stand in a warm place while you prepare the other ingredients. Cut the dates into thirds and combine with the raisins. Pour the boiling water over them. Add the baking soda and let cool.

To the honey-butter mixture, add the eggs, 1 at a time, and beat well. Add the vanilla, orange peel, and half of the date mixture. Combine the wheat and soy flours. Add 1 cup of the flour, then the rest of the date mixture. Add the sprouts and nuts or seeds; then add the rest of the flour. Mix well.

Line the sides of 2 one-pound coffee cans (1 lid removed from each) with parchment paper. Cut circles of parchment paper large enough to line the bottom of each can and run slightly up the sides. (If you prefer to grease the cans rather than use parchment paper, use a mixture of 1 teaspoon liquid lecithin and 1 teaspoon vegetable oil. This will provide a good non-stick surface.)

When the cans have been lined (or greased), divide the batter between the 2 cans. If using cans of different dimensions, simply fill them halfway. Bake at 320 degrees F. for 1 hour, or until a cake tester inserted in the center comes out clean. Let cool slightly, then remove from the cans by tapping on the bottoms. Refrigerate. Absolutely scrumptious with cream cheese. A nutritious after-school snack or lunch box sandwich. Makes 2 breads.

SUPERNUTRITION IN RAW FOODS

One of the greatest virtues of sprouts in that they can be eaten raw, with all their nutrients and enzymes intact. There is something in raw food, according to Dr. Roger Williams, world famous biochemist at the University of Texas, that contributes to *supernutrition*.

Raw foods contain many unknown factors that are destroyed if heated. Scientists at the State University of New York at Buffalo have found in raw vegetables certain elements which may provide a kind of protection against the development of stomach cancer. (*Cancer,* October 1972.)

Dr. Ralph Bircher, of the famous Bircher-Benner Clinic in Switzerland, says, "The natural chlorophyll, abundantly supplied in raw food, stimulates the heart and circulation mildly and works against insidious infections."

It has been found that a diet containing many raw foods tends to lower a too-high blood pressure. A doctor in California actually reduces the insulin requirements of his diabetic patients with such a diet. (*Annals of Internal Medicine,* January 1975.)

At least half of your food intake should be in the raw state. Put the emphasis on big salads, fruits, sprouts of course, and you'll be on the road to renewed vitality.

Spinach, Cauliflower, and Zucchini Salad

As in this recipe, try to use raw spinach in your salads. It's nutritionally far superior to lettuce. According to studies done at Iowa State University, spinach contains 25 times the vitamin A of lettuce, 9 times the vitamin C, 6 times the iron, and twice the B vitamins.

1 *clove garlic, split*
1 *quart fresh spinach*
  leaves, torn into
  pieces
1½ *cups cauliflowerets*
1½ *cups thinly sliced*
  zucchini
1 *medium-sized onion,*
  thinly sliced and
  separated into rings
1 *medium-sized carrot,*
  coarsely grated

½ *cup olive, sesame, or*
  sunflower oil
¼ *cup cider vinegar*
2 *teaspoons prepared*
  mustard
½ *teaspoon crushed*
  basil
¼ *teaspoon salt or kelp*
¼ *teaspoon crushed*
  marjoram
¼ *teaspoon freshly*
  ground white pepper

Rub a large glass salad bowl with the split garlic clove. Discard the garlic. Toss the vegetables together in the bowl. Drizzle a little of the oil (about 2 teaspoons) over all. Mix well, and refrigerate. (The oil seals the pores, preventing oxidation and a loss of nutrients.) Beat together the remaining ingredients and whatever remains from the garlic clove to make a dressing. Place in a covered container and refrigerate. When ready to serve, shake the dressing well and pour over the salad, or serve on the side. Serves 8 to 10.

RAINBOW SALAD

Each colorful vegetable—spinach, carrot, turnip, beet—contributes its special nutrients to this pyramid of natural goodness. Raw spinach is an excellent source of iron; carrots are high in carotene, which the body converts to vitamin A; turnips are a goldmine of calcium; beets contribute trace minerals and the enzyme betaine, which aids digestion.

2 *cups spinach leaves,*
  cut up
2 *medium-sized*
  carrots, grated
2 *turnips, grated*

1 *beet, grated*
  Russian dressing (see
  Index for recipe) or
  your favorite salad
  dressing

Arrange the spinach leaves in the bottom of a large glass salad bowl. Cover with a thin layer of grated carrot. Spread a thin layer of the grated turnip on top, followed by the grated beet. Top the pyramid with a spoonful of the salad dressing and serve. Serves 4.

RADISH SALAD

The radish, valued for its zippy flavor, is an excellent source of vitamin C and is ridiculously low in calories. Highly prized in Egypt in the days of the Pharaohs, as well as in talmudic days, time has not diminished its popularity. This preparation is especially delicious with chopped liver.

1 *black radish, peeled*
1 *onion*
1 *teaspoon vegetable oil or chicken fat*

Salt and pepper, to taste (optional)

Grate the radish and the onion into a small bowl. Add the fat and seasonings (if desired); mix well. Serves 2 to 4.

UNCOOKED BEET RELISH

A wonderful relish for meat or fish. The beets are a good source of calcium, potassium, and phosphorous; they also provide some vitamin A, vitamin C, and sodium. The herbs provide valuable trace minerals. The horseradish is an excellent source of vitamin C, and its pungent aroma helps clear the sinuses.

2 *cups shredded raw beets*
½ *cup lemon juice or cider vinegar*
¼ *cup vegetable oil*
½ *teaspoon mixed herbs (oregano, thyme, basil)*

2 *tablespoons Tamari soy sauce*
2 *tablespoons grated horseradish*

Combine all the ingredients; mix well. Keep refrigerated in a covered jar. Makes approximately 2¼ cups.

RAW CELERY SOUP

This exotic soup boasts an oriental flavor.

1 *cup fresh celery tops*
or ½ cup dried celery
flakes
½ *cup oatmeal*
1 *cup unsweetened*
coconut flakes
½ *cup sunflower seeds*

2 *cups hot water,*
vegetable broth, or
potato water
½ *teaspoon Tamari soy*
sauce
Sliced almonds
Parsley sprigs

Combine the celery and oatmeal in a blender and pulverize. (Use a little hot water or hot vegetable broth if necessary to start the action.) Pulverize the coconut and sunflower seeds separately. Combine the 2 mixtures, then add the hot liquid and the Tamari. Garnish with sliced almonds and parsley sprigs. Serves 4.

RAW APPLESAUCE

An uncooked applesauce with no artificial sweeteners.

1 *cup unsweetened*
pineapple juice

4 *large apples, cored*
and cut into chunks

Pour the pineapple juice into a blender; add the apple chunks in several installments. Blend to desired consistency. Delicious with potato latkes, and a very nice fruit for baby. Makes 4 cups.

APPLE DESSERT FOR TWO

1 *apple, unpeeled (if unsprayed)*
Juice of 1 orange
2 *tablespoons sunflower seeds*

1 *tablespoon unsweetened coconut flakes*

Grate the apple and cover immediately with the orange juice. Scoop it into 2 sherbet glasses and top with sunflower seeds and coconut. When making this for baby, omit the sunflower seeds and coconut or else grind them fine in a seed mill. Serves 2.

FRUIT-NUT UNCOOKED COOKIES

Made from rozhinkes and mandlin (raisins and almonds), with a nutritional boost from wheat sprouts.

½ *cup dried figs, dates, or apricots*
¾ *cup apple juice*
2 *cups finely ground walnuts or sunflower seeds*

2 *cups finely ground almonds*
½ *cup raisins*
½ *cup wheat sprouts*
Unsweetened coconut flakes

Place the dried fruit in a bowl. Cover with the apple juice; soak overnight. Blend the fruit and juice in a blender, in 2 batches if necessary. Mix the fruit mixture with the ground nuts and/or seeds, raisins, and sprouts. Shape like small cookies or into sticks like Tootsie Rolls and roll in the coconut. Makes 36 cookies.

BANANA-PRUNE PIE

Prunes are an excellent natural laxative. They are high in vitamin A, iron, and potassium and provide some of the B vitamins and some C. Search the specialty or health food shops for prunes that are unsulphured and unsprayed with mineral oil, which is used on much of our commercially-dried fruit to present a moist, shiny appearance. Mineral oil interferes with the body's utilization of fat-soluble vitamins: A, D, E, and K. If you have on hand prunes that have been sprayed, wash them in hot water and discard the water before soaking them.

24 *prunes*	2 *tablespoons honey,*
Water to cover	*or to taste*
½ *cup arrowroot starch*	1 *cup granola or*
of whole wheat	*graham cracker*
pastry flour	*crumbs*
¾ *cup orange juice*	*Scant milk*
1½ *cups prune juice*	2 *bananas, peeled and*
3 *tablespoons lemon*	*sliced*
juice	

Cover the prunes with the water and let sit overnight; remove the pits. Combine the arrowroot or flour with the juices and heat to blend; add the honey. Mix the granola or crumbs with a small amount of milk and spread the mixture over the bottom of 2 nine-inch pie plates. Place the slices of 1 banana and half the prunes over the granola or crumbs in each pie plate. Divide the liquid mixture in half and pour over the prunes and banana. Let cool. Serve with whipped cream. Serves 12 to 20.

DATE CONFECTION

The date has been considered one of the most important fruits almost since the dawn of time. It is one of the oldest of cultivated fruits and is renowned for its longevity. Our sages said that "Dates warm the body, satiate, act as a laxative, and strengthen, without adversely affecting the stomach." (*Biblical and Talmudic Medicine,* Sanhedrin Press.)

The date has a high natural sugar content, making it an excellent energy food. It was used as the equivalent of our K ration on the battlefield. Dates also provide some protein, iron, calcium, phosphorous, lots of potassium, vitamin A, a good supply of niacin, and traces of vitamins B1 (thiamine) and B2 (riboflavin).

Dates, pitted   *Sunflower seeds*
Water or fruit juice   *Unsweetened*
to cover   *coconut flakes*

Soak the dates in a little water or fruit juice for a few hours or overnight. Put the dates with the soak water or juice in a blender and purée. Pulverize some sunflower seeds and add enough to the date mixture to make the consistency of dough. Break off pieces the size of a hickory nut, and roll each one in coconut flakes. They satisfy one's sweet tooth in a healthy way, but heed the advice of one of our sages: "Everything in moderation. Eat nothing to excess, not even dates."

OAT-BRAN-ALMOND CEREAL

This cereal provides all the good things rolled into one. The bran provides an important source of fiber which, it has been found, can help you avoid cancer of the colon, diverticulosis, gall bladder problems, hemorrhoids, and other embarrassments you can live very nicely without.

Go creative with this basic recipe: add cinnamon, a banana, or grated apple.

2 *tablespoons bran*   1 *tablespoon raisins*
4 *tablespoons oat*   *Apple or pineapple*
  groats or oat flakes   *juice*
2 *tablespoons chopped*
  almonds

In a bowl, combine all the dry ingredients. Pour the fruit juice over all and let soak overnight in the refrigerator. Eat as is or liquefy in a blender. Makes 1 serving.

SWISS BREAKFAST CEREAL

This very satisfying cereal (the kind served at the Bircher-Benner Clinic, Switzerland) provides sufficient protein, vitamins, and minerals to keep your blood sugar stable for several hours, thus minimizing the craving for *nosherai* and sweets that upset one's metabolism and contribute to overweight.

1 *cup uncooked oat flakes*
1 *cup milk*
2 *oranges*
3 *medium-sized apples, grated*
2 *bananas, peeled and diced*
½ *cup chopped pecans*
2 *cups plain yogurt*
¼ *cup honey*
Raisins
4 *tablespoons wheat germ*

Pour the oats into a large bowl. Cover with milk and let stand for 30 minutes. Combine the rest of the ingredients and add to the oat mixture. Place in 4 bowls and garnish each with a few raisins and a tablespoon of wheat germ. Serves 4.

BANANA-ORANGE RAW JAM

The lively tart orange flavor of this jam complements the sweet mellow banana. No sweetening agent is needed because dried bananas are incredibly sweet. (Bananas are at their sweetest and most flavorful when they are speckled with brown "sugar" spots.)

Dried bananas have a fantastic amount of potassium, the mineral that is your heart's best friend (1,447 milligrams in 3½ ounces). They are very low in sodium, which tends to drive potassium out of body cells (only 4 milligrams in 3½ ounces).

½ *cup banana chips (see Index for recipe)*
¼ *cup orange juice*

Place the chips in a jar or glass and cover with the orange juice. Let soak in the refrigerator overnight. Then mash the soft bananas or whiz in a blender at medium speed for about 1 minute or until the mixture is smooth. Makes ½ cup.

APRICOT-ALMOND RAW JAM

Both apricots and almonds must have been considered by Hippocrates when he said, "Let food be your medicine." A half cup of dried apricots (65 grams) provides 3½ grams of protein; 3½ milligrams of blood-building iron; 8 milligrams of vitamin C; some of the B vitamins (especially niacin, which is very important to maintaining a pleasant disposition); and a whopping 7,000 international units of vitamin A, which helps your body fight infection and has recently been cited as an anti-cancer factor.

The almond has been prized since biblical days, when it was used both as a food and as a source for oil. It is also the symbol of the reawakening of the earth each spring. In Israel it bursts into bloom in January and the trees become delightfully fragrant and beautiful with their masses of pink and white blossoms.

The almond is also the symbol of one of the first miracles. When the rod of Aaron was made to blossom, it bore almonds. (Numbers 17:8).

Nutritionally, too, almonds are a miracle food. They are an excellent source of protein (24 grams per cup), very rich in potassium, iron, calcium, and phosphorous, and are a good source of essential fatty acids of the polyunsaturated type. They make an excellent complement to both apricots and raisins.

½ *cup dried apricots*	*Apple juice to cover*
6 *or 8 whole almonds*	*Grated orange peel*
½ *cup raisins*	*(optional)*

Place the apricots, almonds, and raisins in a jar. Cover with apple juice. Let stand for 24 hours in the refrigerator. Then place all of those ingredients in a blender, add the grated orange peel if desired, and whip until smooth. Makes 1 cup. Great on bread with cream cheese.

2

Kugels, Blintzes & Knishes

If you want to score points with your family, with your college kids home on vacation, with your friends, with your cousins and aunts who drop in—not for dinner, thank you, but maybe just for a little bite—dish up a kugel or some blintzes or knishes. The waves of joyful gustatory nostalgia which these dishes never fail to evoke will warm both their hearts and yours.

But, if you want to do a real good deed, give them some solid nutrition with every bite. You will add to the joy of entertaining when you provide kugels, blintzes, and knishes that are kind to the heart and arteries as well as to the palate.

How? Let me show you.

KUGELS

Let's start with lukshen kugels (noodle puddings).

Whole wheat noodles are available at many health food stores and at cooperatives. Eventually you may learn to use these noodles, but to get started on this adventure without turning your family off, it is better to use the noodles they are familiar with, and to enrich them yourself.

The philosophy behind good-nutrition cooking is simply to add to each food those nutrients which would have been there in the first place if that food had not been emasculated in the refining process.

Since wheat germ and bran have been removed from white flour, unbleached as well as bleached, use those health-builders whenever you use a white flour product. Wheat germ, remember, has the vitamin E and the potassium so necessary for heart health. Bran is an important source of fiber.

Until your family becomes accustomed to bran, start slowly. Kugels provide a good medium for bran for those who refuse to take it in other ways. If you have already provided bran at the breakfast table, you can skip it in your kugels—depending on how much you need. You are the best judge of that.

Dairy noodle kugels call for a lot of fat—butter and sour cream. The human body needs some fat, but not very much. Fat is needed for the utilization of calcium and fat-soluble vitamins such as A, D, E, and K. Fat is a troublemaker when it gangs up in clots in your arteries. In order to help prevent this eventuality, use lecithin granules, soy grits, or soy flour whenever you use fats. It has been shown in many research studies that soy lecithin emulsifies fat, keeps it flowing freely so you can enjoy its benefits without the hazards.

Please don't load your kugels with sugar, which is an enemy to your heart even though your favorite recipe no doubt calls for it. If your family is accustomed to sweet kugels, reduce the amount of sweetener gradually. Switch to honey instead of sugar and use half the amount the recipe calls for. Then gradually reduce the amount of honey as well. Soon your family will be unable to eat those kugels that well-meaning but unenlightened neighbors honor you with on special occasions.

Now, to some recipes.

MAMA'S CREAMY KUGEL

Here is my Mama's recipe for her dairy kugel, only slightly revised.

8 ounces fine noodles	3 tablespoons soy grits
Salted water	or lecithin granules
¼ pound butter	1 cup milk
¼ cup sour cream	3 eggs, well beaten
½ cup plain yogurt	Pinch of sea salt or
8 ounces cottage	kelp, to taste
cheese	Dash of cinnamon
2 tablespoons wheat	Sesame seeds for
germ	garnish

Boil the noodles in salted water and drain. Melt the butter in an 8 x 10-inch baking dish. Add the butter to the noodles, leaving a little in the dish. Add the rest of the ingredients except the sesame seeds; mix to combine well. Put the mixture in the hot baking dish. Sprinkle on some sesame seeds. Bake in a preheated 350-degree F. oven for 1 hour or until nicely browned. Delicious served with sour cream or yogurt and crushed strawberries. Serves 6 to 10.

PINEAPPLE WHOLE WHEAT LUKSHEN KUGEL

Try this dairy kugel made with whole wheat noodles. The noodles cook up almost white and have a more robust, satisfying flavor than the white variety. Of course, this kugel can also be made with white noodles. If so, add 3 tablespoons of wheat germ to the ingredients.

8 ounces medium	3 eggs, beaten
whole wheat noodles	¼ cup honey (or a little
Salted water	less)
1 pound cottage	4 tablespoons butter,
cheese	melted
1 cup sour cream or	½ cup raisins
yogurt	1 teaspoon vanilla
2 tablespoons lecithin	extract
granules (optional)	Cinnamon
1 cup milk	
1 can (20 ounces)	
crushed pineapple,	
drained	

Boil the noodles in salted water and drain. Preheat the oven to 350 degrees F. Combine all the ingredients, including the noodles, in a large bowl. Pour into a well-buttered 11 x 14-inch baking dish. Bake for 1 hour or until the top is golden and crusty. Serves 8 to 10.

Low-Calorie Dairy Kugel

A delicious kugel you can enjoy without committing caloric hara-kiri. The pectin in the apple and the yogurt tend to lower cholesterol levels. Pectin also helps rid the body of lead.

8 *ounces medium noodles*
Salted water
⅔ *cup milk plus 2 teaspoons dry milk powder (use the spray dried)*
1 *cup plain yogurt*
8 *ounces cottage cheese*
1 *unpeeled apple, grated (there's a lot of pectin in the peel)*
2 *tablespoons honey or pure maple syrup*
¼ *cup wheat germ*
½ *teaspoon vanilla extract*
Juice of ½ lemon
½ *cup unsulphured raisins*
4 *eggs*
2 *tablespoons butter*
Cinnamon
3 *tablespoons chopped walnuts*

Boil the noodles in salted water and drain. (Try artichoke noodles if you can find them. They're very low in calories and high in nutrients.) In a bowl, combine the milk, milk powder, and yogurt. Add the cottage cheese to this mixture; mix well. Add the grated apple, honey or syrup, wheat germ, vanilla, lemon juice, and raisins. Fold into the noodles.

Preheat the oven to 325 degrees F. Beat the eggs well and reserve. Heat an 8 x 10-inch baking dish in the oven for 10 minutes. Melt the 2 tablespoons of butter in the heated dish. Pour in the cheese-noodle misture. Pour the beaten eggs on top. Sprinkle with cinnamon and the chopped walnuts. Bake for about 1 hour, until nicely browned. Serves 6 to 10

HIGH-PROTEIN FLEISHIG NOODLE KUGEL

Fantastic with chicken and so easy to make, this kugel is light as a soufflé, with a crunchy crust and a meaty flavor. The wheat germ and bran give this dish extra nutritional value.

8 *ounces fine noodles*
Salted water
6 *eggs, well beaten*
2 *tablespoons bran*
soaked in 4 table-
spoons of the water
drained from the
cooked noodles
½ *cup wheat germ*
2 *tablespoons lecithin*
granules

1 *teaspoon salt or kelp*
Dash of cinnamon
Freshly ground white
pepper, to taste
4 *tablespoons*
vegetable oil or
chicken fat
Sesame seeds

Boil the noodles in salted water and drain. Preheat the oven to 400 degrees F. Add the beaten eggs, the soaked bran, wheat germ, lecithin granules, salt or kelp, cinnamon, and pepper. Mix well. Heat 2 tablespoons of the oil or chicken fat in an 8 x 10-inch baking dish. Pour in the mixture and top with lots of sesame seeds. Drizzle the remaining 2 tablespoons of oil or chicken fat on top. Bake at 400 degrees F. for 15 minutes, then lower to 350 degrees F. and bake for 35 minutes or until browned. Serves 8 to 10.

BLENDER POTATO KUGEL

This crisp-crusted kugel, a perfect partner for roast chicken, is a wonderful Sabbath or holiday side dish. It's moist and savory, but by using a blender you don't have to grate the potatoes and risk bruising your knuckles.

Potatoes are a good source of fiber, are a good energy food, and, believe it or not, are low in calories. There are only 90 calories in a 5-ounce potato, which also provides 20 milligrams of vitamin C, as much as you would get in half a glass of tomato juice, as much protein as you would get in half a cup of milk, and much more iron and niacin. A real nutritional bargain.

3 *eggs, beaten*
1 *medium-sized onion, diced*
3 *large unpeeled potatoes, scrubbed and diced*
⅓ *cup wheat germ or matzo meal (preferably made from whole wheat matzo)*

1 *tablespoon potato flour (optional)*
⅛ *teaspoon white pepper*
1 *teaspoon salt*
3 *tablespoons oil or chicken fat*

In a bowl, combine the eggs, diced onion, and diced potato. Pour a small amount of the mixture into a blender and whiz at high speed until puréed. Empty the purée into a large bowl and repeat the process until all of the egg-onion-potato mixture has been puréed. Add the wheat germ or matzo meal, the potato flour, the seasonings, and the oil or chicken fat. Turn into a well-greased, preheated 9 x 9-inch baking dish. Bake in a 350-degree F. oven for about 1 hour, until brown and crisp. Serve with applesauce. Serves 6 to 8.

POTATONIK

A yeast-risen potato kugel.

3 *tablespoons dry yeast*
1 *cup warm water*
5 *to 6 cups whole wheat bread flour*
3 *large potatoes*
3 *eggs*

1 *onion*
1 *teaspoon salt*
⅛ *teaspoon pepper*
⅛ *teaspoon cinnamon*
4 *tablespoons vegetable oil*

Dissolve the yeast in the warm water. Set aside to proof, then add 1 cup of the flour. Cover and place in warm spot until it doubles in bulk.

Scrub the potatoes and either grate by hand or in the blender or food processor, in installments, with the eggs and onion. Add the seasonings.

Put the remaining flour in a large bowl. Make a well in the center. Add the yeast mixture and the grated potato mixture. Blend everything well. Cover the bowl and set in warm place to rise for 2 to 3 hours.

Heat two 9 x 12-inch baking dishes. Put 2 tablespoons of oil in each till it is very hot. Pour half the mixture into each baking dish and bake in a 375-degree F. oven for about an hour, until nicely browned. Serves 6.

CARROT KUGEL

A sweet kugel created by Shoshana Hayman, of Teaneck, New Jersey. She serves it with chicken and a big salad. Good hot or cold.

2 *large carrots, grated*
½ *cup vegetable oil*
2 *eggs, separated*
½ *cup honey*
1 *cup whole wheat flour*
½ *teaspoon baking powder*

1 *teaspoon vanilla extract*
3 *teaspoons grated lemon rind*
Handful of raisins (optional)
Handful of chopped nuts (optional)

In a bowl, combine the carrots, oil, egg yolks, and honey. Add the flour, baking powder, vanilla, grated rind, and raisins and nuts (if desired). Beat the egg whites until stiff and fold in. Transfer the mixture to an oiled loaf pan. Bake in a preheated 350-degree F. oven for approximately 35 minutes, until nicely browned. Serves 6.

BLINTZES

Blintzes can be enjoyed any day of the year, but it is traditional to enjoy them especially on Shavuot, when dairy foods are stressed. Shavout commemorates the giving of the Torah at Mount Sinai, at which time the Children of Israel were commanded to eat only kosher meat. But they had neither kosher utensils nor kosher meat, so they had to make do with dairy foods. And so the blintz was invented, a dairy food that sustained and delighted.

You will find these recipes a little different from the usual, which are made from white flour and are oversweetened with sugar. These blintzes are made with whole wheat flour and no sugar at all. Only a tiny little bit of honey is added to sharpen the flavors. They are tender, wholesome, and delicious. Enjoy them in good health.

BLINTZES

Nothing says "welcome to our table" like a plateful of snugly-wrapped blintzes (crêpes), each tender crust enfolding a tasty filling of cheese, potatoes, or fruit.

VERY THIN BLINTZ BLANKETS:

4 *eggs, slightly beaten*	½ *cup whole wheat*
1⅓ *cups milk*	*pastry flour*
	3 *teaspoons butter*

In a bowl, beat the eggs, milk, and flour until a smooth batter is formed. Refrigerate for about 2 hours. In a 7-inch skillet heat ¼ teaspoon of the butter over medium heat until it is bubbly but not yet browned. Pour about 3 tablespoons of the batter into the skillet. Tilt the pan to coat the bottom evenly. (Pour excess batter back into the batter bowl.) Cook over medium heat until lightly browned. Bump the bletl (blintz blanket) out onto a tea towel. Fold the towel over it to prevent drying out. Repeat, adding a little more butter to the skillet only when necessary. Makes about 16 very thin bletlach.

NOTE: You can freeze extra bletlach. Separate them with wax paper and place them on a paper plate. Cover with another paper plate, inverted, and staple or clip together.

FILLING: Use the cheese filling in the recipe below, or create a blueberry-cheese filling by adding a tablespoon of blueberries to the cheese filling for each blintz to be made. Or use a potato or kasha filling, or try a mixture of stir-fried vegetables cut into very small pieces and nicely seasoned. Sauté in a greased skillet on both sides until browned or, as an alternative to frying, place the filled blintzes in a single layer in several buttered baking dishes, place dabs of butter atop each blintz and bake at 350 degrees F. for 15 minutes or until golden. (Baking is much more healthful than frying.)

NOTE: You can make any kind of blintz in advance and refrigerate or freeze before the frying or baking stage. It's a good idea to bring them to room temperature before cooking.

COTTAGE AND CREAM CHEESE BLINTZES

For a lovely dairy meal, for a coffee klatch, or for a breakfast that will get sleepyheads out of bed, try these rich, creamy cheese blintzes.

Serve them with yogurt, which has fewer calories, less fat, and more protein than sour cream. (Yogurt also provides helpful bacteria for the colon.) For "I don't like yogurt-niks," mix some yogurt into the sour cream. Gradually increase the proportion of yogurt to sour cream, until you can serve it half and half.

BLINTZ BLANKETS:

4 *eggs*

¼ *teaspoon salt*

1½ *cups whole wheat pastry flour*

1½ *tablespoons butter, melted*

2 *cups milk*

Combine all ingredients in a blender, or with an electric mixer, until a rich batter is formed. If it seems too thick, add a bit more milk. Make the blintz blankets following the directions in the blintz recipe above.

FILLING:

8 *ounces cream*	1 *tablespoon honey*
cheese, softened	1 *teaspoon vanilla*
1 *pound cottage*	*extract*
cheese	*Dash of cinnamon*
2 *egg yolks*	*Grated lemon rind*

Mix all ingredients well and the filling is ready to use. Place 1 rounded tablespoonful of filling in the center of each bletl. Fold over both sides and roll, enclosing the filling in the bletl. Bake at 350 degrees F. for 15 minutes or until golden (or sauté if you wish). Makes 24 to 28 blintzes.

HIGH-PROTEIN, LOW-CALORIE
CHEESE BLINTZES

In this recipe, tender blankets enclose a cinnamon-orange-flavored cheese filling enriched with granola.

BLINTZ BLANKETS:

2 *eggs*	¼ *cup soy flour*
1 *cup plus 2 table-*	½ *cup whole wheat*
spoons water	*pastry flour*
¼ *cup arrowroot starch*	*Butter*

First make the batter, which can also be used for pareve or meat fillings. Beat the eggs; add the water, starch, and flour, and beat until smooth. The batter should have the consistency of light cream. (The batter can also be made in a blender or processor.)

Heat a 6-inch non-stick frying pan over medium heat till a drop of water bounces on it. Rub the pan with a very thin film of butter. That's all the butter you need to make all the bletlach. Drop about 2 tablespoons' worth of batter onto the pan and tip it quickly so the batter spreads thinly over the entire pan. Return any excess to the batter bowl. Cook on 1 side only until the top begins to peel away from the pan. Bump it out, bottom side up, onto a clean towel. Cover immediately with another towel to prevent it from drying out. Repeat this procedure till the batter is used up. Be sure to stir up the batter frequently and add more water as it thickens. Makes about 16 bletlach.

FILLING:

¾ *pound cottage cheese*	½ *teaspoon grated lemon rind*
2 *tablespoons cream cheese*	½ *teaspoon vanilla extract*
1 *egg*	⅛ *teaspoon cinnamon*
1 *teaspoon honey*	1 *tablespoon finely ground granola*
Pinch of salt	

To make the filling, combine the cheeses, egg, and the rest of the ingredients in a blender, or with an electric mixer, or by hand.

To fill the bletlach, place a heaping tablespoonful of cheese mixture onto each, roll once, then fold the sides over toward the center and roll again. The filling should be nicely enclosed. Place in a lightly buttered baking dish, brush with a tiny bit of butter, and bake at 350 degrees F. for 15 minutes. The oven does not have to be preheated. (The blintzes can also be sautéed.) Makes 16 High-Protein, Low-Calorie Cheese Blintzes.

POTATO BLINTZES

These potato-filled blintzes are similar to knishes, but have a softer blanket. They are more robust than cheese blintzes, so serve some of each for variety and balance when entertaining.

FILLING:

2 *eggs*	*Salt and freshly ground pepper, to taste*
6 *medium-sized unpeeled potatoes, scrubbed, boiled, and mashed*	3 *medium-sized onions, minced*
2 *tablespoons wheat germ*	*Butter, vegetable oil, or chicken fat*

Place the eggs in a blender; add the potatoes, the wheat germ, and salt and pepper. Mince the onions and sauté in butter for a dairy meal, in oil for a pareve meal, in chicken fat (you should be so lucky) for a meat meal. Add the onions to the blender and process until the mixture is fluffy. The filling is now ready to use. Makes enough filling for 12 to 16 blintzes.

Make the bletlach (blintz blankets) following any of the preceding recipes, adjusting the quantities of ingredients accordingly. Use a heaping tablespoonful of potato filling on each and roll up. If you want to make a larger quantity, figure on 1 large potato for every 3 blintzes. Serve with sour cream or yogurt for dairy, with gravy for meat, or serve them plain. They're moist and delicious any way.

To bake, brush with butter or appropriate fat and bake in a preheated 350-degree F. oven for about 15 minutes.

FLEISHIG BLINTZES

A meat-meal specialty.

3 *cups chopped meat* *or chicken*	¼ *teaspoon freshly* *ground black pepper*
1 *egg plus 1 egg yolk*	3 *tablespoons chicken* *gravy or soup stock*

Combine the ingredients and proceed as for the Cottage and Cream Cheese Blintzes above, but use water instead of milk and oil instead of butter for the bletlach. Makes enough filling for approximately 24 to 28 bletlach.

APPLE DESSERT BLINTZES

Serve with yogurt or a mixture of yogurt and sour cream for a dairy meal. For a pareve meal, serve with applesauce blended with tofu.

3 *cups apples,*
scrubbed but
unpeeled
2 *egg whites*
½ *cup raisins*

4 *tablespoons chopped*
walnuts or pecans
1 *teaspoon cinnamon*
2 *tablespoons honey*

Core and chop or grate the apples. Beat the egg white lightly. Combine all ingredients and proceed the same as for the Cottage and Cream Cheese Blintzes above. Makes enough filling for approximately 24 to 28 bletlach.

CHERRY OR BLUEBERRY DESSERT BLINTZES

2½ *cups canned sour*
cherries, drained, or
fresh cherries, pitted,
or fresh blueberries
½ *teaspoon cinnamon*
½ *teaspoon almond*
extract

2 *tablespoons*
arrowroot starch or
whole wheat flour
½ *cup unsweetened*
coconut, ground to
a powder
Honey, to taste

Combine the ingredients and proceed as for the Cottage and Cream Cheese Blintzes above. Makes enough filling for approximately 24 to 28 bletlach.

ORANGE-FLAVORED DESSERT BLINTZES

Here, an orange-flavored cheese-and-nut mixture enclosed in an orange-yogurt crêpe is served with a lovely, smooth orange sauce, which adds a touch of elegance that makes this a wonderful party dish.

BLINTZ BATTER:

2 *eggs*
¼ *cup orange juice*
¼ *cup plain yogurt*
¼ *cup milk*

1 *tablespoon vegetable*
oil or melted butter
¼ *teaspoon salt*
(optional)

Combine all ingredients in a blender and process until the batter is smooth—about 1 minute. Scrape down the sides with a rubber spatula and blend for another few seconds or until all the dry ingredients are incorporated. To make the batter using an electric mixing machine or by hand, first beat the eggs in a large bowl; add the rest of the ingredients and beat until smooth. Let stand at room temperature while you prepare the filling and the sauce.

FILLING:

1 *cup cottage cheese*
1 *egg*
1 *tablespoon honey, or to taste*
⅓ *teaspoon grated orange peel*

3 *tablespoons finely ground granola*
⅓ *cup chopped walnuts*

In a medium-sized bowl, mix the cottage cheese, egg, honey, orange peel, and ground granola. Beat until smooth. Add the walnuts. Refrigerate while you make the orange sauce and the blintz blankets.

ORANGE SAUCE:

1 *tablespoon arrow-root powder*
2 *tablespoons orange juice*

1 *cup orange juice*
2 *tablespoons honey*

In a small saucepan, combine the arrowroot powder and the 2 tablespoons of orange juice. Mix to a smooth paste. Add the cup of orange juice gradually, mixing all the while. Add the honey. Cook over moderate heat, stirring constantly until the mixture thickens. Remove from the heat and set aside.

To make the blankets, heat a 7-inch skillet and brush it lightly with butter. Proceed according to instructions in previous recipes. If the batter gets too thick, add more milk and stir it up.

Place a heaping tablespoonful of filling on each blanket and roll up. Brush each filled blintz very lightly with melted butter and bake in a 350-degree F. oven for 15 minutes. Cover with the orange sauce and serve with a dish of yogurt. Makes 12 Orange-Flavored Dessert Blintzes.

Variation: Instead of brushing the blintzes with butter, cover them with the orange sauce and bake until piping hot in a 350-degree F. oven (about 10 minutes).

Blintz Loaf

As a change from individual blintzes, try this delicious dairy loaf. A wonderful addition to a buffet table.

¼ *cup butter, melted*
3 *ounces cream cheese*
1 *pound cottage cheese*
3 *eggs, lightly beaten*
½ *teaspoon lemon juice*
½ *teaspoon vanilla extract*

½ *cup whole wheat pastry flour*
½ *teaspoon baking powder*
4 *tablespoons honey*
Butter for the pan
Cinnamon

Combine the butter, cheeses, and eggs in a blender or with an electric mixer. Add the lemon juice, vanilla, flour, baking powder, and honey. Pour into a buttered 8 x 8-inch baking pan. Dust with cinnamon. Bake in a preheated 325-degree F. oven for 40 to 50 minutes or until nicely browned. Serve with sour cream or yogurt or a combination of both. Serves 6 to 8.

Blintz Soufflé

This is an ideal dish for a company brunch or buffet. The egg sauce makes it easy to reheat previously made blintzes for serving a crowd. It also enhances the protein value, making this a very satisfactory one-dish meal.

¼ *pound butter*

6 *filled blintzes (made*
following any of the
preceding recipes)

3 *eggs, beaten until*
frothy

1 *teaspoon vanilla*
extract

2 *tablespoons honey*

¼ *teaspoon salt*
(optional)

2 *tablespoons orange*
juice

1 *cup sour cream or*
plain yogurt

Melt the butter in a 5 x 9-inch casserole. Roll the filled blintzes in
the butter. Combine the remaining ingredients. Pour this mixture
over the blintzes. Bake in a preheated 350-degree F. oven for 1
hour or until lightly browned. Serves 3 to 6.

BLINTZ MUFFINS

A high-protein snack great for entertaining and for lunch boxes.
The muffins may be served fresh from the oven or at room
temperature.

1 *pound cottage*
cheese

2 *tablespoons sour*
cream

4 *tablespoons butter,*
softened

2 *tablespoons honey*

½ *cup whole wheat*
pastry flour

2 *teaspoons baking*
powder

1 *teaspoon vanilla*
extract

3 *eggs, beaten*

½ *teaspoon vegetable*
oil mixed with ½
teaspoon liquid
lecithin

Preheat the oven to 350 degrees F. In a large bowl, combine the
cheese and sour cream. Blend in the butter and honey. In a
separate bowl, combine the flour and baking powder. Add to the
cheese mixture; add the vanilla and eggs and combine well.
Grease muffin tins with the mixture of oil and liquid lecithin. Fill
and bake for 25 minutes. Makes 12 muffins.

KNISHES

In Israel, knishes are sold by vendors on Purim, when crowds are singing, dancing, and eating in the streets. There's something about the crispy crust and the hot flavorful filling that enhances the mood for merrymaking.

In the United States, knishes are frequently served at cocktail parties and on festive occasions. They are usually made from white flour, which lacks the life-giving nutrients of wheat germ. In addition, they are highly salted and contain too much fat for good health.

If you want to make a meal very special, serve knishes made from whole wheat and soy flours. And cut down on the salt and the fat. Even noneaters—the kind who hang around the table just for the conversation—will eat them. These recipes insure that your knishes will give a nutritional boost along with their irresistible crunch. Whether you fill them with cheese, potato, liver, kasha, or rice, you can use the recipe below for the crust.

KNISH CRUST

This crust is more than a blanket for a savory filling. The combination of wheat and soy make it a wholesome complete protein in its own right.

1½ cups sifted whole wheat pastry flour
2 tablespoons soy flour
½ teaspoon salt (omit if you're on a low-salt diet)
1 egg

¼ cup butter, melted, or vegetable oil
6 tablespoons (⅜ of a cup) warm water
Whole wheat pastry flour

In a large bowl, combine the flours and salt. In a separate bowl, beat the egg; add the fat (butter for dairy fillings, oil for pareve or meat fillings) and water; then add to the flour mixture. Knead lightly until the dough is no longer sticky. Form the dough into a ball and place it in a greased (use oil) bowl slightly larger than the ball of dough. Cover and set in a warm place for 1 hour.

Put an old tablecloth on your kitchen table. Rub some flour into it. Divide the dough in half. Roll out each half as thin as possible. Stretch and pull carefully until the dough is as thin as tissue paper and you can see the pattern of the tablecloth through it. If it should tear, patch it with a piece from the edge and roll it in.

Place filling (see recipes below) in a thick line across 1 end of each sheet of rolled out dough about 4 inches from the edge nearest you. Bend this end over the filling. Raise the tablecloth and let it roll away from you.

Preheat the oven to 375 degrees F. With the edge of your little finger, start to cut the roll into 1-inch pieces. Use a knife to finish the cutting. Pull the ends of the dough over the filling and pat it between your hands. At this point, my mother would say, "Be a knish."

Grease a cookie sheet with a mixture of ½ teaspoon liquid lecithin and ½ teaspoon vegetable oil, or line the cookie sheet with parchment paper. Place the knishes carefully on the prepared cookie sheet—about ½ inch apart. Bake for 45 minutes or until crisp, light brown, and tempting. Makes 12 to 16 knishes; serves 4 to 6.

If you plan to freeze the knishes for later use, bake them for 30 minutes, allow to cool, then freeze.

FILLINGS FOR KNISHES

The recipes below will yield enough filling for the Knish Crust recipe above.

POTATO FILLING (FLEISHIG):

2 *large onions, minced*
2 *tablespoons chicken fat*
Grieben (quantity to taste)

4 *large or 6 medium-sized potatoes, boiled and mashed*
1 *egg*
Salt and freshly ground pepper to taste

Sauté the onions in the chicken fat till golden. Chop the grieben into crumbs in a wooden bowl. Add the hot mashed potatoes, the sautéed onions, egg, and seasonings. Mix well and the filling is ready to use.

POTATO FILLING (MILCHIG):

Follow the same recipe as above but substitute butter for the chicken fat and omit the grieben. Chop some soy nuts in the wooden bowl in place of the grieben, and proceed as above. Soy nuts are a source of lecithin, which emulsifies cholesterol and can prevent large fatty deposits from building up on the artery walls.

CHEESE FILLING (UNSWEET):

3 *tablespoons butter*
1 *large onion, diced*
1 *pound cottage, pot, farmer, or ricotta cheese*
¼ *cup wheat germ*
2 *eggs (if using cottage cheese, use only 1 egg)*

In a skillet, melt the butter. Add the diced onion and sauté lightly. In a bowl, combine the cheese, wheat germ, and eggs; add the sautéed onion, combine well, and the filling is ready to use.

CHEESE FILLING (SWEET):

1 *pound cottage cheese*
1 *egg*
2 *tablespoons wheat germ*
1 *tablespoon soy grits (optional)*
1½ *teaspoons grated lemon rind*
¼ *teaspoon cinnamon*
1 *tablespoonhoney*
½ *cup raisins*
1 *tablespoon plain yogurt or sour cream*

In a large bowl, combine the ingredients in the order given. Mix well and the filling is ready to use.

KASHA FILLING:

Kasha is roasted buckwheat. It is not really a grain, but is related to rhubarb. Kasha is rich in iron, contains almost all the B vitamins, is a good source of calcium, and is considered a curative plant because of its high content of rutin, a bioflavonoid that combats capillary fragility. Many physicians prescribe rutin for circulatory problems, varicose veins, and especially hemorrhoids. It's nice to know that a dish so tasty can do so many good things for you.

1 *cup kasha*	½ *teaspoon salt*
(buckwheat groats)	2 *onions*
1 *egg*	*Butter, vegetable oil,*
2 *cups boiling water*	*or chicken fat*

In a bowl, combine the kasha and egg. Put in a hot oven to brown, or brown in a hot dry skillet. If browning on top of the stove, keep stirring until the kernels are separated and toasted. Add the 2 cups of boiling water and the salt; cover and cook over low heat for about 40 minutes. Meanwhile, mince the onions and sauté in butter, oil, or chicken fat. Add to the kasha, and the filling is ready to use.

3

Meat & Poultry
Main Dishes

Meat on the table used to be a sign of "good times" or special occasions.

Back in the shtetl when Mrs. Bloom asked Mrs. Goldberg over the back fence if she could borrow her meat pot, the immediate reaction was an expression of delight and a mazel tov.

"How did you know?" Mrs. Bloom would ask in surprise. "It only just happened!"

"How did I know? You never have meat except on Shabbos and *yontiff*. This is an ordinary weekday! So you must be celebrating. What could you have to celebrate with your husband sick and your son without a job? So it must be your daughter is engaged. So mazel tov. *Zoll zein mit glick*. Here is the meat pot."

This is a scene from a play we have produced many times here in Allentown, Pennsylvania, depicting Jewish life then and now. We call it *The Swing of the Pendulum*.

Well, the pendulum has swung again. Meat is no longer considered the indispensable food for the good life. And, certainly, for good health one should take the emphasis off meat. Why? Several reasons.

Forty percent of the nation's cancer deaths are tied to the high levels of meat, fat, and calories in the American diet. This is what researchers told a government-sponsored conference on nutritional factors and cancer (October 15-30, 1978).

DES, the synthetic female hormone that was implicated as the cause of vaginal cancer in daughters of women who took it when they were pregnant, was fed to cattle and sheep as a growth stimulant for almost 30 years. For ten years the FDA tried to block its use but was stymied by the drug industry. An FDA ban was finally instituted on November 1, 1979. However, two manufacturers are seeking to overturn the ban.

If the ban is overturned, we will again have DES residues in our meat. And even if DES is successfully withheld, that doesn't insure that our meat is safe. Other potentially dangerous substances are already replacing DES. One of them, Synovex, a hormone-like substance that has been shown to be carcinogenic, is currently being used as a growth promoter. So is Estradiol 17B, a female hormone, and Androgen, a male hormone used to fatten lambs.

Meat from organically-raised animals—free from hormones, antibiotics, and insecticides—is now available at many health food stores. However, though the animals from which this meat comes were tenderly raised, they were not ritually slaughtered. It's a little more difficult to get organic meat that is kosher. But it is possible.

I know of an organic cattle breeder who will sell meat on the hoof and will provide a schochet to do the slaughtering in an approved slaughterhouse. The butchering you must do yourself, or find a butcher willing to cut it up for you.

If you are interested in purchasing the whole animal, kosher and organic, contact the Snow Hill Farm, Coatsville, Pennsylvania 19320. They will buy back from you the cuts of meat that are nonkosher. If you have a large family, or can join forces with other families, it would pay to do this, not only for health benefits but budget-wise.

I suggest, too, that you use less beef and more lamb. Lamb is just about the last of the range-fed animals. Only in the winter are lambs sent to the feed lots to be fattened on hormones. New Zealand lamb is always range fed. But I haven't been able to find any New Zealand lamb with a kosher hechsher.

It is my feeling that any kosher butcher who goes in for organically-raised meat will make himself a fortune and do a great service as well. We talk so much about survival. Let's face it, survival starts in the kitchen.

In general, it is best to cut down on your consumption of meat by making a little go a long way. And put the emphasis on the *organ* meats: they are far more nutritious than the muscle meats.

My butcher, who has been in cahoots with me for years, adds heart to my chuck to make up my special hamburger mix: two parts chuck and one part heart. It makes a juicy, tasty mixture which my children loved (and still do) and so did their friends who came for homework and stayed for dinner. I must confess, I never told them what was in it. Many people have an emotional hangup when it comes to eating organ meats. But, it is possible to serve hamburger every night in a different guise and never hear a complaint.

When you add heart to your hamburger, you greatly reduce the amount of fat, improve the quality of the protein, increase the vitamin content, and lower the calorie count. Chuck loads you up with ten times more fat than heart, half as much iron, and half as much vitamin A. Heart is also much richer in the B vitamins. Add up all these values and heart is far better for *your* heart.

HEART IN TOMATO SAUCE

Try this old-fashioned recipe for sweet and sour heart. It's delicious served with kasha varnishkas or mamaligge (cornmeal mush).

2 veal hearts (the younger the animal, the less chance of its having been to the feed lot for hormone feeding)

2 tablespoons vegetable oil or chicken fat

1½ cups tomato, cut into chunks

¼ cup water or stock

½ cup cider vinegar

¼ cup honey

2 tablespoons whole wheat pastry flour or arrowroot starch

3 tablespoons water

2 tablespoons lecithin granules

¼ teaspoon paprika

Trim away the gristle and cut the heart into cubes. Heat the oil or chicken fat in a heavy pot like a Dutch oven. Sauté the heart over moderate heat for 5 minutes. Add the tomato, water or stock, vinegar, and honey. Cover and simmer for about 40 minutes or until the heart is fork-tender. Mix the flour or arrowroot with the 3 tablespoons of water; add this mixture to the heart mixture. Cook and stir until the gravy thickens. Add the lecithin and paprika. Serves 8 very nicely.

HAVE YOU HAD ANY MILTZ LATELY?

You won't find it on the menu of your favorite restaurant, and you won't find it mentioned in most cookbooks. Too bad. Miltz is one of the most nutritious of meats, very rich in iron and in the B vitamin niacin. It is also delicious. You can actually feel its strengthening effects as the juices titillate your taste buds. I admit that not everybody likes it as much as I do.

Miltz is the spleen of the animal. When I make it, I always have an alternate dish ready for those who just can't stand the stuff. Miltz is that kind of dish, as evidenced by the cheers and boos for it that poured into Craig Claiborne of the *New York Times* when he mentioned it in one of his columns.

"When I saw the word *miltz*,"wrote one reader, "my body reacted with a joyful gustatory nostalgia."

So did mine!

STUFFED MILTZ

This is the way I was taught to make it—rich and hearty.

1 *miltz*	2 *cups water or stock*
1 *egg*	1 *large or 2 small*
1 *cup raw coarse or*	*onions, minced*
medium kasha	1 *tablespoon chicken*
(buckwheat groats)	*fat*

Ask the butcher to make a pocket in the miltz. Mix the egg with the kasha and toast it in the oven or in a skillet on top of the stove. In a saucepan, bring 1 cup of the water or stock to a boil. When the kasha is toasted, pour ½ cup of the boiling water or stock over it and let it steam over low heat or in a warm oven for 10 minutes. Sauté the onion in the chicken fat; add half to the kasha. Stuff this mixture into the miltz and sew tightly.

Put the remaining sautéed onion in a roasting pan. Put the stuffed miltz on top and add the remaining 1 cup of water or stock. Cover and place in a preheated 325-degree F. oven. Baste occasionally with the pan drippings, adding more of the boiling water as necessary. Bake for 2½ hours or until brown and tender. With a salad this is a memorable meal for 6 to 8 miltz-lovers.

A BALEBUSTA USES BRAINS

When I ask my butcher if he has any brains, he usually says, "If I had any brains, would I be a butcher? Maybe next week I will find a calf with some brains. I'll save them for you."

If you're a smart balebusta, you'll use brains. They contain protein of a superior quality and are one of the richest sources of the B vitamin choline, which plays an important role in the way you utilize cholesterol.

Adelle Davis, in her book *Let's Cook It Right*, cites an experiment in which a group of children were given brain daily over a five-year period starting in infancy. They were fed no other meat. When they entered school, they had the highest I.Q.'s ever recorded in the school they attended, and each one ranked in the genius class.

Now, new research at M.I.T. reveals that choline has a direct effect on brain function, bringing about almost immediate effects on memory.

So, the smart thing to do is to use brains. They're good for your heart and your head.

I concede that many people, even members of my family, recoil at the idea of eating brains. So I cook the brains in chicken or vegetable soup, then I purée them with some of the soup in the blender and watch with secret glee as they spoon the soup down, getting smarter with every mouthful. There are many ways to fix brains, ways that hide their identity but don't disguise their virtues.

Many recipes call for brains that have been precooked. Whether you use calf, lamb, or beef brains, the method is the same. Put them in a saucepan with cold water to cover. Add ½ teaspoon of salt and 2 tablespoons of vinegar. Cook for 25 minutes over moderate heat. Remove from the water, cool slightly, then remove the membrane.

Try some of these recipes on your family.

BRAIN FRITTERS

2 eggs
⅓ cup whole wheat
  flour
3 tablespoons cold
  water
¼ teaspoon paprika
¼ teaspoon kelp

Pinch of white
  pepper
1 set (approximately
  ½ pound) cooked
  brains
Vegetable oil

In a bowl, beat the eggs. Stir in the flour and water to make a batter. Add the seasonings and mix. Slice the brains and dip the slices into the batter. Sauté in hot oil until browned. Serves 4.

BRAINS IN TOMATO SAUCE

A rich and flavorful dish.

2 tablespoons chopped
  onion
2 tablespoons
  vegetable oil
1 cup tomato sauce
¼ pound mushrooms,
  sliced

½ cup chopped celery
Sea salt or kelp and
  white pepper, to taste
1 tablespoon rice flour
  (optional)
1 pound cooked
  brains, cubed

In a pot, cook the onion in the oil until transparent. Add the tomato sauce, mushrooms, and celery. Cover and cook over medium heat for about 20 minutes. Season and thicken with rice flour if necessary. Add the brains to the sauce. Simmer until completely heated. Serves 4.

BRAINS VINAIGRETTE

Smooth, rich, and savory.

⅓ *cup wine vinegar*
⅓ *cup olive oil*
¼ *teaspoon prepared mustard*
1 *teaspoon Tamari soy sauce*
1 *set (approximately ½ pound) cooked brains, calf or lamb*

1 *hard-cooked egg, finely chopped*
1 *teaspoon chopped fresh dill*
1 *teaspoon chopped fresh chives*

Mix a marinade of equal parts wine vinegar and olive oil; stir in the mustard; add the Tamari. Slice the brains and marinate them for several hours. Serve slightly chilled. Sprinkle on the chopped egg, dill, and chives immediately before serving. Serves 4.

MOCK OYSTER COCKTAIL

A nutritious food however eaten, brains contain rare amino acids when eaten raw. This recipe is suggested by Pat Conolly in *A Mini Guide to Living Foods,* published by the Price-Pottenger Nutrition Foundation (P.O. Box 2614, La Mesa, California 92041). This dish is believed to be remarkably similar to oyster in taste.

1 set (approximately ½ pound) brains—calf, lamb, or beef—raw and partially frozen

⅔ cup homemade catsup (see Index for recipe)

4 tablespoons prepared white horseradish

2 teaspoons Tamari soy sauce

A few grains of cayenne pepper

Rinse the brains and pat dry with paper towels. Remove the thready veins and cut into bite-sized pieces. Mix the remaining ingredients together in a bowl. Place alternating layers of brains and sauce in each serving cup. Serves 4 to 6.

SWEETBREADS

Sweetbreads are the thymus gland of the calf and are highly perishable. Use them right away or freeze them. They are prepared much the same way as brains. Cook sweetbreads as follows:

Cover with water to which 2 tablespoons of vinegar and a dash of salt have been added. Simmer for 20 minutes. Drain and allow to cool a little, then remove the membrane and tube.

To broil, brush them with a little oil or chicken fat and broil gently until browned on both sides.

SWEETBREADS AND MUSHROOMS

This is the delicate dish served at lavish weddings. The sweetbreads and mushrooms are a Fountain of Youth combination, rich in nucleic acids, which help your cells stay young longer. Interestingly, a new hormone extract derived from the thymus gland of the calf has been found by the Weizmann Institute, in Israel, to combat dangerous infections in children. The thymus hormone aids and strengthens defective immunity systems.

1 cup sliced fresh mushrooms or 2 small cans (8 ounces each) sliced mushrooms, drained (reserve the liquid)

3 tablespoons vegetable oil or chicken fat

5 tablespoons whole wheat pastry flour

2 cups liquid from mushrooms or vegetables, or chicken stock

2 teaspoons Tamari soy sauce

¼ teaspoon white pepper

¼ teaspoon onion powder

1 pound cooked sweetbreads

1 cup mung bean sprouts

Whole grain toast, patty shells, or brown rice

In a deep skillet, brown the mushrooms in hot oil or chicken fat. Stir in the flour. Add the liquid slowly, then the Tamari, pepper, and onion powder. Cook for about 5 minutes over medium heat until thickened, stirring constantly. Break the sweetbreads into small pieces and add to the mushrooms. Add the sprouts last and just heat through. Serve over whole grain toast, in patty shells, or over brown rice. Serves 6 to 8 very elegantly.

OTHER MEAT DISHES

CHOPPED LIVER

Liver, another organ meat, is also highly nutritious. This traditional favorite is rich in folic acid and vitamin B_{12}, so necessary to maintain good blood.

1 *pound lamb or baby*
beef liver or 8
chicken livers
Salt
½ *of a medium-sized*
onion
1 *teaspoon lecithin*
granules
2 *hard-cooked eggs*

Toasted soy nuts
(optional)
3 *crisp lettuce leaves*
2 *tablespoons chicken*
fat
Salt and freshly
ground pepper, to
taste

Wash the liver, salt on both sides, then broil under a flame on a wire rack for 5 to 10 minutes or until light brown on both sides. Wash again, then put everything except the fat through a food chopper or processor, or chop with a hock-messer in a wooden bowl. Add the chicken fat; then season to taste. Serve with grated white radish, or serve on crackers or stuffed into celery. Also good on turnip slices. Serves 6.

PITCHA
(Calves'-Foot Jelly)

Some like it hot, some like it cold. It's delicious either way. Served hot on a bleak wintry day, there's nothing like it for making you feel like June in January. You can almost feel its strength bringing new vigor to your bones and vital organs.

You will need calves' feet, which your friendly butcher will provide, all washed and chopped. If he doesn't have feet, settle for knee or shin bones.

2 *calves' feet (or more,*
if you're lucky)
Cold water
1 *or 2 onions, minced*
2 *or 3 cloves garlic, to*
taste, minced
2 *tablespoons vinegar*
2 *bay leaves, crushed*
Hard-cooked eggs
(for cold pitcha)

1 *raw egg (for hot*
pitcha)
Juice of 1 lemon (for
hot pitcha)
Day-old bread,
sliced (for hot
pitcha)
Garlic cloves, split
(for hot pitcha)

First make sure the *feeselach* (feet) are clean. Put them in a pot with cold water to cover by 2 inches. Bring to a boil and skim off the foam. Add the onion, garlic, vinegar, and bay leaves. Cook over low heat for about 3 hours—until the meat separates easily from the bones. Add more water if necessary.

For cold pitcha, remove the feet from the pot. Remove the meat from the feet and cut it into small pieces; strain the liquid over it. Add slices of hard-cooked eggs. Or do like my Mom used to do: bury whole hard-cooked eggs in the mixture and chill it in a loaf pan. Serve with vinegar. We served this way at one of our Bar Mitzvah celebrations and it made a hit. Everyone had a story about how "Mamma used to make it."

To make hot pitcha, beat up an egg; add the lemon juice and beat it well. Add a tablespoon's worth of the hot liquid and continue beating. Add a little more hot liquid and beat. Add this mixture to the pot and mix it all up to prevent curdling. To serve, toast some day-old bread or challah—a slice for each person—in the oven till crispy. Rub both sides with garlic. Put a piece of garlic toast in each bowl. Serve the bones and liquid broth on top. *Es gezunte hait*. Serves 6.

STUFFED CABBAGE
(Holopches)

It is customary to serve this cabbage dish during the festival of Sukkot because of the ease with which it can be carried to the Sukkah. This recipe captures the spirit and fragrance of Grandma's kitchen, but has extra nutritional benefits.

There is another reason for using cabbage, not only on Sukkot but frequently throughout the year. It has been determined in a study by Dr. Saxon Graham and others that vegetables of the cabbage family provide a certain protection against cancer of the colon. In this study, those whose diets included lots of vegetables had the lowest rate of this kind of cancer, and the vegetables which afforded the most protection were cabbage, brussel sprouts, and broccoli. (*Journal of National Cancer Institute,* September 1978.)

1 *large head of cabbage*
  (4 to 5 pounds)
  Water
1 *pound ground meat*
  (¾ pound chuck and
  ¼ pound heart, if
  possible)
2 *tablespoons wheat*
  germ
2 *eggs*
2 *onions, grated*
1 *clove garlic, minced*

Salt and freshly
ground white pepper
½ *cup raw brown rice*
1 *can (28 ounces)*
  tomatoes
2 *onions, sliced*
  Meat bones or a few
  lamb riblets
2 *tablespoons honey,*
  or to taste
  Juice of 1 lemon
2 *bay leaves*
1 *sour apple, quartered*

Using a sharp knife, remove the core from the cabbage. Remove as much as possible of the center. (Chew on the core while you prepare the dish: it's got some good nutrients in it!)

Bring a big pot of water to a boil. Place the cabbage in the boiling water; boil for a few minutes and remove. Take off each leaf with a fork and return the leaves to the water to soften a little. Turn off the heat. Now prepare the filling.

Combine the meat, wheat germ, eggs, grated onion, garlic, salt and pepper to taste, and rice. Mix well. Lay out each cabbage leaf flat and cut off the hard part. Put a heaping tablespoon of filling on each leaf. Roll up like a blintz.

In a large heavy pot like a Dutch oven, or in a roaster, mix the tomatoes, a dash of salt and pepper, the sliced onions, and the meat bones or lamb riblets. Put any remaining odds and ends of cabbage in, too. Lay the cabbage rolls in gently, seam side down. Cover the pot and bring to a boil. Lower the heat and cook for 1 hour. Add the honey, lemon juice, bay leaves, and apple; continue to cook for 45 minutes more. Taste-check for seasoning. Add more honey or lemon juice as needed. This dish can also be baked in a preheated 350-degree F. oven for about 2 hours. It freezes well. When you reheat, you may have to add some tomato sauce. Heat it gently to avoid burning. Serves 6 as a main dish; 10 to 12 as an appetizer.

VARIATION: Ground cooked meat or chicken may be used instead of raw meat.

KARNATZLACH

This spicy hamburger mixture shaped to resemble frankfurters contains no nitrites and no artificial colors or flavors.

1½ *pounds ground meat mixture (chuck or neck with heart, if possible)*
1 *onion, grated*
1 *large carrot, grated*
1 *clove garlic, minced*
3 *tablespoons soy powder*
Pinch of thyme, marjoram, and oregano or 2 teaspoons poultry seasoning

2 *eggs, lightly beaten*
Dash of kelp
½ *cup wheat germ*
2 *tablespoons nutritional yeast*
½ *teaspoon paprika*
3 *tablespoons sesame seeds*
Hot tomato sauce

In a bowl, combine all ingredients except the last 5. Mix well and form into rolls about the diameter of a frankfurter and about 3 inches long, tapering at each end. Roll each in a mixture of the wheat germ, yeast, paprika, and sesame seeds. Broil under moderate heat on a lightly oiled rack. Turn to brown on all sides. Serve with hot tomato sauce. Makes 24; serves 8. As a variation, use this recipe to make a nutrition-packed meat loaf.

MEATBALLS—
SWEET AND SOUR STYLE

Here, tangy, succulent meatballs are laced with onion, the perfect accompaniment for meat dishes. Onions contain a substance that helps the blood vessel walls dissolve clots. Onion also lowers high cholesterol levels and provides important nutrients such as selenium, which spares vitamin E, thus increasing your supply of available oxygen.

2 *large onions*
1 *pound chopped meat mixture (¾ pound chuck and ¼ pound heart, if possible)*
1 *egg*
1 *tablespoon wheat germ*
1 *tablespoon lecithin granules*
1 *eggshell's worth of water*

Vegetable oil or chicken fat
2 *teaspoons honey Juice of ½ lemon*
⅓ *cup ketchup (preferably the sugar-free variety available at health food stores)*
½ *cup water*

Grate 1 onion into a bowl and mix together with the meat, egg, wheat germ, lecithin granules, and the eggshell's worth of water. Combine well. Form meatballs the size of a walnut.

Slice the other onion. In a heavy skillet, sauté the onion in a little oil or chicken fat until transparent. Add the meatballs, honey, lemon juice, ketchup, and ½ cup of water. Bring to a boil, then simmer for 1 hour, adding a little more water if necessary. Taste-check the lemon and honey content and adjust as necessary. Serve with whole wheat spaghetti, macaroni, or brown rice. Serves 4 to 6.

GOULASH

A hearty, economical dish that fills the house with an appetizing aroma. The lecithin emulsifies the fat and lowers the cholesterol levels of the beef.

2 *small onions, sliced*
1 *clove garlic, minced*
2 *tablespoons vege-*
  table oil or chicken fat
1½ *pounds stewing*
  beef, cubed
1 *cup cooked or canned*
  tomatoes, cut up

2 *tablespoons lecithin*
  granules
1 *cup water*
1 *teaspoon paprika*
½ *teaspoon kelp*
3 *medium-sized*
  potatoes, scrubbed
  but unpeeled

In a skillet, sauté the onion and garlic in the oil or chicken fat until golden. Place the beef, tomatoes, lecithin granules, and water in a pot; add the onion and garlic. Season with the paprika and kelp. Cover and cook in a 350-degree F. oven for 1 hour. Slice the potatoes lengthwise, add to the stew, and simmer for another 30 minutes. Taste-check and adjust the seasoning. Serves 4 to 6.

SPICY STEW

This rich, full-bodied stew is more than a culinary treat: the spices contribute many rare trace minerals.

2 *pounds lean beef,*
  cut into chunks
2 *cups water*
1 *can (6 ounces)*
  tomato paste
3 *tablespoons wine*
  vinegar
1 *teaspoon salt*
  (optional)

½ *teaspoon pepper*
1 *teaspoon minced*
  garlic
2 *cinnamon sticks*
8 *whole cloves*
2 *onions, cut into*
  chunks
2 *tablespoons lecithin*
  granules

In a heavy pot, brown the meat in a 325-degree F. oven. In a bowl, combine the rest of the ingredients. Add the mixture to the meat. Cover the pot and bake at 325 degrees F. for 2½ hours. Remove the cinnamon sticks and cloves before serving. Serve with kasha or mamaligge (cornmeal mush). Serves 4 to 6.

LONDON BROIL

Flank steak is a protein bonanza—as much as 30 grams in 3½ ounces. It is also high in phosphorous, iron, and niacin. The steak is low in fiber and calcium, however, so serve crisp baked potatoes, a tossed salad, and broccoli along with it. These will fill your body's fiber and calcium need.

The leftover marinade from the preparation of this dish may be refrigerated and re-used.

1 *flank steak (about 1½ pounds), scored*
¾ *cup vegetable oil*
1 *tablespoon vinegar*
1 *clove garlic, minced*
¼ *teaspoon white pepper*

1 *tablespoon Tamari soy sauce*
1 *tablespoon lecithin granules*

Place the flank steak in a shallow dish. Combine the rest of the ingredients; pour over the steak. Cover and let stand at room temperature for 3 hours or in the refrigerator overnight. Turn the steak several times during the marinating period. Preheat the broiler. Broil 3 inches from the heat source for about 5 minutes. Turn and broil the other side. Remove to a heated platter. Carve very thin slices across the grain of the meat. Serves 4 to 6.

STUFFED FLANK STEAK

The potatoes, scallions, parsley, and pecans provide needed fiber and a whole gamut of vitamins and enzymes to enhance the digestibility of the high protein content of the flank steak. A very substantial stick-to-your ribs meal.

1 *large beef flank (2 to 3 pounds) with pocket*
2 *cups diced raw potato*
3 *scallions, chopped (white parts only)*
½ *cup coarsely chopped pecans*
2 *teaspoons chopped fresh parsley*
3 *eggs beaten with 1 teaspoon lecithin granules*
Vegetable oil

Have the butcher cut a pocket in the beef. In a bowl, mix the potato, scallions, pecans, and parsley with the beaten eggs. Stuff the pocket with the mixture. Roast in a preheated 325-degree F. oven, basting frequently with oil, for about 1 hour and 45 minutes. Serves 6.

BREAST OF LAMB
WITH
BROWN RICE STUFFING

Because the lamb is the last of the range-fed animals, its meat is the safest in terms of toxic additives. Only in the very cold months is the lamb sent to the feed lots to be fattened on hormones.

To this very *geshmache* dish brown rice contributes lots of vitamins and minerals and parsley contributes lots of iron.

1 *breast of lamb (2 to 3 pounds) with pocket*
1 *clove garlic, cut*
¾ *cup brown rice, parboiled for 15 minutes in salted water*
1 *teaspoon Tamari soy sauce*
¼ *cup chopped raw peanuts, pecans, or any mixed-nut combination*
2 *tablespoons minced parsley*
4 *tablespoons whole wheat pastry or bread flour*
4 *tablespoons vegetable oil*
2 *cups boiling rice water or soup stock*

Rub the cut clove of garlic on the inside and outside of the meat. Trim the fat from the meat and discard. Drain the rice and reserve the liquid. To make the stuffing, in a bowl combine the rice, Tamari, chopped nuts, and parsley. Fill the breast of lamb pocket with the stuffing and fasten the opening with skewers, or sew it up with strong white thread. Pat the bottom and top with the flour. Heat the oil in a roasting pan and place the stuffed breast in the center, spooning some of the oil over the meat. Add the 2 cups of rice water or soup stock. Roast in a preheated 325-degree F. oven, allowing 30 to 35 minutes per pound of meat. Baste occasionally with the gravy in the pan. Serves 4 to 6.

VARIATION: Omit the chopped nuts. Add 1 pound of chopped beef, prepared as for hamburger, to the ingredients. Proceed as in the basic recipe. Serves 4 to 6 generously.

LAMB AND LIMA BEANS

A superb combination of taste and texture. The lima beans contribute some of the nutrients deficient in the lamb, such as vitamin A, calcium, and fiber. They also contribute a goodly portion of protein—as much as 19.7 grams in 3½ ounces.

¼ *pound dry lima beans*
Water
1½ *pounds shoulder lamb, cubed*
1 *clove garlic, minced*
1 *onion, chopped*
2 *tablespoons vegetable oil*
1 *cup tomato sauce*
1 *cup boiling water*
1 *teaspoon paprika*
1 *teaspoon minced parsley*

Wash the lima beans. Allow to soak overnight in water; drain, reserving 1 cup of the liquid. In a large pot, sauté the lamb, garlic, and onion in the oil. Add the drained beans and tomato sauce. Bring the 1 cup of water (in which the beans were soaking) to a boil; add to the pot. Add the paprika and parsley. Cover and simmer for 1½ to 2 hours, until tender. Serves 4 to 6.

VARIATIONS: Instead of dried beans, add string beans, Brussels sprouts, dandelion greens, and/or potatoes after the lamb has been sautéed. Or add diced eggplant 30 minutes before the lamb is tender.

CONTINENTAL LAMB STEW

Lamb is an excellent source of body-strengthening protein, magnesium, iron, and phosphorous. Although it lacks fiber, in this stew the fiber is well supplied by the potatoes, celery, and bean sprouts.

2 *pounds neck lamb*
Water
2 *bay leaves*
2 *tablespoons chopped fresh parsley*
½ *teaspoon dried crushed thyme*
⅛ *teaspoon white pepper*
1 *teaspoon Tamari soy sauce*
3 *medium-sized onions, quartered*
2 *potatoes, quartered*
½ *cup chopped celery*
½ *clove garlic*

6 *carrots, cut into chunks*
1 *cup fresh peas or mung bean sprouts*
¼ *pound mushrooms, sliced*
2 *tablespoons rice flour, arrowroot, or whole wheat pastry flour*
2 *tablespoons cold water*
½ *tablespoon lemon juice*
Chopped dill weed, fresh or dried

Cut the lamb into 1 to 1½-inch pieces. Place in a large pot and half cover with water. Add the bay leaves, parsley, thyme, pepper, and Tamari. Simmer for 30 minutes. Add the onions, potatoes, celery, garlic, and carrots. Cover and simmer until the vegetables and meat are almost tender—about 1½ hours. Add the peas or sprouts and mushrooms; cook for an additional 15 minutes. Combine the flour or arrowroot with the cold water; flavor it with the lemon juice, and add it to the stew to serve as a thickening agent. Garnish with dill. Serves 4 to 6.

POULTRY DISHES

Chicken is not just for Shabbos any more. And that's all to the good. Poultry is less costly, less fatty, and higher in nutritional value in proportion to calories than either beef or lamb.

Yesterday's utopian promise of a chicken in every pot is today's reality. Most of us are consuming more than twice as much chicken now than we did in the 1930s.

Gone are the days when we bought chickens live and took them to the schochet. Gone are the little *eyerlach* (eggs without shells) that we used to find inside the chickens; they were cooked with great care and doled out to the children with love and chicken soup. And very rarely can you find a chicken with feet, which add gelatin and that indescribable "Shabbos taste" to the soup.

In order for chickens and turkeys to grow and develop naturally, they should be allowed to run and scratch on the ground. Today's marketplace poultry never tasted the joys and perils of life in the barnyard. They are hatched in incubators and raised in tight little cubicles in high-rise apartment henhouses.

Both chickens and turkeys that lived a normal lifestyle, that pecked for their food and consumed no antibiotics or arsenic, are available in some health food stores—but not with a kosher hechsher. I know of no source for organically-raised kosher chickens and turkeys unless you raise your own or buy from a natural farmer and have it ritually slaughtered.

Duck, which is less in demand, is raised in a more natural setting. And the goose, which has so far escaped exploitation, is still raising goslings in the good old-fashioned way. However, chickens and turkeys, no doubt because of intensive farming and industrial technology, are much more plentiful and generally available. They are also higher in protein and lower in fat than ducks and geese.

As little as 3½ ounces of chicken or turkey provides an impressive 28 to 31 grams of protein. (The light meat has the higher protein value and less fat than the dark, though the differences are slight.) Also provided are potassium, iron, phosphorus, and some calcium. Some vitamin A is found in chicken and some B vitamins in both chicken and turkey, with a real high in niacin, the vitamin that makes every day a holiday.

CHICKEN IN LEMON AND WINE

My favorite chicken recipe. It's simple, quick, moist, tender, and tasty, and can be prepared in less than an hour. It is also lower in calories than most chicken dishes.

2½ to 3 pounds chicken thighs and pulkes (drumsticks) or other parts (according to your family's preference)
Juice of 1 lemon
1 clove garlic, crushed
½ teaspoon ground ginger
½ teaspoon dry mustard
¼ teaspoon crushed thyme
¼ teaspoon sage
1 teaspoon paprika
½ cup dry white wine
Mushrooms (optional)

Clean the chicken pieces and pat them dry. Sprinkle on the lemon juice; rub with the crushed garlic. Combine the spices in a shaker-top jar and sprinkle the mixture over the chicken, coating all sides. Place the chicken in an electric skillet preheated to 250 degrees F. Cover and cook. After 20 minutes, turn over the chicken pieces and add the wine. (You can also add the mushrooms at this point.) Reduce the heat to 220 F. and let simmer till done—about 40 minutes. Meantime, you can make a kugel. Serves 4 to 6.

CHICKEN AND PINEAPPLE

A sweet-tart chicken dish with a distinctly Polynesian flavor.

1 can (20 ounces) unsweetened pineapple chunks, with juice
3 tablespoons Tamari soy sauce
2 tablespoons lemon juice
2 tablespoons honey
½ teaspoon ground ginger
1 tablespoon minced onion
1 broiler chicken, cut into 8 parts

In a bowl, combine all ingredients except the chicken. Pour this marinade over the chicken in a deep bowl. Refrigerate for 1 hour. Remove the chicken parts and place in a large baking pan. Pour the marinade over them and bake in a preheated 350-degree F. oven for about 1 hour. Serves 4 to 6.

CHICKEN-NAHIT DELIGHT

As in the recipe above, pineapple gives this dish a Polynesian flavor. Garbanzos, also known as chickpeas or nahit, are an important food in Israel and Arab countries, where they are ground and mixed with garlic, lemon, and tahina to make hummous. Garbanzos are high in protein and contain twice as much iron as other legumes. When they are sprouted, they multiply their vitamins and enzymes and develop vitamin B12, which is hard to find in foods outside the animal kingdom.

½ cup orange juice
¼ cup barbecue sauce
  (see Index for
  recipe)
2 tablespoons
  vegetable oil
2 cups cooked
  chicken, cut up

1 can (20 ounces)
  unsweetened
  pineapple chunks,
  drained except for 3
  tablespoons of the
  juice
1 cup garbanzo
  sprouts
  Brown rice
  (optional)

Combine the orange juice, barbecue sauce (preferably home-made), and oil (I use sesame) in a saucepan. Heat gently for 3 minutes. Add the cut-up chicken, pineapple, and juice. Continue simmering, but do not boil. Turn off the heat and add the garbanzo sprouts. Mix them in carefully. Let them absorb some of the heat and juices. When you heat the sprouts this way, you don't destroy any of their valuable enzymes. Serve this dish over brown rice and greatly increase protein values. This will serve 4 adults or 2 hungry teenagers.

CHICKEN BALLS

Here, baylick (white-meat chicken) is made to taste remarkably like gefilte fish.

1 *slice rye bread*	¼ *teaspoon white*
Scant water	*pepper*
1 *chicken breast,*	2 *cups water*
uncooked	1 *carrot, sliced*
3 *large onions*	*Dash of freshly*
1 *egg, beaten*	*ground pepper*

Soak the rye bread in a little water. In a wooden bowl, chop the soaked rye bread, chicken, and 1 onion until fine; mix well. Add the beaten egg and pepper; mix well and set aside.

Dice the remaining 2 onions into a large pot. Add the water and bring to a boil. Shape the chicken mixture into 1-inch balls and drop into the boiling onion water. Add the carrot slices and dash of pepper. Let it simmer for 1 hour. Add more water, if necessary. Turn the heat off and let the balls cool in the broth. Remove them with a slotted spoon. Strain the broth and pour it over the balls. Garnish with carrots and onions from the broth and serve with horseradish. Delicious hot or cold. Makes 6 Chicken Balls. Serves 2 as a main dish; 6 as an appetizer.

CHICKEN OR TURKEY WITH CASHEWS

A great way to make a nutritious party dish using leftovers. Especially good served over steaming brown rice.

½ cup unsalted cashew
nuts
2 tablespoons chicken
fat or vegetable oil
1 onion, diced
1 cup fresh sliced
mushrooms or ½ cup
canned sliced
mushrooms, drained
1 green or red pepper,
diced

2 cups chicken soup or
stock
¼ teaspoon curry
powder
1 tablespoon
arrowroot starch
2 tablespoons water
2 cups leftover cooked
fowl, cut up

Warm the cashews in a low oven (250 degrees F.). In a large deep skillet, heat the chicken fat or oil; add the onion, mushrooms, and pepper, and sauté. Add the soup or stock and curry powder. In a bowl, mix the arrowroot with the 2 tablespoons of water; add this to the skillet mixture when it comes to a boil. Add the cut-up fowl. Heat through. Sprinkle in the warmed cashews. Serves 4 to 6.

CHICKEN AND WHOLE WHEAT (OR SPINACH) NOODLES

Another way to use leftover chicken. The parsley gives this dish the taste of spring plus lots of potassium, iron, calcium, and vitamin A.

2 tablespoons chicken
fat
1 large onion, diced
4 fcups cooked and
drained whole wheat
(or spinach) noodles

2 cups cooked chicken,
cut up
2 tablespoons minced
fresh parsley
½ teaspoon paprika
Parsley sprigs

Melt the chicken fat in a deep skillet; add the diced onion and sauté. Add the cooked, drained noodles. Add the chicken and minced parsley. Sprinkle with the paprika. Turn into a 2-quart baking dish. Cover and bake for 20 minutes in a preheated 350-degree F. oven. Uncover and let brown for 10 minutes. Garnish with parsley sprigs. Serves 4 to 6.

4

Dairy Specialties

Milk has long been a symbol of the good, the plenty, the natural. Throughout history, the products of milk have played a major role in the Jewish diet. Back in the shtetl, many families owned a cow or a goat to keep the family well supplied with cheese for blintzes and with sour cream, buttermilk, and butter. Those who did not could avail themselves of the wares of a local version of Tevye, Sholom Aleichem's dairyman, who hawked his wares, talked to God, and longed to be a rich man.

In a sense, Tevye enjoyed nutritional riches that are not generally available to us today. His milk came directly from the herd, its rich store of nutrients undiminished by factory processing. His milk was not homogenized, pasteurized, or fortified. It was natural and *raw*.

What's wrong with today's factory processed milk? Plenty. Kurt A. Oster, M.D., emeritus chief of cardiology at Park City Hospital, Bridgeport, Connecticut, on the basis of extensive studies of milk-drinking societies, maintains that homogenized milk may be a major cause of heart disease. Homogenized milk has been processed to break up its fat content into tiny particles. The fat in milk contains an enzyme (xanthine oxidase) that is destructive to the arteries. When milk is not homogenized, the body metabolizes this enzyme. But, says Dr. Oster, when milk is homogenized, new vesicles that contain liposomes (fat bodies) are formed. Liposomes act like a Trojan horse carrying the enzyme into the arterial wall and causing damage in these alien locations. The cholesterol buildup that is usually blamed seems to be nature's way of trying to heal the damage caused by the enzyme.

Dr. Oster's views are admittedly controversial, but so are all new theories. It is said that it takes 30 years from test tube to table. Until all the evidence is in, much harm can be done.

If you must use homogenized milk, I suggest you follow these simple precautionary measures suggested by Dr. Oster. Simmer the milk (don't boil it) for ten seconds, then cool it and refrigerate. The heat knocks out the destructive enzyme. Homogenized milk used in cooking and baking need not be preheated.

For those in whom arterial damage has already been done, Dr. Oster suggests large doses of folic acid, a B vitamin which is a potent inhibitor of xanthine oxidase. He has used it in dosages of 40 to 80 milligrams daily on 180 patients and noted a significant decline in angina pectoris and recurrent myocardial infarction in the treated group, compared with controls.

It cannot be denied that milk contains a remarkable concentration of nourishing ingredients especially important to growing children—in particular, protein, calcium, and riboflavin (vitamin B_2). But, however great the nutritional content, there are considerations other than homogenization for exercising moderation or even abstinence in some instances.

Many allergic conditions are attributable to milk. Postnasal drip, constant throat clearing, stomachaches, headaches, various muscle aches, ear and tonsil infections, especially in children, are sometimes caused by homogenized pasteurized milk, warns Dr. Lendon Smith. (*Feed Your Kids Right*, McGraw Hill, 1979.)

But, says Dr. Smith, "Some people find that raw milk or goat's milk will not cause this syndrome, which suggests that the processing of milk or the additives are at fault."

Not many of us today keep cows in our backyards, but somewhere in your area there may be a dairy farm to which you can go for safe raw milk. Many health food stores are now carrying raw milk and goat's milk. The health advantages are many.

MILK INTOLERANCE

There are numerous people, about half the human race and including many Ashkenazic Jews, who lack the enzyme lactase and therefore have difficulty digesting lactose, or milk sugar. For these people, milk can cause severe intestinal distress, diarrhea, flatulence, and cramps. Too frequently, these ailments are not diagnosed as milk intolerance.

Those who cannot drink regular milk because of lactose intolerance should have no problem with cultured milk products such as yogurt and buttermilk so long as no milk solids have been added. Cottage cheese and hard cheeses are usually well tolerated. So are such cultured products as kefir and piima, which can be made by incubation at room temperature, thus conserving valuable enzymes. Kefir is similar to yogurt but is sweeter and more custardlike. Freeze-dried cultures for making kefir, if not available at your health food store, may be ordered from The International Yogurt Company, 628 North Doheny Drive, Los Angeles, California 90069.

Piima is a cultured milk of Finnish origin. It is even milder than kefir and can be used as a substitute for milk in any recipe. Mix it with fruit juice for a delicious, nutritious milkshake. The virtue of piima is that it can be tolerated by some people who can't handle any form of milk, even the usual cultured products. And, because it is very mild in flavor, hardly tart at all, it can be used in recipes that call for milk without affecting the flavor.

Piima can be made in new batches from a previous batch, just like yogurt and kefir. If your health food store does not yet carry piima culture, it can be ordered from PIIMA, Box 2614, LaMesa, California 92041.

Butter, because it contains none of the proteins of the milk, can usually be tolerated even by those who cannot tolerate other dairy products. Use raw butter if possible. If this is unavailable, use the unsalted butter. All fats should be used in moderation. When using butter in cooking, warm it very gently to prevent browning. Butter provides the fat-soluble vitamins A, D, and E.

CHEESE

Cheese is an important source of calcium, phosphorus, and protein. Ounce for ounce, some cheese contains seven times as much protein as the milk from which it is made. Cheese also contains the fat-soluble vitamins A, D, E, and K and water-soluble vitamins of the B complex kind.

Look for cheese made from raw milk, sometimes available at natural food stores. Health Valley Natural Foods puts out 15 varieties of raw milk cheese, all except the Swiss made without rennet, an animal product which is not acceptable to vegetarians and to strict observers of kashrut.

Avoid process cheese: it contains emulsifiers, flavoring, coloring, and water. All so-called "American cheese" is process cheese.

Enjoy your natural (as opposed to process) cheese in moderation. It can be high in fat and in calories. You'll get the most protein for the least amount of fat and calories from uncreamed cottage cheese and mozzarella. Highest in protein are cottage cheese, ricotta, Parmesan, and Romano. Highest in fat and calories are cream cheese, Gruyère, and Cheddar.

The dairy dishes featured in this chapter are perfectly wonderful all year 'round, but are especially good on the dairy holiday of Shavuot. Dairy dishes are served during this festival both because the Torah is compared to milk and honey and because the Land of Israel is described in the Bible as a "land flowing with milk and honey" (Exodus 3:8). It is customary to welcome Shavuot with an all-night study session and then partake of cheesecake and coffee.

Potato Soup

Caraway gives this rich, creamy soup a pleasantly spicy flavor. With a lovely salad and the Ambrosia Cream Dessert (recipe appears later in this chapter), it makes a delightful meal for family or friends. For a more expansive buffet dinner, include blintzes on the menu.

3 *tablespoons butter*
2 *large onions, sliced thin*
2 *ribs celery with leaves, sliced*
6 *medium-sized unpeeled potatoes, scrubbed and cubed*
½ *teaspoon salt*

½ *teaspoon kelp*
1 *tablespoon caraway seeds (optional)*
⅓ *cup egg barley or macaroni*
1 *quart water*
1 *quart milk*
Paprika

In a sturdy pot, melt the butter and sauté the onion and celery very lightly; do not brown. Add the potato cubes, salt, kelp, seeds, egg barley or macaroni, and water. Cook until the potatoes are soft— about 20 minutes. Pour 2 cups of this mixture into a blender and whiz until smooth. Return it to the pot, add the quart of milk, and bring to a boil. Dust with paprika and serve with sour cream or yogurt. Garnish with parsley or chopped chives. Serves 8 to 10.

BLUEBERRY SOUP

Rich in manganese.

1 *quart blueberries*
1½ *cups water*
1 *stick cinnamon*

2 *slices lemon*
2 *tablespoons honey*
1 *cup plain yogurt*

Place all ingredients except the yogurt in a pot. Bring to a boil, turn the heat down immediately, and let simmer for 12 minutes. Blend in the 1 cup of yogurt or serve with yogurt as a topping. Garnish with a few blueberries. Serves 3 or 4.

Sweet Potato Soup

1 quart scrubbed
  sweet potatoes, cut
  into chunks
3 onions, thickly sliced
3 carrots, cut into
  chunks
3 ribs celery, cut into
  large chunks
2 quarts water
  Sea salt, to taste

Freshly ground
  pepper, to taste
1 tablespoon butter
¼ cup milk
2 tablespoons sesame
  seeds
1 tablespoon caraway
  seeds
2 tablespoons chopped
  parsley

Place all the vegetables and the water in a large kettle. Add the salt and pepper. Bring to the boil. Cover and simmer for 30 minutes. With a slotted spoon, remove half of the carrots, celery, and sweet potatoes and set aside. Purée the remainder of the soup until smooth; return to the kettle. Add the reserved vegetables, the butter, milk, sesame and caraway seeds, and parsley. Reheat. Taste-check for seasoning. Serves 8.

Mamaligge and Soy Grits

A bean and grain combination with high protein value.

½ cup soy grits
  Boiling water
⅓ cup noninstant dry
  milk powder or
  whey powder
1 cup yellow cornmeal
1 teaspoon kelp

3 cups milk
  Sesame seeds or
  ground sunflower
  seeds (or a
  combination)
2 tablespoons butter

Put the soy grits in a bowl and cover with boiling water. Combine the milk or whey powder, cornmeal, and kelp. Combine the 2 mixtures. Add 1 cup of the cold milk gradually. Heat the other 2 cups of milk not quite to the boil. Stir the cornmeal mixture into the hot milk, stirring constantly for 5 minutes or until the mixture is thick and smooth. You can serve it this way with butter, cottage cheese, or yogurt. Or you can pour it into a 9 x 13-inch buttered dish and cool it, then cut it into squares or, with a cookie cutter or the edge of a glass, make rounds, for a change of shape. Dip the squares or rounds into sesame seeds or ground sunflower seeds and fry in butter on both sides or dot with butter and toast them in the oven. For a delicious change, serve with a poached egg on top. Serves about 6.

Potato-Herring Casserole

Ideal for those who love herring and potatoes. Wonderful to serve as the main attraction on the buffet table to break the Yom Kippur fast. With a salad and a good whole grain bread, this is a well-balanced meal.

4 *tablespoons butter*	2 *matjes herring fillets*
1 *large onion, thinly sliced*	*Paprika*
3 *large potatoes, scrubbed*	1 *tablespoon wheat germ*
	½ *cup light cream*

Melt 1 tablespoon of the butter in a skillet. Add the onion and sauté lightly for about 6 minutes, until limp and golden. Meanwhile, slice the scrubbed potatoes into ⅛-inch slices. Butter a 1½-quart baking dish with ½ tablespoon of the remaining butter. Arrange a layer of potatoes in the dish. Cut the herring fillets into ½-inch diagonal slices and arrange a layer of herring over the potatoes; top with a layer of the sautéed onion. Make alternating layers, ending with potato; as you do, sprinkle each layer with paprika and dot with a little butter. Sprinkle the top layer with the wheat germ and dot with more butter.

Heat the ½ cup of light cream almost to boiling and pour over all. Bake in a preheated 350-degree F. oven for 1 hour, or until the potatoes are cooked through. Serve from the baking dish. Serves 6.

SALMON QUICHE

Salmon, a high-protein food, provides a bonanza of health-building nutrients. The most polyunsaturated fatty acids is provided by *pink* salmon, which is also the most economical variety. Fish and fish oil in general tend to lower the amount of fat in the blood, thus improving its overall quality. Be sure to use the skin and bones of the salmon. They contain lots of calcium and other important minerals.

1 10-*inch unbaked pie shell*
½ *cup chopped onion*
1 *tablespoon butter*
1 *can (15½ ounces) pink salmon, drained and mashed (do not discard the skin or bones)*
1 *package (10 ounces) frozen chopped spinach, unthawed*
4 *eggs, lightly beaten*
2 *cups small curd cottage cheese*
1 *teaspoon crushed oregano*
¼ *teaspoon salt*
⅛ *teaspoon grated nutmeg*
¼ *cup grated Parmesan cheese*

Preheat the oven to 400 degrees F. Prick the pie shell with a fork and bake for 8 minutes. In a skillet, sauté the onion in the butter until transparent; add the salmon and combine well. Spoon the mixture into the pie shell. Cook the spinach briefly and drain. In a bowl, combine the spinach with the eggs, cottage cheese, oregano, salt, and nutmeg. Spoon the mixture over the salmon in the pie shell. Sprinkle with Parmesan cheese. Bake in a preheated 350-degree F. oven for 40 minutes. Serves 6.

SALMON KEDGEREE

Serve this quick-to-prepare meal over whole grain toast or in patty shells.

¾ cup raw brown rice
1 can (16 ounces)
  salmon (use the
  liquid and the
  bones)
1¼ cups milk

4 hard-cooked eggs,
  chopped
¼ cup snipped parsley
2 tablespoons butter
½ teaspoon salt
½ teaspoon paprika

In a pot, cook the rice (or use leftover rice) according to package directions. Combine the rice with the rest of the ingredients in a saucepan and heat through. Serves 6.

RHODA'S VEGETARIAN CHEESE LASAGNE

A savory blend of cheeses, tomato, mushrooms, and spices enriched with wheat germ. Excellent for the vegetarian who eats cheese.

6 tablespoons butter
½ cup choppen onion
1 garlic clove, minced,
  or ¼ teaspoon
  garlic powder
2 cans (2 pounds, 3
  ounces each) Italian
  tomatoes
½ pound fresh mush-
  rooms, sliced
½ cup wheat germ
¼ cup milk
2 eggs, lightly beaten
1 cup grated Romano
  or Parmesan cheese
½ cup chopped fresh
  parsley
1 teaspoon salt
  (optional)

½ teaspoon white
  pepper
2 cans (6 ounces each)
  tomato paste
3 cups water
1 tablespoon honey
1½ teaspoons crushed
  dried basil
1 pound lasagne
  noodles (preferably
  whole wheat),
  cooked and drained
1 pound ricotta or
  cottage cheese
1 pound mozzarella
  cheese, sliced

Melt 4 tablespoons of the butter in a large saucepan. Add the onion, garlic, and tomatoes. Simmer and stir until some liquid has evaporated—about 10 minutes. Meanwhile, in a bowl combine the mushrooms, wheat germ, milk, eggs, ¼ cup of the grated cheese, ¼ cup of the chopped parsley, ½ teaspoon of the salt (if desired), and the pepper. Mix well. Melt the remaining 2 tablespoons of butter in a skillet; pour in the mushroom mixture and brown.

Add the mushroom mixture to the tomato mixture. Add the tomato paste, water, honey, the remaining ¼ cup of parsley, the basil, another ¼ cup of the grated cheese, and the remaining ½ teaspoon of salt (if desired). Simmer for 45 minutes.

Pour 1 cup of this sauce into a 15 x 10 x 2-inch baking dish. Cover with a layer of the drained noodles, a third of the mozzarella cheese, a third of the ricotta or cottage cheese, and 2 tablespoons of the grated cheese. Cover with sauce. Repeat, making 2 more layers, ending with sauce. Sprinkle the remaining grated cheese on top. Bake in a preheated 350-degree F. oven for 30 minutes. Serves 10 to 12.

Tuna Whole Wheat Lasagne

Use whole wheat lasagne noodles and boost the nutritive value of this elegant, economical dish. If you don't have whole wheat lasagne on hand, substitute whole wheat broad egg noodles or giant shells. If all you have available is white lasagne noodles, sprinkle a mixture of ¼ cup bran and ¼ cup wheat germ over the noodles during the layering process.

1 onion, chopped
2 cloves garlic, minced
2 tablespoons
vegetable oil
1 can (28 ounces)
tomatoes, cut into
chunks
1 can (12 ounces)
tomato paste
½ cup water
½ teaspoon salt
½ teaspoon crushed
oregano
¼ teaspoon crushed
thyme
¼ teaspoon crushed
basil
¼ teaspoon paprika
2 cans (7 ounces each)
tuna
5 quarts water
1 teaspoon salt
1 pound whole wheat
lasagne noodles
1 pound cottage
cheese
1 cup grated cheese
(Parmesan or another
hard-grating cheese)
½ to 1 cup shredded
mozzarella or
Muenster cheese
for topping

In a deep skillet, sauté the onion and garlic in the oil until the onion is light brown. Add the tomatoes, tomato paste, ½ cup water, and the herbs and seasonings. Cover and simmer for 1 hour. Stir in the tuna.

In a large pot, bring the 5 quarts of water to a boil. Add the 1 teaspoon of salt to the rapidly boiling water. Gradually add the lasagne strips, allowing the water to continue to boil. Cook till tender. Drain in a colander.

Spread a third of the sauce from the skillet into a 4-quart oblong ovenproof dish. Add a layer of cooked lasagne noodles. Dot with a third of the cottage cheese; sprinkle on some of the grated cheese. Repeat this sequence twice more, ending with grated cheese. Sprinkle the mozzarella or Muenster cheese on top. Bake uncovered for 30 minutes in a preheated 350-degree F. oven. Serves 8 to 10.

TUNA-MUSHROOM QUICHE

When it's your turn to entertain, especially to break the Yom Kippur fast, try this quiche and you'll enjoy many compliments. Note that mushrooms are a good source of vegetable protein and are the only non-animal food source that provides vitamin D, the sunshine vitamin, which is essential to the proper utilization of calcium.

9-inch pie shell	1 large tomato, sliced
Raw beans (any variety)	1¾ cups milk
1 egg, separated	½ cup grated Swiss cheese
¼ cup fresh sliced mushrooms or 1 can (4 ounces) sliced mushrooms, drained	½ cup grated Cheddar cheese
	½ teaspoon paprika
	1 teaspoon grated onion
1 tablespoon butter	3 eggs
1 can (6½ or 7 ounces) tuna	

Line a 9-inch ungreased pie plate with pastry, making sure that the sides are 2 inches high. Prick holes in the bottom of the shell and line the bottom with beans to keep the shell from buckling. Bake in a preheated 400-degree F. oven for 5 minutes. Remove the beans to a bowl and bake the shell for another 5 minutes. Cool slightly. Beat the egg white lightly and brush it over the shell.

To make the filling, sauté the mushrooms in the butter until tender. Line the pastry shell with a layer of mushrooms, then a layer of tuna, then a layer of sliced tomato; set aside. Heat the milk in a saucepan and add the cheeses. Stir over moderate heat until the cheeses have melted. Add the paprika and onion. Remove from the heat and beat in the 3 eggs and the remaining egg yolk, 1 at a time.

Pour the cheese mixture over the tomato-tuna-mushrooms in the pastry shell and bake in a preheated 325-degree F. oven for 40 minutes, or until the custard is set and the tip of a knife inserted in the center comes out clean. This will feed 6 happy people.

ONION QUICHE IN BROWN RICE SHELL

A favorite dairy meal or nosh at our house. The crunchy brown rice shell provides the "feel good" B vitamins and a nice contrast in texture to the smooth, custardy cheese filling, which is rich in vitamin A and calcium.

1½ *cups cooked brown rice (½ cup brown rice to 1 cup boiling water and ¼ teaspoon sea salt)*
3 *eggs*
1¼ *cups milk*
½ *teaspoon sea salt*
Dash of freshly ground white pepper
Dash of cayenne pepper

Dash of freshly grated nutmeg
1 *tablespoon potato flour*
1¼ *cups shredded sharp Cheddar cheese, or Swiss and Cheddar mixed*
1 *medium-sized onion, thinly sliced*

To make the brown rice shell, pat the cooked brown rice onto the bottom and sides of a lightly oiled 9-inch pie plate. Place in a preheated 375-degree F. oven to dry, but not brown, for 5 minutes. Remove from the oven and let cool.

To make the filling, in a medium-sized bowl beat the eggs until light and fluffy. Add the milk, salt, pepper, cayenne, and nutmeg. Continue to beat until thoroughly mixed; set aside. In a separate bowl, toss the potato flour with the shredded cheese; toss lightly but thoroughly. Place the cheese in the cooled rice shell, spreading it to the edges of the crust. Place the thinly sliced onion over the cheese and pour the egg-milk mixture over all. Place in a preheated over (375 degrees F.) and bake for 10 minutes. Reduce the heat to 325 degrees F. and continue to bake for 25 to 30 minutes, or until the filling puffs up and is golden brown. Remove from the oven and allow to set for about 5 minutes. Cut into wedges and serve. Serves 6.

CHEESE STEAKS

We enjoyed these in Israel. They taste like blintzes but are much easier to prepare.

1 *pound cottage cheese*
2 *eggs, beaten*
4 *tablespoons whole wheat bread flour*

½ *teaspoon salt*
½ *teaspoon cayenne pepper*
2 *tablespoons butter*

Drain the excess moisture from the cheese. Combine the cheese and eggs, then add the flour and seasonings. Melt the butter in a skillet. Drop 2-tablespoon portions into the hot buttered skillet. Cook over low heat until golden brown on both sides. Makes a nice meal for 4. Serve with sour cream, yogurt, or applesauce.

SPINACH-RICOTTA PIE

The nutrients in this wholesome pie will put stars in your eyes and vitality in your step. Spinach is fantastically rich in vitamin A, providing as much as 15,000 international units per cup (cooked), and it comes escorted by an honor guard of minerals—especially calcium, iron, magnesium, and zinc. The cheese and eggs provide excellent protein patterns and a gift of selenium, the mineral that helps retard the aging process, making this is an excellent pie for the vegetarian who eats cheese and eggs.

CRUST:

⅓ *cup sweet butter*
1 *cup whole wheat pastry flour (⅘ whole wheat and ⅕ soy is nice)*

¼ *teaspoon salt (optional)*
3 *tablespoons cold buttermilk, water, or orange juice*

Using a pastry blender or 2 forks, cut all but 1 tablespoon of the butter (reserve the 1 tablespoon for later use) into the flour; add the salt if desired. When the mixture is blended, gradually add the buttermilk, water, or orange juice—add only enough so the mixture holds together. Chill the dough in the refrigerator for at least 1 hour. Roll the dough out between 2 sheets of wax paper and place it in a 10-inch pie plate. Soften the remaining 1 tablespoon of butter, and brush this butter over the crust. Refrigerate while you prepare the filling.

FILLING:

1 *pound ricotta or cottage cheese, whizzed in the blender until smooth (about 30 seconds)*

3 *eggs, beaten*

½ *pound spinach, sautéed in butter with a little pepper, salt, and basil, and 1 small onion, diced*

3 *tablespoons whole wheat pastry flour*

½ *cup grated sharp Cheddar cheese Dash of nutmeg*

1 *cup sour cream or yogurt, or half of each Paprika*

Preheat the oven to 375 degrees F. Mix all but the last 2 ingredients in a bowl, blending well. Spread the mixture in the unbaked pie shell. Top with the sour cream or yogurt. Dust with a generous amount of paprika. Bake for 35 to 40 minutes. Serve piping hot. Serves 6 to 8.

SPINACH-CHEESE DUMPLINGS

A beautiful blend of nutritious ingredients. Serve these tasty dumplings over whole wheat noodles and you have all the flavors of lasagne without the lengthy baking.

4 cups finely chopped
 fresh spinach
1½ cups ricotta or
 cottage cheese
¾ cup whole wheat
 bread crumbs
¼ cup wheat germ
2 eggs, beaten
1 clove garlic, minced
¼ cup chopped onion
¼ cup grated Parmesan
 or mozzarella cheese

½ teaspoon salt
 (optional)
1 teaspoon dried basil
 Dash of allspice
½ cup whole wheat or
 soy flour
2 quarts boiling water
1 teaspoon Tamari soy
 sauce
 Tomato or mushroom
 sauce

Combine the first 11 ingredients. Form into 1-inch balls and roll lightly in the flour. Chill. Bring the water to a boil in a deep saucepan. Add the Tamari and lower the heat to simmer. Drop the spinach dumplings into simmering water and cook until they rise to the top—about 4 to 5 minutes. Remove with a slotted spoon and serve with tomato or mushroom sauce. Makes 6 to 8 servings.

PECAN-CHEESE CASSEROLE
WITH
CREAMY MUSHROOM SAUCE

Crunchy with pecans and sunflower seeds, fortified with wheat germ and flavored with cheese, this epicurean preparation can be baked like a meatloaf. It is favored by meat-eaters as well as vegetarians for its blend of flavors and its meaty texture.

PECAN-CHEESE CASSEROLE:

1 cup coarsely
    chopped pecans
1 cup finely chopped
    sunflower seeds
1½ cups fine whole
    wheat bread crumbs
½ cup wheat germ
    (preferably raw)
¾ cup finely chopped
    onion

4 eggs, beaten
½ cup grated Cheddar
    cheese
2 tablespoons butter,
    melted
1 tablespoon Tamari
    soy sauce
1 cup milk

Combine all the ingredients in a bowl. Mix thoroughly. Place in a buttered 1½ to 2-quart casserole and bake in a preheated 325-degree F. oven for 30 minutes. Serve with Creamy Mushroom Sauce.

CREAMY MUSHROOM SAUCE:

3 tablespoons butter
1 cup sliced fresh
    mushrooms
½ cup diced onion
½ cup chopped celery

2 tablespoons whole
    wheat pastry flour
1 cup hot water
½ cup light cream

Melt the butter in a saucepan and sauté the mushrooms, onion, and celery briefly. Blend in the flour; add the hot water and cream. Cover the pan. Let it steam for about 5 minutes, or until the vegetables are crisp-tender. Add more water if necessary. Season to taste. Serve with the Pecan-Cheese Casserole. Serves 8 to 10.

VARIATIONS: Peanuts may be substituted for the pecans. Tomato sauce may be substituted for the Creamy Mushroom Sauce. For Vegetarian Cheeseburgers, chill the Pecan-Cheese loaf then slice. Top each slice with a slice of mozzarella cheese and place under the broiler until the cheese melts.

Cottage Cheese-Potato Casserole

If you've never blended cheese with a potato, you have a delightful surprise awaiting you in this easy-to-prepare loaf that brings you a blintz taste with an extra dimension. An excellent protein dish, especially for those who can't eat eggs.

Butter
6 *medium-sized potatoes, cooked and sliced*
2 *cups cottage cheese*
2 *tablespoons butter, softened*
2 *tablespoons whole wheat pastry flour*
¼ *cup wheat germ*
2 *tablespoons chopped fresh parsley or 1 teaspoon dried parsley flakes*

½ *teaspoon sea salt*
½ *teaspoon kelp*
½ *teaspoon paprika*
1 *teaspoon crushed thyme*
2 *teaspoons nutritional yeast*
⅓ *cup milk*
2 *tablespoons grated Parmesan cheese (optional)*
4 *tablespoons sesame seeds (optional)*

Place a layer of the sliced potatoes in a buttered 1½-quart casserole. In a bowl, combine the cottage cheese and the butter; mix till fluffy. In a separate bowl, combine the flour and wheat germ with the seasonings and yeast. Cover the potatoes with a layer of the cottage cheese mixture. Sprinkle with the flour mixture. Repeat this layering. The top layer should be sliced potatoes. Pour the milk over all.

Combine the grated cheese and/or sesame seeds. Sprinkle this mixture on top. Bake in a preheated 350-degree F. oven for 30 minutes. Serve with a salad and cold borscht. Serves 6.

Ambrosia Cream Dessert

A favorite dairy dessert, especially for Yom Kippur night. Yogurt helps to maintain the necessary flora in the intestinal tract and has been found to lower cholesterol levels. It is much lower in calories than sour cream, is more digestible, and it tastes good. Gradually decrease the amount of sour cream you use in this dessert and increase the amount of yogurt in proportion.

1 *can (20 ounces)*
unsweetened
crushed pineapple
2 *oranges*
1 *pint plain yogurt*
½ *pint sour cream*
½ *cup coarsely*
chopped walnuts

½ *cup unsweetened*
coconut flakes
1 *pound seedless*
grapes plus any
fruit in season,
cut up

Drain the pineapple; reserve the juice for another use. Peel, section, and pit the oranges. Combine the yogurt and sour cream; add the rest of the ingredients, reserving a few orange sections as garnish. Serves 8 to 10.

HEAVENLY FRUIT DESSERT

Here, chewy sprouts and sweet and tart fruits are surrounded by luscious whipped cream.

¾ *cup heavy cream*
2 *cups pitted fresh*
cherries or peaches,
or 1 can (20 ounces)
unsweetened crushed
pineapple or pitted
tart cherries

¼ *cup honey*
½ *teaspoon vanilla*
extract
1½ *cups wheat sprouts*

You can substitute any fruit for those listed above (try nectarines). In a large bowl, whip the cream and fold in the rest of the ingredients. Serve in sherbert or parfait glasses. Serves 6.

VARIATION: Garnish with shredded coconut, sunflower seeds, or chopped walnuts.

PINEAPPLE CHEESECAKE

It's so good to be able to enjoy luscious cheesecake without conscience qualms. This one provides wholesome nutrients in every palate-pleasing bite. Cottage cheese is low in fat and high in protein, calcium, and selenium, the fantastic nutrient that works with vitamin E to preserve youth. Pineapple provides the protective vitamins A and C and an enzyme which helps in the digestion of protein.

Enjoy this cheesecake on the festival of Shavuot, as we do.

CRUST:

1 *cup whole wheat pastry flour*
¼ *cup butter, softened*
1 *tablespoon vegetable oil*
1 *egg, beaten*
2 *tablespoons sour cream or yogurt*
2 *tablespoons honey*
1 *tablespoon baking powder*
Pinch of salt

To make the crust, work the flour, butter, and oil together. Add the egg and the rest of the ingredients. Mix well, then roll the dough out and line the bottom and sides of an ungreased 10-inch spring-form pan. Bake in a preheated 350-degree F. oven for 10 minutes. Remove from the oven and let cool.

FILLING:

1 *pound cottage cheese*
1 *can (20 ounces) unsweetened crushed pineapple, drained*
4 *egg yolks, beaten*
¼ *cup honey*
Dash of cinnamon
4 *egg whites*
Pinch of cream of tartar
2 *tablespoons honey*

In a bowl, mix the cottage cheese, pineapple, egg yolks, the ¼ cup of honey, and cinnamon; blend well. Spread the mixture over the crust. Bake for 15 minutes in a preheated 400-degree F. oven. While the cake is baking, make a meringue by beating the 4 egg whites with the pinch of cream of tartar until stiff. Very gradually add the 2 tablespoons of honey. Remove the cake from the oven.

Spread the meringue on top. Return to the oven and bake till golden brown—about 15 minutes. Serves 8 to 10.

FROZEN STRAWBERRY-HONEY CHEESECAKE

An elegant dessert for Chanukah—and easy to make.

CRUST:

1 cup granola
½ cup wheat germ
1 egg, beaten

2 tablespoons butter, melted
Additional butter for pan

Preheat the oven to 350 degrees F. In a bowl, mix the granola and wheat germ. Mix in the beaten egg and the butter. Press the mixture into a well-buttered 11 x 7-inch pan and bake for 8 minutes. Let cool completely.

FILLING:

4 eggs, separated
8 ounces cream cheese, softened
⅓ cup honey
½ teaspoon vanilla extract

1 cup heavy cream
¾ cup purée of strawberries, fresh or frozen

In a large bowl, beat the egg yolks; add the softened cream cheese, honey, and vanilla. Beat until the mixture is smooth and light. In a separate bowl, whip the cream. Fold the whipped cream into the cheese mixture. In another bowl, beat the egg whites until stiff peaks form. Fold the beaten egg whites into the cream and cheese mixture. Pour the mixture into the cooled crust. Spoon the strawberry purée onto the fluffy cheesecake and swirl it through with a knife. Freeze the cake. When it is frozen solid, cover it and return to the freezer.

To serve, allow the cake to thaw in the refrigerator for 1½ hours, or at room temperature for 10 minutes. Serves 8 or more.

COTTAGE CHEESE CAKE
WITH MUERBE TEIG CRUST

This luscious cake with a rich, sweet, tender crust embracing a creamy filling is wonderful as a dessert for a light dairy meal. The crust can also be used for fruit pies.

MUERBE TEIG CRUST:

1 *cup minus 2 table-spoons whole wheat pastry flour*
2 *tablespoons soy flour*
Tiny pinch of salt
¼ *cup butter*

2 *teaspoons honey*
1 *egg yolk*
2 *tablespoons lemon juice, ice water, or brandy*

Combine the flours and the salt. Cut in the butter using a pastry blender or 2 knives until the mixture has the consistency of cornmeal. In a bowl, combine the honey and egg yolk; add it to the other mixture and stir. Add the liquid of your choice, drop by drop, using only enough to hold the mixture together. Pat into a 10-inch pie plate or spring-form pan and chill until it is ready to be filled.

FILLING:

¼ *cup butter, softened*
¼ *cup honey*
3 *eggs*
2 *cups dry cottage cheese (or 1 cup cottage cheese and 1 cup cream cheese)*

1 *tablespoon arrowroot starch*
Grated rind of 1 lemon

In a large bowl, cream the butter. Add the honey and mix thoroughly. Beat in the eggs, 1 at a time. Rub the cottage cheese through a sieve or put it in a blender with the arrowroot and lemon rind. Whiz till blended and add to the butter mixture.

Turn the filling into the pie plate or spring-form pan lined with the Muerbe Teig pastry. Bake in a preheated 425-degree F. oven for 10 minutes; then lower the heat to 325 degrees F. and bake for 25 to 30 minutes more, or until nicely browned. Remove the cake from the oven and let cool; then refrigerate. Serves 6 to 8.

Coconut Cream Pie

This pie, which makes its own crust, cozies up to your palate like whipped cream.

2 *cups milk*	4 *eggs*
½ *cup honey*	¼ *cup butter, softened*
½ *cup whole wheat pastry flour*	1½ *teaspoons vanilla extract*
2 *teaspoon baking powder*	1 *cup unsweetened coconut flakes*

Blend all ingredients except the coconut at low speed for 3 minutes. Place in a buttered 10-inch pie plate. Let stand for 5 minutes. Sprinkle the coconut on top. Bake in a preheated 325-degree F. oven for 40 minutes. Serves 6 to 8.

Pineapple Frozen Yogurt

A dairy treat featuring yogurt. Yogurt creates a healthy intestinal environment, which helps the body manufacture the whole family of B vitamins. Many people who are allergic or sensitive to milk can tolerate yogurt. Ancient tradition holds that an angel taught Abraham how to make yogurt, and some believe that yogurt contributed to his longevity and his ability to father a child at an advanced age. A lovely Shavuot dessert.

1 *can (20 ounces) unsweetened crushed pineapple*	1 *medium-ripe banana, peeled and cut into chunks*
1 *envelope kosher gelatin*	½ *cup unsweetened coconut flakes*
2 *cups plain yogurt*	1 *teaspoon vanilla extract*
	2 *teaspoons honey*

Drain the pineapple, reserving the juice in a small saucepan. Sprinkle the gelatin over the juice. Heat over a low flame until the gelatin is dissolved. Combine the yogurt and banana in a blender; whiz till smooth. Continue to whiz while you slowly add the gelatin mixture. Add the pineapple, coconut, vanilla, and honey as well. Whiz just to blend. Pour into a large bowl and freeze for 2 hours, stirring once or twice. Then remove from the freezer and beat the mixture with an electric mixer until smooth. Return to the freezer until "softly" frozen—1 to 2 hours. Makes 6 servings.

BETTY'S OUT-OF-THIS-WORLD CAKE

Pineapple-cream cheese filling rests between the layers of this crunchy pecan-coconut-cookie crumb cake, making this a treat that is truly "out of this world."

BATTER:

½ *cup honey*
½ *cup butter, softened*
4 *eggs*
1 *teaspoon baking power*
1 *pound graham crackers, finely crushed (Health food stores carry sugarless graham crackers, or use 2½ cups of your own good cake and cookie crumbs.)*

1 *cup plain yogurt or buttermilk*
1 *cup chopped pecans*
1 *cup unsweetened shredded coconut*

In a bowl, cream the honey with the butter; add the eggs, 1 at a time. In a separate bowl, sprinkle the baking powder over the cracker crumbs and stir. Add the crumb mixture to the creamed ingredients alternately with the yogurt or buttermilk, blending well. Add the chopped nuts and coconut to the batter and mix well with a wooden spoon.

Spoon the batter into 3 greased and floured 8-inch round pans. The batter will be thick. Bake in a preheated 350-degree F. oven for 40 minutes. Cool the cakes in their pans for 15 minutes before turning out. Cool completely before spreading the filling between layers.

FILLING:

1 *can (20 ounces) unsweetened crushed pineapple*

3 *ounces cream cheese or 1½ ounces cream cheese and 1½ ounces cottage cheese*

2 *tablespoons honey*

Drain the pineapple. Cream the cheese; add the honey, then the pineapple, and mix well. Spread between the cake layers when they are absolutely cool. Serves 10 to 12.

5

To Be Kosher & Vegetarian

Recipes to help you be a healthy vegetarian. They present a good balance of amino acids comparable to what you would get in meat or fish. Any of the recipes that do not contain dairy ingredients can be served as pareve dishes.

Last Saturday night we were honored by the local Jewish Day School at a black-tie dinner-dance. Featured as the main course were thick slabs of prime roast beef with kishke. Two guests at our table asked if they could have a vegetarian alternative.

"I'll see what I can do," the waitress said uncertainly, "we've had so many vegetarian requests, we're running out of eggplant."

There is no longer any doubt that vegetarianism is a way of eating whose time has come—again, even for many who were brought up on brisket, chicken soup, and cholent. I say "again" because no meat was eaten in the Garden of Eden. Meat was not introduced as food for humans until the time of Noah when God said: "Every moving thing which is alive is given to you for eating, like the vegetation and grasses I give you everything." Some see this license to eat meat as a concession on the part of God to human weakness. Others reason, if it is imperative that the schochet observe kindness and mercy in the act of slaughter, how much more kind and merciful to spare the animal's life?

119

Which reminds me of a very funny story about Leo Tolstoy. A Russian woman accepted with delight the famous author's invitation to dinner. When she entered the dining room, she let out a *ge'shrai*. There was a live chicken tied to her chair. "My conscience forbids me to kill it," Tolstoy, a committed vegetarian, told his visitor. "As you are the only guest taking meat, I would be greatly obliged if you would first undertake the killing."

The abhorrence of killing animals is one factor which is swelling the ranks of the vegetarians, who now number 10 million in this country alone. Other factors are an increasing awareness of the food shortages facing a large part of the hungry world and the possible link between cancer and the various chemicals and hormones fed to animals to fatten them up.

Quite a few college students of my acquaintance have announced a switch to vegetarianism, much to the consternation of their parents, who fear their kids will waste away from malnutrition, consumption, or pernicious anemia. Actually, if they are avoiding junk foods and planning their diets wisely, keeping in mind the importance of complementary proteins, these young people are reducing their risk of heart disease, cancer, high blood pressure, overweight, and in fact enjoying better odds for living to see their grandchildren grow up than the average gedempte flaish enthusiast.

The word vegetarian is not, as one might think, derived from vegetable, but from the Latin *vegetus,* which means "whole, sound, fresh, lively." Statistically, vegetarians in the United States are thinner, healthier, and live longer than meat-eaters.

Switching to greater use of grains, vegetables, fruits, seeds, and nuts can actually increase your intake of essential nutrients while reducing your consumption of calories and saturated fats.

Be it for reasons of health, economics, ethics, or ecology, the number of vegetarians in the United States has almost doubled since 1970. At some colleges so many students follow a vegetarian diet that the food service contractor is instructed to provide good vegetarian meals. At Purchase College in New York State, vegetarian main dishes that combine beans and grains, nuts, seeds, and greens for proper amino acid patterns are on the menu every day.

The rise in vegetarianism is particularly notable at colleges with large Jewish populations, Arlene Pianko Groner points out in her excellent article "Can Vegetarianism Become the Ultimate Dietary Law?" (*The National Jewish Monthly,* April 1976.)

Some of these new Jewish vegetarians are committed halachic Jews who see vegetarianism as the ultimate form of kashrut. Outstanding among them is Jonathan Wolf, a teacher who frequently hosts vegetarian galas to mark the Jewish festivals in the eight-room Manhattan apartment he shares with two other vegetarians and which serves as an eating center to share views on halachic vegetarianism. At one TuB'Shevat meal, 60 guests celebrated the beginning of the Jewish agricultural year with a taste of each of the biblical Seven Fruits of the Land.

In Judaism the killing of animals is justified only with great hesitation—and some misgivings. The schochet sheds a tear.

The Talmud, referring to Deuteronomy 14:26, says, "Man should not eat meat unless he has a special craving for it, and even then, only occasionally and sparingly."

Also in the Talmud: "The longevity of the generations from Adam to Noah is due to their vegetarian diet."

Zerubbabel attributes the good morals and keen intellect of the Hebrews to their scant eating of meat.

But, there are Jewish traditions which make it hard to be both an observant Jew and a vegetarian. Also in the Talmud is a description of the ways a Jew celebrates Passover, Shavuot, and Sukkot: "There is no happiness without meat."

One could define the word "meat" in its figurative sense, meaning food in general, but the association of meat with celebrations is so strong that some halachic vegetarians do eat a symbolic piece of chicken on festive occasions. Michel Abehsera, a committed halachic vegetarian and author of *Cooking For Life* and *Our Earth Our Cure,* (Swan House, Brooklyn, New York), told me that on the Sabbath he eats a little bit of chicken or fish, and his wife, also a vegetarian, prepares chicken for the many guests at their Shabbos table who might feel deprived without it.

Whether you are a halachic vegetarian, an ethical vegetarian, the mother of a vegetarian, or a meat-eater who would like to reduce meat consumption, or if you would simply enjoy a change of pace in your diet, let me assure you that it is possible to maintain health and vigor on a purely vegetarian diet. It's also possible to enjoy some great meals, but you must know what you are doing. You must have at least a rudimentary knowledge of protein patterns.

HOW TO BE A HEALTHY VEGETARIAN

If you were to make a chart of protein foods—such as meat, eggs, milk, soybeans—and list them according to their desirable amino acid patterns, which food do you think would head the list? Did you answer meat? You are wrong. I know that the cattle industry ballyhoos meat as the superior protein. But meat does *not* top the list. The egg—the incredible edible egg—tops the list. Eggs are the perfect protein food and, in fact, the standard by which proteins are measured. Even milk is superior to meat. Soybeans are very close to meat. If you include eggs and dairy products in your diet, no problems will result. You can just omit the meat, use some form of these foods, and you're in business.

If you should plan a meal without these components, the key words are complementary proteins. Suffice it to say, for our purposes, that there are eight essential amino acids or protein-building blocks.

One of the dangers inherent in the vegetarian diet is the possibility of an imbalance in amino acids. Not only must all the essential aminos be supplied in adequate amounts, they must be supplied at the same time. Eggs, dairy products, meat, and fish are complete proteins, which means they contain all the essential amino acids in the correct proportions. Because amino acids depend upon each other to make body tissue, if one is absent, none of them is used. It's like trying to make brick without straw.

The tryptophan you consume in the morning in your oatmeal does not sit around waiting for a delivery of lysine to come from your brown rice eaten at dinner.

Laboratory animals that were fed a diet consisting of all the essential amino acids except one could not maintain growth, even if the missing amino was fed several hours after the incomplete mixture.

When people in the Deep South lived mainly on a diet of corn, pellagra became endemic. Corn is low in tryptophan, which the body uses to manufacture niacin, an essential B vitamin.

O.K. So what's the secret formula? Do you have to have a speaking acquaintance with all those aminos and jiggle them around every time you sit down to a meal? Must you keep a slide rule or a calculator in your pocket? Not necessary. Here is a simple guide, courtesy of Dr. Roger J. Williams of the University of Texas, author of *Nutrition Against Disease* (Pitman, New York, 1971):

"Don't restrict yourself to one part of a living organism, try to get the whole works. In the plant world do not restrict yourself to green leaves (spinach, kale, romaine, endive) or to roots (parsnips, turnips, carrots, potatoes) or to seeds (corn, wheat, rye) or to fruit (apples, tomatoes). Each of these is in itself incomplete. A combination diet containing leaves, roots, tubers, seeds, and fruits is a vast improvement. Early in the history of animal nutrition it was found that seeds and leaves have a profound supplementary action.

Helpful hint: Nuts, seeds, avocados, whole grains, and legumes are considered incomplete proteins. But, according to Dr. Williams' formula, when eaten with raw, green, leafy vegetables, they provide a complete protein well utilized by the body.

Raw foods such as salads, fresh fruits, and sprouts are important in everyone's diet, vegetarian or not, but they have particular importance to the vegetarian because some essential aminos, particularly lysine, are heat sensitive. The higher the heat or the longer the cooking period, the more lysine is lost. The one food that improves its protein picture with cooking is the soybean. It contains a protein inhibitor which is destroyed by heat.

To insure yourself a complete amino acid pattern, make sure you have with every meal of cooked foods either raw fruit, raw salad greens, raw sprouts, or unroasted seeds.

Here are some more helpful hints:
● Nutritional yeast, sometimes called brewer's yeast, is rich in the amino acids that are low in soy and peanut flour. When using these flours, add a little nutritional yeast. If you are avoiding dairy products and using soy milk, add a little yeast to it. Start with very small quantities and gradually increase

until you can take one tablespoon in one glass of milk. This practice would guarantee you some excellent protein.
- Beans and grains have complementary protein patterns. Whenever you use whole wheat flour (made from a grain), one-fifth should be soy flour (made from a bean). Remember the ratio: five parts grain to one part legume.
- When you cook brown rice (a grain), add some lentils, split peas, or mung beans to the pot. About three tablespoons of beans to one cup of rice.

Here are some more good combinations:
- Cook lentils with barley or rice.
- Cook split peas with cracked wheat or bulgur wheat.
- Add cracked wheat to chili beans.
- Serve chili beans with polenta (cornmeal).

Remember that eating a mixture of protein sources multiplies the protein value of the meal. Here is a case where the whole is greater than the sum of its parts.

- If you use dry skim milk, make sure you get the spray dried kind. When skim milk is subjected to the intense heat process, these important amino acids are destroyed: lysine, methionine, and valine (*Modern Nutrition,* October, 1960).
- When you eat nuts, mix them up. Cashews are high in lysine. Brazil nuts are a good source of methionine, as are sunflower and sesame seeds. Combine nuts with raisins for a more complete protein pattern. Remember rozhinkes mit mandlin? The old folks knew their aminos.

GET SOME B$_{12}$

The one essential vitamin sometimes in short supply in a vegetarian diet is B$_{12}$, which is associated with animal proteins. Lacto-ovo vegetarians, who eat eggs and milk in generous amounts, are not quite so vulnerable as are vegans, who avoid all animal by-products. Remember that pernicious anemia in vegetarians frequently escapes diagnosis. That is because the vegetarian diet is rich in the green vegetables which provide lots of folic acid. The folic acid, an essential nutrient, keeps the blood picture looking normal and masks the evidence so that irreparable nerve damage can occur before the B12 deficiency is discovered.

Nutritional yeast, wheat germ, soybeans, sunflower seeds, and sprouted garbanzos do have some B12. But, to be nutritionally safe, it would be wise for everyone on a vegetarian diet to take a daily vitamin B supplement that provides B12, thereby avoiding the possibility of neurological damage which might not show its symptoms for five years. B12 is made from molds. It is not synthetic or of animal origin when you get it as a supplement.

Can you enjoy a vegetarian diet and still get back to your ancestral roots? Indeed you can. Back in the shtetl, where meat was a rare commodity, many delicious meatless dishes were devised—kugels, blintzes, kreplach, and kasha varnishkas are all examples of complete protein dishes. But, remember, in those days flour was not refined. Everything was made with the coarser whole grain flour which provided important values that are lacking in today's commercial version of flour and therefore lacking in the foods you make from it.

If you use whole wheat soy noodles or add wheat germ and a little soy to a lukshen kugel made with cheese and eggs, it will provide more and better protein than you get in a pastrami sandwich.

The helpful chart below indicates the protein combinations that can be used as alternatives to meat. Use any food from one column with any food from another.

Protein Combinations as Alternatives to Meat

Grains, Cereals, Flours	Legumes	Nuts, Seeds	Dairy
whole wheat, whole wheat flour	soybeans	pine nuts	milk
rye, rye flour	soy grits	pumpkin seeds	yogurt
corn, cornmeal	soybean curd	squash seeds	cottage cheese
barley	(tofu)	sunflower seeds	powdered milk
buckwheat kasha	mung beans	sesame seeds	ricotta cheese
buckwheat flour	whole or split	peanuts	natural cheese
bulgur wheat	peas	peanut butter	(Swiss, Edam,
oatmeal	kidney beans	sesame butter	Cheddar, Brie, etc.)
brown rice	cowpeas	(tahina)	eggs
wheat bran	black beans	almonds	
wheat germ	garbanzos	cashews	
noodles, macaroni, spaghetti,	lentils	brazil nuts	
preferably whole grain	other common	black walnuts	
whole grain bread	beans		

So, in summary, whether you are a halachic vegetarian, an ethical, health-minded or ecologic vegetarian, or the mother of a vegetarian, or if you simply want to cut down on your consumption of meat, you can enjoy the taste and health values of the delicious vegetarian dishes in this chapter. They are all nutritionally balanced to give you complete proteins.

VEGETARIAN BOUILLON
(STOCK)

This stock has a thick consistency, is pleasant to the taste, and is rich in minerals and strengthening nutrients. Particularly good for growing children and convalescents.

1 *tablespoon wheat grains*	1 *tablespoon corn or cornmeal*
1 *tablespoon whole oat grains (use oatmeal if you don't have oat grains)*	1 *tablespoon bran*
	1 *tablespoon dry lentils*
1 *tablespoon uncooked barley*	1 *tablespoon dried white beans*
1 *tablespoon rye grains*	3 *quarts water*

Place all ingredients in a large soup pot with 3 quarts of water. Bring to a boil and let simmer until the stock is reduced to 1 quart— about 3 hours. Blenderize and season to taste. Makes 1 quart.

VEGETABLE SOUP WITH PECAN DUMPLINGS

Pecan dumplings, seasoned with such aromatics as garlic, parsley, sage, and marjoram and fortified with the yolk of an egg, give this hearty vegetable soup an extra culinary dimension.

1 carrot

2 tablespoons vegetable oil

2 quarts water or vegetable stock

1 parsnip or parsley root

3 small potatoes

2 ribs celery

1 clove garlic

2 onions, with skin

1 teaspoon vegetable salt (Vegit or Spike)
White pepper, to taste

1 teaspoon celery seeds

2 tablespoons finely minced onion

¼ cup whole wheat or rye flour

¼ cup bread crumbs or wheat germ

1 egg yolk

½ cup cold water
Pinch of garlic salt
Pinch of freshly ground black pepper

1 slice whole grain bread soaked in water, then pressed out and torn into small pieces

2 tablespoons finely chopped pecans

1 tablespoon finely chopped fresh parsley
Pinch of sage or marjoram

1 egg white, beaten to soft peaks

3 cups water

Scrub the carrot and grate 2 tablespoons. In a large soup pot, heat 1 tablespoon of the oil; add the grated carrot. Heat and stir for 1 minute. Add the water or stock, the rest of the carrot, and the next 8 ingredients. Cover, bring to a boil, and simmer for 1½ hours.

While the soup is cooking, make the dumplings. Heat the remaining 1 tablespoon of oil in a medium-sized skillet, then add the minced onion and sauté till golden. Sprinkle the flour and bread crumbs or wheat germ over the onion and sauté briefly.

In a bowl, beat the egg yolk with the cold water; add the garlic salt and pepper. Add this mixture to the onion mixture. Add the soaked bread, the chopped pecans, parsley, and sage or marjoram. Let stand for 15 minutes, then fold in the beaten egg white.

In a saucepan, bring the 3 cups of water to a boil. With a small spoon, take ½ tablespoon of the dumpling mixture and ease it into the vigorously boiling water. Repeat until the mixture is used up. Reduce the heat and simmer for 15 minutes, till the dumplings are light and fluffy. Remove the dumplings with a slotted spoon, place a few in each soup bowl, and spoon the vegetables and soup over them. Serves 6 to 8.

CREAMY SQUASH SOUP

A smooth, creamy soup that tastes rich but is very low in calories and very high in vitamin A.

1 *large onion, sliced*	6 *cups water*
3 *tablespoons vegetable oil*	1 *teaspoon sea salt (optional)*
4 *cups washed and sliced butternut squash*	*Chopped parsley*

In a soup pot, sauté the onion in the oil until transparent. Add the squash and cook for 5 minutes. Add the water and salt. Bring to a boil, then reduce the heat immediately and simmer for 30 minutes. Purée the contents of the pot in a blender until creamy. Add chopped parsley as garnish. Serves 8.

SCHAV
(Sorrel or Sourgrass Borscht)

1 *pound schav (sorrel)*	*Juice of 2 lemons (or less, to taste)*
1 *quart water*	
½ *teaspoon salt (optional)*	2 *egg yolks or 1 whole egg*
1 *small onion, chopped*	*Sour cream or yogurt*
2 *tablespoons honey*	

Wash the sorrel leaves very carefully. Drain and chop fine. Add the water and salt (if desired). Bring to a boil. Add the onion and lower the heat to simmer. Allow to cook slowly for 10 minutes. Add the honey and lemon juice. Simmer a few minutes longer. Beat the egg yolks or whole egg. Add a little of the hot liquid to the egg mixture and beat. Add a little more and beat. Add the egg mixture to the pot and beat to prevent curdling. Let cool and refrigerate. Serve cold with sour cream or yogurt. Serves 8.

COLD FRUIT SOUP

1 *cup prunes*	1½ *tablespoons*
1 *cup dried apricots*	*arrowroot starch*
2 *quarts warm water*	*Cold water*
1 *stick cinnamon*	3 *apples, unpeeled (if*
2 *tablespoons honey*	*unsprayed) and*
	diced

Soak the dried fruit with the cinnamon stick overnight in the warm water. In the morning, strain out the fruit. Remove the prune pits and cinnamon stick. Add the honey to the juice. Mix the arrowroot starch with a little cold water and add it to the juice. Boil for a few minutes to thicken; add all the fruit and let stand till cool. Chill in the refrigerator. Serve with a dollop of yogurt, sour cream, or whipped cream. A nice dessert, too. Serves 8.

MILLET SOUP

Millet is one of the most well-balanced and least allergenic of all the grains. It is rich in protein, minerals, vitamins, and lecithin.

Osborne and Mendel, of Yale University, found that millet was the only grain able to supply experimental animals with all the essential amino acids and vitamins when fed as an exclusive food.

Dr. Ernst Krebs, of California, feels that the decreased use of millet has contributed to the increase in cancer. Millet is one of the richest sources of nitrilosides which, says Dr. Krebs, are a natural cancer preventative. The popular grains in this country, like wheat and rye, do not contain an appreciable amount of this anti-cancer factor, unless the grains are sprouted.

When millet is cooked, a mucilaginous substance rises to the surface. This substance exerts a bland healing action in cases of gastrointestinal inflammation and ulceration. It is one of the most easily digested of all grains. Great for babies, too!

Millet cooked with other vegetables as a soup or stew can be a meal in a dish. Toss a salad, add some fresh fruit, and you have a perfectly delectable, well-balanced, high-protein meal.

½ *cup diced onion*
½ *cup diced celery*
1 *garlic clove, minced*
2 *tablespoons safflower oil*
2 *cups sliced fresh mushrooms*
½ *cup diced carrot*
¼ *cup minced fresh parsley*
1 *tablespoon minced fresh dill or ½ teaspoon crushed dill seed*
½ *cup millet*
2 *cups vegetable stock*
2 *cups water*

2 *teaspoons Tamari soy sauce*
1 *teaspoon Italian seasoning (a mixture of crushed oregano, basil, rosemary, thyme, and paprika)*
2 *teaspoons nutritional yeast*
¼ *teaspoon celery seed*
¼ *teaspoon allspice*
1½ *cups skim or whole milk*
½ *cup powdered nonfat milk (spray dried)*

In a large soup kettle, sauté the onion, celery, and garlic in the oil for 3 minutes. Add the mushrooms and stir for 3 minutes. Add all remaining ingredients except the milk and milk powder. Cover and cook over low heat for 30 minutes. Combine the liquid and dry milk; add to the soup, stirring constantly; mix thoroughly. Serves 8 to 10.

LENTIL-MILLET LOAF

The combination of lentils and millet makes this a simple yet nicely-balanced meal. The lentils and millet are complemented by the apple, carrot, and soy granules.

1½ cups cooked lentils (½ cup brown lentils to 1½ quarts water and ¼ teaspoon salt, cooked for 30 minutes)

1 cup cooked millet (1 cup water to ¼ cup of millet and ¼ teaspoon salt. Bring the water to a boil. Gradually add the millet, stirring constantly. Cook over low heat for 30 minutes or until all the water is absorbed.)

2 eggs

1 unpeeled (if unsprayed) apple, shredded

½ cup grated carrot

2 tablespoons sesame oil

½ cup soybean granules

1 teaspoon kelp

¼ teaspoon savory

¼ teaspoon dried parsley or chives

½ teaspoon Spike or a good seasoning salt

2 tablespoons toasted sesame seeds

Combine all the ingredients except the sesame seeds and mix thoroughly. Pour the mixture into a lightly oiled 9 x 5-inch loaf pan and sprinkle with the sesame seeds. Bake for 45 minutes in a preheated 375-degree F. oven. Serves 6 to 8.

VEGETARIAN CHOPPED LIVER

While enjoying this vegetarian dish, you will benefit from the eggplant, which is rich in potassium, very low in calories, and tends to lower cholesterol levels.

1 *medium-sized eggplant*
1 *egg, well beaten*
2 *tablespoons whole wheat flour*
1 *tablespoon milk or light cream*
Salt and freshly ground pepper
2 *onions, chopped*
Butter
1 *tablespoon vegetable oil or butter*
2 *hard-cooked eggs, chopped fine*

Slice the eggplant into ¼-inch-thick slices; set aside. In a bowl, make a paste of the beaten egg, flour, and milk or cream. Add salt and pepper to taste. Dip the eggplant slices, 1 at a time, into this mixture; place the eggplant in a buttered baking dish, and bake at 350 degrees F. until brown and soft. Meantime, sauté the onions in the tablespoon of oil or butter. Remove the eggplant from the oven. When cool enough to handle, chop it fine. Add the chopped hard-cooked eggs and the sautéed onion; mix well. Chill and serve. Serves 4 to 6 as an appetizer.

FALAFEL

Just like in Israel! Serve this treat in whole wheat pita garnished with tomatoes, lettuce, olives, and tahina. Or serve with brown rice, a salad, and applesauce for a change of pace.

2 cups cooked
chickpeas (about 1
cup dried)
⅓ cup cooking water
(necessary only if
using a blender to
purée)
Crumbs from 1 slice
whole wheat bread
1 tablespoon soy flour
2 cloves garlic, finely
minced
1 egg, lightly beaten
2 tablespoons chopped
fresh parsley
¾ teaspoon salt

¼ teaspoon ground
cumin
¼ teaspoon basil
¼ teaspoon marjoram
¼ teaspoon cayenne
pepper (or less, to
taste)
White pepper, to
taste
1 tablespoon tahina
(sesame butter)
Whole wheat or soy
flour for coating
5 tablespoons
vegetable oil

Mash or grind the chickpeas or put them through a blender with the ½ cup water. Combine the chickpeas and all the remaining ingredients except the flour for coating and the oil. The mixture will be soft. Form it into 1-inch balls, coat with the flour, and sauté in the oil until crisp. Then turn the balls and sauté on the other side. Serves 4 to 6.

Mamaligge

The dish every Rumanian would walk a mile for—in the rain.

2 cups yellow
cornmeal
1 cup cold water
3 cups boiling water
½ teaspoon salt

2 tablespoons wheat
germ
2 tablespoons
vegetable oil (or
chicken fat or
butter)

Combine the cornmeal with the cup of cold water. Stir well. Pour the boiling water into the top pot of a double boiler. Add the salt to the boiling water; stir in the cornmeal mixture. Cook over moderate heat for 5 minutes, stirring constantly. Now place over boiling water in the bottom pot of the double boiler and continue to cook for 20 to 30 minutes, stirring occasionally. Stir in the wheat germ. Add the vegetable oil (or chicken fat or butter). For a fleishig meal, serve with gravy. For a milchig meal, serve with pot cheese or sour cream. Serves about 6.

Mock Wild Rice

½ *cup raw brown rice*
2 *tablespoons vegetable oil (or butter or chicken fat)*
1¼ *cups vegetable bouillon (or chicken broth)*

¼ *teaspoon sea salt*
⅓ *cup finely chopped walnuts*
½ *cup finely chopped fresh mushrooms*

Cook the rice in the fat until it is well browned. Add the bouillon (or broth). Cover and cook until all the liquid is absorbed—about 40 minutes. Add the salt, chopped nuts, and chopped mushrooms. Serves 4.

Kasha Varnishkas

The very fragrance of kasha cooking will quicken your appetite and bring back memories of those golden days of childhood.

This recipe is a little different from the one you might have grown up with. It has protein complements in the sesame seeds and the mushrooms. It's from Ellen Sue Spivack's very helpful guide for vegetarians called *A Beginner's Guide for Meatless Casseroles* (Deep Roots, Lewisburg, Pennsylvania 17837).

1 cup raw kasha
(buckwheat groats)
1 egg
½ teaspoon salt
(optional)
2 cups boiling water
1 package (12 to 16
ounces) whole grain
noodles, preferably
bow ties. If you
can't find the whole
wheat, use the white
ones and add 3
tablespoons of wheat
germ after cooking
and draining.

1 large onion, thinly
sliced
Vegetable oil for
sautéeing
1 cup sliced or
chopped fresh
mushrooms
4 tablespoons butter,
melted
⅔ cup sesame seeds
Salt and white
pepper, to taste

Place the kasha in a large skillet. Add the unbeaten egg and mix well. Place over low heat and stir constantly until each grain of kasha is coated. Add the ½ teaspoon salt (if desired), and pour in the boiling water. Cover and cook for 30 to 40 minutes, or until the water is absorbed and the grains are tender. Cook the noodles according to package directions. While the noodles and kasha are cooking, sauté the onion in oil until golden. Add the mushrooms and cook for 5 more minutes.

Drain the noodles (save the water for stock). Add to the noodles 3 tablespoons of the butter, the sesame seeds, a little salt and pepper. Combine this mixture with the cooked kasha. Add the sautéed vegetables and mix well. Serve it this way or put the whole mixture in an oiled casserole, top with the rest of the butter and bake at 350 degrees F. for 15 minutes. With a salad, good bread, and cheese, and maybe fruit or a pudding for dessert, you've got a nutritionally balanced meal. Serves 4 to 6.

VEGETARIAN KISHKE

2 *stalks celery with
    leaves, chopped*
1 *carrot, grated*
1 *large onion, chopped*
1 *teaspoon salt*

½ *cup vegetable oil*
1½ *cups whole wheat
    flour*
2 *teaspoons paprika*

Blend all ingredients except the flour and paprika in the blender. Do not blend too smooth: a coarse texture will make a more interesting kishke. When blended, add the flour and paprika. Spoon half of the mixture onto a large piece of heavy duty aluminum foil. Shape like a cylinder. Fasten the foil securely at the top and the sides. Do the same with the other half of the mixture. Place both rolls on a baking sheet (there might be some leakage). Bake in a 350-degree F. oven for 45 minutes. Carefully turn the kishke rolls over (to prevent burning on one side) and bake for approximately 45 minutes more. If additional browning is desired, turn the kishke rolls over once again and open the foil a bit. Remove the foil, slice, and serve. Serves 6 to 8 as a side dish.

VEGETABLE LOAF

Shoshana Hayman, wife of Rabbi Peter Hayman of Teaneck, New Jersey, who keeps an all-natural mostly-vegetarian kitchen, knows how to combine wholesome ingredients into appetizing dishes. She graciously shares this recipe with us. The loaf is good served hot or cold.

1 *cup chopped onion*
1 *cup chopped celery*
1 *cup grated carrot*
1 *cup ground walnuts*
  Vegetable oil

1 *cup whole wheat
    bread crumbs*
2 *eggs*
1 *teaspoon mixed
    seasonings*
1 *cup milk or stock*

Sauté the onion, celery, carrot, and walnuts in vegetable oil for 15 minutes. Add the remainder of the ingredients; combine well. Pour into an oiled loaf pan. Bake in a preheated 350-degree F. oven for approximately 45 minutes, until nicely browned. Serves 6

FRESH RUTABAGA PUFF

Rich in vitamin A, which is so good for your complexion, and in potassium, which is especially important to your heart muscle. This puff also wins plaudits for its mild turnip flavor and its velvety texture.

1 *large or 2 medium-sized rutabagas*	½ *teaspoon salt*
3 *tablespoons butter, softened*	⅛ *teaspoon freshly ground white pepper*
⅓ *cup milk*	¼ *teaspoon crushed dried tarragon leaves*
⅓ *cup chopped onion*	4 *eggs, separated*

Quarter the rutabagas and steam them over hot water or cook in a little water until fork-tender. (Reserve the cooking liquid for use in a soup or vegetable cocktail.) Peel and mash the cooked rutabagas in a large mixing bowl. Add 2 tablespoons of the butter and the milk. Beat with an electric mixer at low speed until smooth. Sauté the onion in the remaining tablespoon of butter until tender. Add to the rutabaga; add the seasonings.

Beat the egg yolks, then beat the egg whites until stiff and fold both into the rutabaga mixture. Turn into a buttered 1½-quart baking dish. Bake in a preheated 350-degree F. oven for 50 minutes or until lightly browned. Serves 6 to 8.

NOTE: Using this basic technique, you can make a delicious puffy kugel from any vegetable.

VARIATION: Use half rutabagas and half potatoes or carrots.

BROCCOLI-YAM OR SWEET POTATO PIE

Broccoli is one of the finest nutritional bargains on the market. It contains twice as much vitamin C as orange juice and also beats the orange in the potassium department. Broccoli contains substantial amounts of calcium, some of the B vitamins, and is an excellent source of vitamin A—as much as 2,500 international units in 3½ ounces. Be sure to use the broccoli leaves, for they are nutrient-rich. Broccoli provides all this goodness at a "cost" of only 26 calories in 3½ ounces.

The yams or sweet potatoes in this recipe contribute minerals, complementary proteins, and a delicious sweetness and consistency.

1 *onion, chopped*
½ *cup sliced mushrooms*
1 *tablespoon butter*
2 *cups chopped cooked broccoli*
1 *egg, lightly beaten*
2 *tablespoons sesame seeds*

1 *cup yams or sweet potato, steamed in ½ cup pineapple, apple, or orange juice in a pot with a tight-fitting lid*
1 *9-inch pie shell, prebaked for 10 minutes (recipe below)*

Pastry strips for lattice topping (recipe below)

In a skillet, sauté the onion and mushrooms in the 1 tablespoon of butter. In a bowl, mix this with the cooked broccoli. Add the lightly beaten egg. Place this mixture in the prebaked pie shell and sprinkle with 1 tablespoon of the sesame seeds. Mash the yams or sweet potato with the juice in which they were cooked and spread over all. Sprinkle with the other tablespoon of sesame seeds. Make a lattice crust. Bake at 400 degrees F. for 30 to 40 minutes, until the crust is browned. Serves 8 very nicely.

VARIATIONS: Omit the yams and place slices of mozzarella cheese over the broccoli. Or, substitute carrots or pumpkin for the yams or sweet potato.

WHOLE WHEAT PIE CRUST:

1½ cups whole wheat
 pastry flour
¼ teaspoon salt
 (optional)
¼ cup butter

6 to 7 tablespoons cold
 plain yogurt, sour
 cream, or Half-and-
 Half

In a small bowl, combine the flour and the salt (if desired). Add the butter and cut it in using a pastry blender or 2 knives until the mixture is crumbly. Add the yogurt, sour cream, or Half-and-Half a little at a time. Use only as much as you need to hold the dough into a ball.

Chill the dough for about an hour. Remove a piece of dough about as big as a tangerine. Roll out the large piece of dough to fit a 9-inch pie pan. Roll out the other piece and cut into strips to make a lattice top.

CHEESELESS ONION QUICHE

The onions in this custardy pie provide far more than the zesty flavor so favored by the ancient Hebrews. Many folk cures based on onions have been authenticated by recent scientific evidence. It seems that onions contain a substance called cycloallin, which helps the blood vessels dissolve clots, thus helping to prevent and alleviate heart disorders. Tests conducted in Newcastle, England, at the Royal Victoria Infirmary, show that this substance found in onions remains active even when the onions are boiled or sautéed.

⅓ cup butter
1 cup whole wheat
 pastry flour
3 to 4 tablespoons ice
 cold orange juice or
 water
3 tablespoons butter
2 cups chopped onions

3 eggs
1 cup sour cream or
 plain yogurt
½ cup milk
 Freshly ground
 pepper and paprika,
 to taste

Make a pie crust from the first 3 ingredients: Cut the butter into the flour using a pastry blender. Add the liquid a little at a time, using only enough to hold the dough together. Roll the dough out to form a 10-inch diameter circle. Place it in a 9-inch pie plate and crimp the edges. Prick the dough generously with a fork and bake it in a preheated 425-degree F. oven for 8 minutes.

To make the filling, heat the 3 tablespoons of butter in a skillet and add the chopped onions. Cook gently until soft; let cool. In a bowl, beat the eggs; add the sour cream or yogurt, milk, and seasonings, then the cooled onions. Pour the mixture into the pie crust. Bake at 350 degrees F. for 25 minutes or until the center is firm. Serves 6 to 8.

SWEET POTATO-APPLE PUDDING

Superb for the vegetarian as well as an excellent side dish for chicken, this pudding is exceptionally nutritious. The sweet potatoes will provide you with enough vitamin A to battle infection. The apples provide valuable fiber and many essential minerals, including magnesium, manganese, selenium, and zinc. Apples are also an excellent source of pectin, which binds with many toxic elements and ushers them out of your body.

4 *medium-sized sweet potatoes or yams*	2 *tablespoons water*
	2 *tablespoons honey*
3 *medium-sized apples*	½ *cup granola or*
1 *cup apple, orange, or pineapple juice*	*wheat germ*
	Chopped nuts
1 *tablespoon arrowroot starch*	*(optional)*
	Cinnamon

Steam the sweet potatoes or yams for 15 to 20 minutes, until tender. Peel and slice each lengthwise, about ½-inch thick. Layer the sweet potato or yam slices in a 9 x 9-inch ungreased casserole. Wash and core the apples. Slice the apples about ¼-inch thick and layer the slices on top of the sweet potatoes.

In a saucepan, heat the fruit juice to a boil. Combine the arrowroot and water and add it to the juice, cooking until the sauce has thickened. Add the honey and stir. Pour the sauce over the sliced apple, then top with the granola or wheat germ. If using wheat germ, add some chopped nuts. Dust with a little cinnamon. Bake in a preheated 325-degree F. oven for 45 minutes to 1 hour, until the apple slices are tender. Makes 6 to 8 servings as a side dish.

VARIATION: To make this dish for Passover, substitute potato starch for the arrowroot and use Passover Granola (see Index for recipe) for topping.

SUNFLOWER PATTIES

The sunflower seed is like a little sunlamp in your digestive system. It is one of the few foods that provides the sunshine vitamin D, so necessary to the utilization of calcium and phosphorous, both of which are plentiful in the sunflower seed. Its high protein content (24 percent) makes it an excellent substitute for meat. These meatless patties taste a lot like hamburgers.

2 tablespoons
vegetable oil
or butter
3 tablespoons chopped
onion
1 clove garlic, crushed
½ cup finely chopped
fresh mushrooms
½ cup chopped celery,
including leaves
½ cup grated raw
carrot
2 tablespoons chopped
green pepper
½ cup water
1 egg
1 cup ground
sunflower seeds
2 tablespoons wheat
germ
1 tablespoon
nutritional yeast

2 tablespoons chopped
fresh parsley or 1
teaspoon dried
parsley flakes
½ teaspoon kelp
¼ teaspoon chili
powder
¼ teaspoon dry
mustard
1 teaspoon finely
chopped fresh basil
or ½ teaspoon
crushed dried basil
2 teaspoons Tamari
soy sauce
¼ cup tomato sauce, or
as much as needed
to bind the
ingredients

Heat the oil or butter in a large skillet. Sauté the onion, garlic, mushrooms, celery, carrot, and pepper for 2 minutes. Add the ½ cup of water, cover the skillet, and allow to steam-sauté over medium heat for 3 minutes more. Turn the skillet ingredients into a large bowl and add the rest of the ingredients. Preheat the oven to 350 degrees F. Mix well. Form into flat patties about the size of hamburgers. Arrange in an oiled or buttered shallow baking dish about 10 x 6 inches. Bake until brown—about 20 minutes. Turn and brown the other side—about 10 minutes. Makes 8 patties.

VARIATIONS: (1) Coat with sesame seeds before baking. (2) Patties may be sautéed or broiled. (3) Try broiling with Cheddar cheese on top.

CEREAL BURGERS

1 *cup cooked cereal (variety of your choice)*
1 *onion, chopped*
½ *cup homemade or natural peanut butter*
1 *stalk celery, chopped*
½ *cup wheat germ*
2 *tablespoons soy flour*
¼ *cup whole grain bread crumbs*
2 *tablespoons milk or light cream*
½ *teaspoon dried sage*
¼ *teaspoon garlic powder*
Sesame seeds
Butter

Combine all but the last 2 ingredients and form into patties. Coat with sesame seeds and broil or sauté in butter. You can serve them like hamburgers with hot tomato sauce or you can put them in a casserole, cover with diluted soup of any kind and bake at 375 degrees F. until bubbly. Serves 4.

VEGETARIAN CHOLENT

There's no meat in this bean-barley-potato medley, which is nicely seasoned with spices and wine. But beans and barley have complementary amino acids that make this a high-protein dish with the same value to your body as meat. The flavors meld as the dish cooks slowly all night, filling the house with an appetite-stimulating aroma.

½ pound kidney beans
(1¼ cups)
½ pound navy beans
(1 cup)
Water
2 medium-sized
onions, sliced
2 cloves garlic, minced
½ cup sliced fresh
mushrooms
¼ cup vegetable oil
½ cup whole barley
1 teaspoon finely
chopped fresh basil
or ½ teaspoon
crushed dried basil

½ teaspoon chopped
dill weed
Salt, pepper, paprika,
cayenne, to taste
2 large carrots, sliced
4 large potatoes,
scrubbed and
quartered
1 cup dry red wine
2 teaspoons Tamari
soy sauce
1 bay leaf
Boiling water or
vegetable stock

If the beans have not been presoaked, wash them carefully, discarding any that are broken or discolored. Place in a large pot, and cover with water. Bring to a boil. Remove from the heat and allow to soak for about 1 hour.

In a large heavy pot, sauté the onions, garlic, and mushrooms in the oil. Add the beans, barley, herbs, and seasonings. Add the carrots, potatoes, the wine, Tamari, and bay leaf. Add boiling water or stock to about 1 inch above the contents. Adjust the seasonings to taste.

Before sundown on Friday, cover the pot tightly and allow to simmer slowly in a 225-degree F. oven or over very low heat on top of the stove. Let it cook all night until time to enjoy it for Sabbath (or any) lunch. Serves 6 to 8 hearty eaters.

BARLEY-MUSHROOM CASSEROLE

Barley is said to be the very first grain utilized by man, so I often serve it on Rosh Hashanah, the beginning of the New Year. Barley is a highly nutritious food: high in protein; rich in calcium, phosphorus, iron, potassium, and niacin; and it's very easy to digest. A wonderful side dish for fowl.

1 *cup whole barley*
1 *teaspoon sea salt*
8 *cups boiling water*
½ *cup chopped onion*
¼ *cup chopped green pepper*

½ *pound fresh mushrooms, sliced*
¼ *cup vegetable oil*
Dash of freshly ground pepper
¼ *teaspoon ground sage*

Add the barley and salt to a pot filled with the boiling water. Reduce the heat and cook uncovered over low heat for 1 hour, stirring occasionally; drain and reserve. Lightly brown the onion, green pepper, and mushrooms in the oil in a large skillet, stirring occasionally. Stir in the dash of pepper, sage, and cooked drained barley. Cook over low heat for 5 minutes. Place the mixture in a 1½-quart casserole. Bake uncovered in a preheated 350-degree F. oven for 25 to 30 minutes. Serves 6 to 8.

MANDARIN RICE PILAF

Cinnamon, cloves, orange, and toasted almonds bring a delightful combination of flavors to this raisin-and-rice dish. A Sukkot favorite.

1 *onion, finely chopped*
¼ *cup butter or vegetable oil*
2 *cups raw rice*
2 *cups orange juice*
2 *cups boiling water*

12 *whole cloves*
1 *small stick cinnamon*
¼ *cup sliced almonds*
3 *tangerines or oranges, peeled, sectioned, and pitted*
½ *cup raisins*

Sauté the onion in 2 tablespoons of the butter or oil in a large saucepan for 5 minutes. Add the rice and continue cooking for 5 minutes, stirring constantly. Combine the orange juice and 2 cups of boiling water. Pour the orange juice-water mixture over the rice; add the cloves and cinnamon. Cover and simmer for 40 minutes, or until all of the liquid is absorbed. Remove the cloves (count them) and cinnamon from the cooked rice.

Sauté the almonds in the remaining butter or oil until golden. Reserve a few tangerine or orange segments for garnish. Stir in the other segments and the raisins. Add this mixture to the cooked rice, stirring lightly to blend. Top with the reserved orange segments. Serves 6.

LENTIL-RICE CASSEROLE

Lentils and rice complement each other's amino acids, making this a high-protein dish. Lentils are rich in minerals (especially iron and calcium) and contain vitamin A and some of the B vitamins. Brown rice contains four times as much zinc as the white variety and is very rich in B vitamins, especially niacin, which tends to dissolve blood clots and is used in the treatment of phlebitis.

1 *cup lentils (orange or brown)*	1 *garlic clove, crushed*
2 *tablespoons butter*	1 *cup raw brown rice*
2 *medium-sized onions, finely chopped*	1 *teaspoon salt*
	1 *teaspoon turmeric*
½ *inch piece of fresh ginger, peeled and chopped very fine*	*Boiling water*
	2 *tablespoons milk*
	Sautéed onions for garnish (optional)

Wash the lentils. Melt the butter in a large saucepan. Add the onion, ginger, and garlic, and sauté until the onion is golden. Add the rice and lentils and sauté gently, stirring constantly for 2 minutes. Add the salt and turmeric; toss lightly and cook for 5 minutes.

Pour in enough boiling water to cover the rice and lentils by ½ inch. When the water bubbles vigorously, cover the pan, reduce the heat to very low, and cook for 30 to 35 minutes, or until the rice and lentils are cooked and all the water has been absorbed. Transfer to a heated serving dish. Drizzle the milk on top. Garnish with sautéed onions, if desired. Serves 4 to 6.

Carrot, Nut, and Rice Loaf

Serve with a salad and a good whole grain bread for a light meal that's high in essential nutrients.

3 *carrots*
1 *onion*
1 *cup peanuts or sun-flower seeds (or ½ cup of each)*
2 *eggs*
1 *cup cooked brown rice*

2 *tablespoons nutritional yeast*
1 *teaspoon Tamari soy sauce*
¼ *teaspoon crushed dried basil or thyme*

Grind or grate the carrots and onion into a bowl. Using a blender or seed mill, grind the nuts and/or seeds. Add this to the carrot mixture. Add the eggs, rice, yeast, Tamari, and basil or thyme. Coat a bread pan or a 9 x 5-inch baking dish with a mixture of oil and lecithin (½ teaspoon of each). Pour the carrot-nut mixture into the pan and bake for 30 minutes in a preheated 350-degree F. oven. Serves 4 to 6.

Meatless Chop Suey

Rice and beans eaten together provide superior quality protein and give this chop suey a satisfying, meaty texture and taste at a cost of a few dimes per serving. The sprouts contribute a fresh, lively quality.

2 tablespoons
vegetable oil
2 green peppers, diced
2 onions, thinly sliced
2 cups diced celery
3 cups mung or soy
sprouts
1 cup hot water or
vegetable stock (or
use water in which
you have soaked
seeds for sprouting)

½ teaspoon vegetable
seasoning (try Vegit,
a natural low-sodium
product available at
gourmet and health
food shops)
2 tablespoons
arrowroot starch
1 tablespoon Tamari
soy sauce
Scant water
Brown rice, cooked
Alfalfa sprouts

Heat the oil in a skillet and sauté the pepper, onion, celery, and sprouts for about 2 minutes. Add the water or stock and seasoning. Cover and cook gently for about 10 minutes. Combine the arrowroot, Tamari, and a little water to make a paste. Stir this paste into the vegetable mixture and cook for 2 minutes. Serve over brown rice. Top with a handful of alfalfa sprouts. Serves 4 to 6.

6

Tofu: The Pareve Wonder

Did you ever dream of eating your fill of luscious blueberry cheesecake without a worry about calories, cholesterol, or chemicals—and after a chicken dinner, yet?

I have great news for you. You can make luscious cheeseless cheesecake from tofu, a remarkable oriental food that marries well with Jewish cuisine.

I have used tofu in kugels, blintzes, gefilte fish, hamburgers, karnatzlach, stuffed cabbage, and in terrific creamy desserts. I can serve them with pride at any meal or occasion with never a worry about mixing meat and dairy.

Tofu is a natural wholesome alternative to the ubiquitous non-dairy concoctions that are loaded with chemicals and are potentially dangerous to your health. Derived from soybeans, tofu provides the protein of meat and fish and the versatility of whipped cream and eggs. It also provides lots of lecithin, which dissolves cholesterol, and the B vitamin choline, a substance needed by the brain.

Not only is tofu free from cholesterol, it has the remarkable ability of lowering cholesterol in those who have chronically high levels. This was demonstrated in a study by medical researchers in Milan, Italy, published in *The Lancet*, February 5, 1977. "The cholesterol-lowering effect of soybeans was remarkable," the researchers reported. "It was achieved within a few weeks and

149

Comparative Nutritional Evaluation Chart

(For reference, Carbo. = carbohydrates; Cal. = calories; Sod. = sodium; Vit. A = vitamin A; Thia. = thiamin; Ribo. = riboflavin; Nia. = niacim; and Vit. C = vitamin C.)

Food	Water %	Energy cal.	Protein gm.	Fat gm.	Carbo. gm.	Cal. mg.	Iron mg.	Sod. mg.	Vit. A I. U.	Thia. mg.	Ribo. mg.	Nia. mg.	Vit. C mg.
Soybean curd, 16 ounces..........	85	327	35	19	11	581	8.6	32	0	0.27	0.14	.5	0
Milk, whole 16 fluid ounces..........	87	318	17	17	24	576	0.2	244	700	0.14	0.82	.4	4
One-Serving Basis													
Soybean curd (Tofu), 1 (4-ounce) package.....	85	86	9.4	5.0	2.9	154	2.3	8	0	0.07	0.04	.1	0
Pressed Soybean curd, 3½ ounces..........	69	135	16.2	7.3	—	210	7.1	38	233	0.04	0.05	14.2	0
Soybean milk, 8 ounces..........	—	75	7.7	3.4	—	47	1.8	—	90	0.18	0.06	.5	0
Milk, whole, 8 ounces..........	87	159	8.5	8.5	12.0	288	0.1	122	350	0.07	0.41	.2	2

was probably superior to that expected even from several months' treatment with a low-cholesterol diet."

Tofu is also a terrific food for waist-watchers. An eight-ounce portion contains 147 calories, as opposed to 648 calories in an equal amount of hamburger and 320 in an equal amount of eggs.

Tofu is also a boon to your budget. This relatively inexpensive pareve wonder is available in oriental food stores, in many health food stores, in some supermarkets and, of course, in tofu shops, which are springing up all over the country.

Try the recipes given here by all means. But, don't stop there. Go creative. Freeze some tofu and it will have a different texture. Put a few frozen chunks in a jar of gefilte fish and let it marinate in the juices overnight. Eat it with horseradish and see if it doesn't taste just like gefilte fish. Even has the same spongy quality.

Last Friday, I blended a chunk of tofu with the potatoes for the Shabbos kugel. It was delicious, light in color and texture, and very tasty, too. Last night we had stuffed cabbage. I put a few chunks of tofu in the pot and darn if it didn't taste like chunks of meat.

Like a chameleon takes on colors, so does tofu take on flavors. Every time you prepare a meal, ask yourself, "Can I put some tofu in this dish?" Usually the answer is a big "Yes" and you are on the road to some delightful culinary discoveries.

Some of the wonderful recipes that follow were developed with the help of Andy Schechter and Greg Weaver, who run the very successful Tofu Shop in Rochester, New York.

GARLIC-FLAVORED TOFU DIP OR SALAD DRESSING

Garlic has a long and venerable reputation for killing germs. In fact, the Russians use a garlic vapor in their hospitals and as an antibiotic. It is rich in potassium, low in sodium, and provides some of the B vitamins and vitamin C. You get all these benefits to some degree in this pungent appetite-stimulating dip, which can easily be converted into a salad dressing.

1 *pound tofu*	½ *teaspoon chopped*
1 *clove garlic, crushed*	*dill weed*
2 *teaspoons prepared*	2½ *tablespoons lemon*
mustard	*juice*
1 *tablespoon sesame,*	1 *tablespoon finely*
sunflower, or olive	*chopped onion*
oil	3 *tablespoons Tamari*
	soy sauce

Purée all ingredients in a blender and you have a creamy dip that is kind to your waistline even though it tastes like it has a thousand calories. This makes 2 cups. Serve it as a dip in a pretty bowl surrounded by all kinds of vegetables in the raw. To use this dip as a salad dressing, simply thin it with a little water.

TOFU SPREAD

Tahina, or sesame butter, contributes linoleic acid, important to the body's utilization of fats, to a glowing complexion, and to the health of the prostate gland. Tahina also boasts a delicate nutty flavor, which is a perfect counterpoint to the other ingredients in this zippy spread.

1 *cake (8 ounces) tofu*	*Garlic powder*
2 *tablespoons tahina*	*(optional)*
1 *teaspoon Tamari soy*	*Lemon juice*
sauce	*(optional)*

Blend all ingredients with a fork. If you like, season with garlic powder and lemon juice. Spread on crackers, bread, or pita, or stuff into celery sticks. Makes a very nice dip for parties. Makes 1 cup.

TOFU AND GROUND BEEF

Here's a dish that gives you the flavor of meat with half the calories and fat. It tastes beefy, yet is made with only a half pound of ground beef.

1 *tablespoon vegetable oil*
½ *pound ground beef*
1 *clove garlic, minced*
2 *tablespoons finely chopped scallions or onions*
2 *cups sliced fresh mushrooms*

3 *cups tofu, cut into ½-inch cubes*
2 *tablespoons Tamari soy sauce*
1 *teaspoon honey*
1 *tablespoon arrowroot starch*
½ *cup water or stock*

Heat the oil in a heavy skillet or wok. Add the meat, garlic, scallions or onions, and mushrooms and sauté until the meat changes color. Drain off the fat.

Add the tofu, Tamari, and honey. Cover and cook slowly for 10 minutes. Stir the arrowroot into the water or stock; add to the tofu mixture. Cook over low heat until the mixture thickens. This is a high-protein, mineral-rich dish that provides only 180 calories in a ½-cup serving. Makes a meal for 6.

MARINATED TOFU WITH VEGETABLES

The vegetables are just crisp-tender in this delightful vegetarian dish that has the flavor of London Broil without the calories, cholesterol, or sodium.

4 *cakes (8 ounces each) tofu*
½ *cup Tamari soy sauce*
½ *cup vegetable oil*
2 *tablespoons lemon juice*
3 *tablespoons wine vinegar*
4 *cloves garlic, minced and sautéed*

⅛ *teaspoon black pepper*
1 *eggplant, cubed and steamed*
Cherry tomatoes
1 *onion, sliced*
Several whole mushrooms
3 *medium-sized green peppers, sliced*

First, press the tofu: Cube it, and place the cubes on a towel on the counter. Place another towel on top. Place a cookie sheet over all; add 3 pounds of weight to the cookie sheet, evenly distributed (use jars of beans or water). Let stand for 10 minutes.

While the tofu is being pressed, make a marinade by combining the Tamari, oil, lemon juice, vinegar, garlic, and black pepper in a bowl. Add the pressed tofu to the marinade. Allow to marinate for at least 30 minutes or up to 5 hours. (You can do this early in the day.) Right before cooking, add the vegetables to the bowl; toss well.

Place everything in a shallow 12 x 16-inch pan and broil 4 inches below the heat source. Baste and turn twice. When the tofu appears crisp, it is done. Serve over Baked Rice. Serves 10 to 12.

BAKED RICE:
>   2 *cups raw brown rice*
>   4 *cups water*
>   ½ *teaspoon sea salt*

Place the rice, water, and salt, in a casserole. Cover and bake in a preheated 350-degree F. oven for about 45 minutes, until the water evaporates. Serves 10 to 12.

TOFU CHOP SUEY

Tofu is sometimes referred to as the steak without a bone. It is an excellent source of high-quality protein—almost 12 grams in an 8-ounce serving—the same amount as supplied by 5½ ounces of hamburger or ¾ ounce of steak. And the hamburger or steak costs you much more in calories, cholesterol, and cash. Tofu is low in calories—only 190 in 8 ounces. It is also very low in sodium and has only one-fortieth the pesticide level of meat.

2½ cups tofu, cut into
½-inch cubes
¼ cup butter or
vegetable oil
1½ cups sliced onion
1½ cups celery, cut into
1-inch strips
1 cup water, vegetable
broth, or stock
2 teaspoons arrowroot
starch or potato
starch

1 tablespoon cold
water
1 can (8½ ounces)
water chestnuts or
an equal amount of
cubed watermelon
rind
1½ cups mung bean
sprouts
3 tablespoons Tamari
soy sauce
Brown rice, cooked

In a skillet, sauté the tofu in the butter or oil until lightly browned.
Remove the tofu from the skillet and cook the onion and celery for
2 minutes. Add the water, broth, or stock and the sautéed tofu and
cook slowly for 5 minutes, uncovered.

Blend the starch with the 1 tablespoon of cold water. Stir into the
tofu mixture, stirring constantly until the mixture thickens. Add
the water chestnuts or watermelon rind cubes (see Index for
recipe), the bean sprouts, and Tamari. Heat thoroughly. Serve
over brown rice. Makes 6 servings. A satisfying meal—and only
270 calories per serving including the rice; 180 without the rice.

Tofu Manicotti

½ pound fresh spinach
¼ cup minced onion
1 tablespoon vegetable
oil
2 pounds tofu
3 cloves garlic, pressed
2 tablespoons chopped
fresh parsley

1 teaspoon salt
¼ teaspoon pepper
Pinch of nutmeg
Manicotti shells
(preferably whole
wheat)
Tomato sauce

Cook the spinach briefly in water; drain and purée in a blender.
Sauté the onion in the oil. Combine the spinach, onion, tofu, garlic,

parsley, and spices, mashing until well mixed. Stuff the manicotti shells with the filling. Layer the tomato sauce, shells, then more tomato sauce in a casserole. Cover and bake for 40 minutes in a 350-degree F. oven. Serves 4.

TOFU STIR-FRY WITH WALNUTS

To this nicely spiced dish, the walnuts contribute a rich share of protein, bone-building calcium, vitamin A, vitamin B, and a most pleasant contrast in textures.

1 *large onion, chopped*
3 *tablespoons sesame or sunflower oil*
4 *large mushrooms, sliced*
1 *cup string beans, cut into 1-inch pieces*
1 *teaspoon powdered ginger*
1 *tablespoon finely chopped fresh ginger (optional)*
1 *large clove garlic, crushed*
1½ *tablespoons arrowroot starch*
⅔ *cup water*
2 *tablespoons Tamari soy sauce*
1 *tablespoon cider vinegar*
1 *teaspoon honey*
1 *pound tofu, cut into 1-inch cubes*
½ *cup chopped walnuts*
Chopped fresh parsley

In a heavy skillet or in a wok, sauté the onion in the oil over medium heat. Then add the sliced mushrooms and string beans (any vegetable may be substituted). Cover the pan and steam for 5 minutes. Add the ginger (optional) and garlic. Stir in the arrowroot. Add the water, soy sauce, vinegar, and honey. Turn the heat to high and stir vigorously as you bring to a boil. Lower the heat to simmer; add the tofu and the walnuts. Simmer for a few minutes, until the sauce thickens. Serve as is or over brown rice and garnish with parsley. Beautiful to look at and a lovely medley of flavors. Tastes very oriental. Serves 4 as a side dish; 2 as a main dish.

TOFU STROGANOFF

Stroganoff is usually made with meat and sour cream, a combination not acceptable to those who observe kashrut. But everyone can enjoy this pareve stroganoff enriched with miso, a soybean paste produced by lactic fermentation, which aids digestion and adds a robust flavor.

1½ *pounds tofu*
2 *tablespoons sesame or sunflower oil*
6 *medium-sized onions, chopped*
1 *tablespoon Tamari soy sauce*
Hot water
Lukewarm water
3 *tablespoons dark miso*
¼ *cup water*

1 *tablespoon vegetable oil*
2 *bay leaves*
½ *teaspoon caraway seeds*
1 *medium-sized potato, chopped*
1 *carrot, sliced*
1 *small stalk celery, sliced*
¼ *teaspoon crushed thyme*

Cut the tofu in half. Arrange on a plate, leaving at least ½ inch between pieces. Place in the freezer for at least 48 hours. (Once frozen, the tofu may be transferred to sealed plastic bags.)

Heat the oil in a skillet; add the onions and soy sauce. Cook over very low heat for a long time (90 minutes ideally), stirring occasionally. Place the frozen tofu in a heatproof bowl and cover with hot water. Let stand for 3 to 5 minutes. Gently pour off the water and cover again with lukewarm water. Press the tofu lightly between your palms to expel milky water. Change the water and repeat. Press the tofu once more to expel as much water as possible. Cut into ¾-inch cubes.

Cream the miso with the ¼ cup water. Place the cooked onions, miso mix, vegetable oil, bay leaves, caraway seeds, potato, and sliced vegetables in a saucepan. Add water to make a consistency like thick soup. Bring to a boil, lower heat, and simmer for about 1 hour. Remove the bay leaves; add the thyme. May be served immediately. Flavor will improve if kept in the refrigerator overnight. Serves 4.

TOFU AMBROSIA

A creamy dessert that can be served with meat or dairy. It's extremely high in protein and a powerhouse of the minerals that strengthen bones and come to the aid of your heart muscle.

1 cup orange juice
2 tablespoons honey
1 tablespoon arrowroot starch
1 heaping teaspoon grated orange peel
3 drops almond extract
¾ pound tofu, drained and cut into ½-inch cubes

2 oranges or tangerines, sectioned and pitted
2 tablespoons unsweetened coconut flakes
2 tablespoons sliced almonds, slightly toasted

Reserve 2 tablespoons of the orange juice and combine the remaining juice and honey in a small saucepan. Heat gently to simmer. Meanwhile, dissolve the arrowroot starch in the 2 tablespoons of orange juice and add this to the saucepan, stirring until the mixture thickens—about 30 seconds. Add the grated orange peel and the almond extract; stir to blend. Combine the tofu and orange or tangerine sections in a glass bowl. Add the orange juice mixture and the coconut; stir gently to blend. Cover and chill for at least 1 hour. Serve in attractive stemware or parfait glasses. Garnish with the toasted almonds. Makes 4 servings.

CREAMY CAROB-TOFU PIE

For lovers of chocolate cream pie, here's a taste-alike with a big nutritional difference. This pie is low in fat, low in calories, high in protein, free of harmful additives, very easy to digest, and rich in protease, an enzyme which according to recent studies can help prevent the development of malignancies.

This recipe was developed by the New England Soy Dairy, Inc., in Greenfield, Massachusetts. They graciously share it with us.

FILLING:

⅓ cup cashew nuts and
⅔ cup water (cashew
milk) or 1 cup milk
2 pounds tofu
½ cup pure maple
syrup or honey

3 teaspoons vanilla
extract
½ teaspoon cinnamon
⅓ cup carob powder
½ cup chopped
walnuts or coconut

First make cashew milk (for pareve) by blending at high speed the ⅓ cup cashew nuts and ⅔ cup water; or pour 1 cup of regular milk into a blender (for dairy).

To the cashew or dairy milk in the blender add the rest of the ingredients except for the walnuts or coconut; blend at high speed. Now stir in the walnuts or coconut. Set aside while you prepare the pie crust. Preheat the oven to 400 degree F.

PIE CRUST:

1 cup whole wheat
pastry flour
½ teaspoon salt

⅓ cup butter or
vegetable oil
4 tablespoons ice
water

In a bowl, combine the flour and salt. Cut in the butter or add the oil and combine well. Add the water, 1 tablespoon at a time, until the dough forms a ball and leaves the sides of the bowl. Roll out and place in a 10-inch pie plate. Flute the edge. Pour in the filling and bake for 13 minutes. Let cool, then chill or freeze before serving. If frozen, remove the pie from the freezer 10 minutes before serving. Serves 8.

TOFU CHEESELESS "CHEESECAKE"

Enjoy a "cheesecake" splurge that's stingy on calories: it only tastes fattening. Although this cake contains no cheese, it has a creamy consistency that improves with age. On the fifth day it tastes like Lindy's. If you want to put a festive hat on this cake, top it with a fruit glaze made from blueberries, strawberries, or pineapple.

FILLING:

1 *cup raisins*	1 *tablespoon vanilla*
½ *cup apple juice*	*extract*
2 *teaspoons grated*	4 *pounds tofu*
lemon rind	3 *tablespoons lemon*
3 *tablespoons tahina*	*juice*
(sesame butter)	½ *cup light honey*

Soak the raisins in the apple juice until soft—about 2 hours. In a blender purée the raisins with the apple juice and grated lemon rind. Remove this mixture from the blender and whiz the rest of the ingredients to make a tofu purée. You may have to do this in several batches. Combine the raisin purée with the tofu purée and stir thoroughly. Set aside while you prepare the cheesecake crust.

CRUST:

½ *cup ground*	3 *tablespoons butter,*
sunflower seeds	*softened*
or raw cashews	½ *teaspoon cinnamon*
½ *cup wheat germ*	¼ *teaspoon allspice*
2 *teaspoons honey*	

In a medium-sized bowl, combine all the ingredients and mix with your fingers until the mixture feels crumbly. Pat the mixture into a 9-inch spring-form pan, covering the bottom and about 1½ inches up the sides. Now spoon in the filling.

Preheat the oven to 350 degrees F. and bake for 25 to 30 minutes, until the top begins to brown delicately. Remove from the oven and allow to cool. Using a knife, separate the cake from the sides of the pan; then remove sides. When the cake is completely cool, chill in the refrigerator. Glaze it if you wish. Serves 10 to 12.

CHEESECAKE GLAZE:

2 *cups fresh or thawed frozen blueberries, strawberries, or pineapple*
1 *cup fruit juice or water*
¼ *cup honey*

1½ *tablespoons arrowroot starch dissolved in 3 tablespoons of the fruit juice or water*
1 *tablespoon lemon juice*

In a saucepan, combine all ingredients except the lemon juice. Cook over medium heat, stirring constantly until thickened— about 15 minutes. Stir in the lemon juice and cook for 2 more minutes. Chill. This makes 2 cups.

7

Sabbath & Festival
Specialties

The warm memories associated with the Jewish Sabbath and festivals are bathed in the tantalizing aromas and tastes of the special foods which marked each celebration.

Our grandmothers were very wise in that they did not allow certain choice dishes to become commonplace by frequent use, but reserved them to bring a special quality of joyful anticipation to holiday meals. In time, each holiday acquired its own delights and aromas.

I remember well the lovely spicy odor of honey cake studded with toasty almonds, hot out of the oven the day before Rosh Hashanah; the savory appetite-stimulating fragrance of gefilte fish on Fridays; the rich aroma of coffee cake and blintzes on Shavuot; the sharp, tingling fragrance of onion-accented crisp potato latkes on Chanukah.

Many of us are searching for our roots, the fountainhead from which we evolved. If you want to understand some of the forces that shaped you, try digging into your culinary roots. At the same time, plant some roots for your children to cherish. It's a very nice, warm, meaningful thing to do, and there's no better time to do it than on the Sabbath and during festivals.

When these foods first evolved, before the advent of the technology which has robbed many basic foods of the nutrients with which nature endowed them, they were not only heart-warming, they were body-building and wholesome. Not so today, unless we add to each food that which would have been there in the first place, before it was removed during the refining process.

For that reason, you may find the recipes in this chapter a little different from the ordinary. Try them. They will add a very special glow to your holiday and contribute new nutrition to an old tradition.

Try the recipes for gefilte fish and chicken soup with that special "Sabbath taste." Enjoy carrot tsimmes on Rosh Hashanah and have a sweet New Year; serve kreplach for the pre-Yom Kippur meal for their special significance; invite your favorite people to enjoy the easy-to-prepare delicious potato latkes on Chanukah; delight the children with hamantaschen on Purim.

Note that included in this chapter are Sabbath and festival *specialties* only. Consult the Index and other chapters for more dishes you might want to include on your Shabbos or *yontiff* menu.

This chapter does not include a section devoted to either Sukkot or Shavuot. Sukkot is a thanksgiving holiday, also known as the Festival of Ingathering, which celebrates the bounty of the harvest. The biblical injunction, "You shall rejoice in your festival" (Deuteronomy 6:14), makes one obligated to enjoy festive meals. Because they are easy to carry to the Sukkah, festive casserole dishes are customarily prepared on Sukkot. You'll find many casserole recipes throughout the book.

Shavuot, also called the Feast of Weeks, originally celebrated the spring harvest. Now, it commemorates the revelation of the Law on Mount Sinai. Two blintzes are traditionally served at Shavuot meals to represent the Scrolls of the Law. (For blintz recipes see Chapter Two—Kugels, Blintzes, and Knishes.)

It is also customary to serve dairy meals on this lovely holiday. Therefore, Shavuot is often referred to as "the dairy holiday." Be sure to consult Chapter Four, Dairy Specialties, for many suitable recipes.

THIS IS SHABBOS

Our Irish neighbor used to say, "This house is a little bit of heaven every Friday night."

I can see it yet—the soft glow of the Shabbos candles, reflected a hundred times in everybody's eyes, in the highly-polished metal of the parlor stove, making shadows flicker on the round oak table—the look of peace on Mama's face and pride in Dad's. We could be little devils all week, but on Shabbos we became, in their eyes, little angels and they called us by our diminutives—Bessela, Jennela, Zeenala for the boys. This always meant that whatever we had done to try their patience, it was forgiven the instant the candles were lit.

CHICKEN SOUP WITH FLANKEN

Hot chicken soup does fight colds!

We knew it all the time. Now the doctors know, too. How do they know? They used a device called a bronchofiberscope and cineroentgenograms, and measurements of mucus velocity, believe it or not, to prove what every Jewish mother has known all along—that chicken soup can help cure a cold. (*Medical World News*, July 10, 1978.)

Dr. Marvin A. Sackner, director of medical services at Mount Sinai Medical Center in Miami Beach, tested the effects of hot chicken soup as well as those of hot and cold water. Cold water actually lowered nasal clearance. Hot water improved it, but not nearly so much as did hot chicken soup.

To negate the effects of the steam, the same fluids were sipped from covered containers through a straw. Hot water had little effect this way, but hot chicken soup still had some benefit.

It might be the aroma, it might be the taste, Dr. Sackner said. But, whatever it is, there's "something extra" in chicken soup.

Could it be the Sabbath taste?

3 *quarts water or*
vegetable stock or
water from soaking
seeds for sprouting
1 *piece of flanken*
(approximately 1½
pounds)
Marrow bones (as
many as you can get
from the butcher)
1 *pullet (about 4*
pounds), cut into
quarters. Be sure to
use the giblets,
gorgel, and especially
the feet.
3 *small onions*

2 *carrots*
2 *stalks celery, with*
leaves
1 *parsley root*
1 *bay leaf*
¼ *teaspoon chopped*
fresh dill or dill
seeds
Several sprigs of
parsley
¼ *teaspoon ground*
ginger
1 *tablespoon*
nutritional yeast
Salt and white
pepper, to taste
(optional)

Boil the water in a large pot. Add the flanken and bones. Simmer for 30 minutes, then skim. Add the chicken, the vegetables, and the seasonings. Simmer for 1 hour, or until the chicken and meat are tender. Serve with brown rice, noodles, or knaidlach. Serves 6 to 8.

NOTE: If your family doesn't particularly relish boiled chicken, remove the chicken after 45 minutes of cooking in the soup. Put it in a baking dish, rub with garlic, sprinkle with lemon juice, paprika, ginger, thyme, dried mustard, and a little bit of sage. Roast in a preheated 350-degree F. oven, uncovered, until delicately browned.

MUSHROOM, BARLEY, AND BEAN SOUP

Prepare this on Friday and you'll have an excellent meal in a dish for Shabbos. The barley gives this soup a hearty, creamy, chewy texture that makes you think it's fattening. Not so. It actually has less fat than brown rice and more iron, and you can enjoy a half cup of cooked barley—with all its calcium, potassium, and niacin—at a cost of only 52 calories.

Mushrooms add much more than a touch of class and incomparable flavor to this soup. Mushrooms are rich in pantothenate, the antistress vitamin that helps you cope. They are also rich in niacin and riboflavin, are a good source of copper and selenium, the stay-young-longer mineral, and provide trace amounts of iron, magnesium, and zinc. And there are only 20 calories per cup of mushrooms.

The nutritional (brewer's) yeast contributes fabulous nutrients. It is rich in all the B vitamins, even B_{12}, which is very hard to come by in non-animal foods. Nutritional yeast is 50 percent protein and is the richest dietary source of chromium, which helps the body regulate blood sugar and may help prevent diabetes as well as treat it.

½ *cup large dry lima beans*
¼ *cup mung beans*
¼ *cup coarse barley*
2 *quarts water or stock*
1 *pound soup meat*
3 *marrow bones*
2 *tablespoons dried mushrooms*
1 *large onion, sliced*
2 *ribs celery, sliced*
1 *cup finely chopped carrot*
1 *turnip or ½ rutabaga, finely chopped*

½ *teaspoon chopped dill weed*
2 *tablespoons dried parsley or ½ cup chopped fresh parsley*
½ *teaspoon celery salt*
2 *tablespoons nutritional yeast*
1½ *teaspoons Tamari soy sauce*
1 *teaspoon kelp*
Salt and pepper, to taste (optional)

Wash the beans and barley and place in a soup kettle with the water or stock and remaining ingredients. Cover; bring to a boil. Allow to simmer gently for about 2 hours, until the beans are soft. Remove the meat, cut it, and serve the soup with a piece of the meat in each bowl. Serves 8 to 10.

VARIATION: For a vegetarian soup, omit the meat and bones. Sauté the onion in a little oil before adding. With potato latkes, it's a meal.

GEFILTE FISH

No wonder we sing when we eat gefilte fish, the traditional Sabbath dish. The carp in gefilte fish is higher in protein and much lower in calories than most cuts of meat. Moreover, it provides polyunsaturated fatty acids, the kind that dissolve cholesterol, but it does not provide cholesterol. Carp also contains vitamin A and many B vitamins (especially niacin) and bone-building minerals (calcium, phosphorus, magnesium).

3 *pounds fish (carp,* | ½ *cup water*
pike, white) | 3 *tablespoons whole*
2 *onions, grated* | *wheat matzo meal*
2 *carrots, grated* | 2 *onions, sliced*
2 *eggs* | 2 *carrots, sliced*
Salt and white | *Water*
pepper

Fillet the fish or have it filleted at the fish market. Retain the skin, bones, and heads. Using a grinder, grind the fish fillets and place in a bowl; add the grated onions, grated carrots, eggs, salt and pepper to taste, and the ½ cup of water; mix thoroughly. Add the matzo meal; mix well. The mixture should feel slightly sticky.

Put the bones, heads, and skin in the bottom of a large pot lined with the sliced onions and sliced carrots. Shape the fish mixture into balls about 1¼ inches in diameter. Flatten them a little and place them in the pot. Add water to cover, a little salt and pepper, and cook over a low flame for 1 hour. Let cool.

Using a slotted spoon, remove the fish to a serving dish. Strain the broth, and pour it over the fish. Good hot or cold. If you intend to serve the fish cold, refrigerate the broth until it jells. Serves 6.

Tuna Gefilte Fish

For those who don't care for the taste of carp, pike, or whitefish, this Tuna Gefilte Fish is ideal.

1 *can (7½ ounces) white meat tuna*
2 *eggs, lightly beaten*
1 *small onion, grated*
4 *teaspoons matzo meal*
Salt and white pepper

1 *quart water*
2 *medium-sized onions, sliced*
2 *carrots, sliced*
⅛ *teaspoon white pepper*
1 *teaspoon salt*

Flake the tuna into a bowl; add the eggs, grated onion, and matzo meal. Season to taste with salt and pepper, mix well, and shape into balls. In a pot, boil the water; add the sliced onions, carrots, ⅛ teaspoon of pepper, and 1 teaspoon of salt. Place the tuna balls into the boiling water. Cover and simmer over low heat until the vegetables are soft—about 30 minutes. Serves 4 as an appetizer.

Salmon Gefilte Fish

Although it tastes like the kind you spend hours preparing, this version of gefilte fish is very simple to make, and it brings you the extra nutrients and polyunsaturates found in salmon. Serve it as a change of pace on Shabbos or, as I do, on Sukkot.

4 onions
3 cups water
1 stalk celery, with
  leaves
3 sprigs fresh parsley
  or 1 tablespoon
  dried parsley flakes
1 can (16 ounces) pink
  salmon, drained and
  mashed (reserve the
  liquid and be sure to
  include the bones
  and skin when you
  mash the salmon)

2 eggs, beaten
¼ teaspoon white
  pepper, or to taste
1 teaspoon powdered
  kelp
2 tablespoons wheat
  germ
1 teaspoon nutritional
  yeast
2 parsnips
4 carrots

Slice 3 of the onions and put them in a large pot with the water. Add the celery and parsley and bring to a slow boil. Place the salmon in a bowl. Grate the remaining raw onion into the salmon. Add the beaten eggs, pepper, kelp, wheat germ, and nutritional yeast to the salmon; combine all ingredients well. Form into balls, the size of golf balls, then flatten the balls slightly. Add a little matzo meal if necessary to hold them together.

Slice the parsnips and carrots, first in halves, then lengthwise. Place them in the pot. Add the reserved salmon liquid. Add the salmon balls and cook, covered, for 30 minutes. Allow them to cool in the sauce. Serve hot with tomato sauce or cold with horseradish. Ladle some of the sauce over each portion. Makes 12 portions.

CHOLENT

Cholent is a meal-in-one stew. During the long cooking time the flavors of the barley, beans, potato, and meat blend, forming a flavorsome repast. Traditionally, cholent cooks all Friday night and is enjoyed by the entire family after attending synagogue services on Saturday. There is a theory that the word "cholent" is a contraction of the German words *Shule ende* (synagogue services have ended), and that means it's time to eat!

½ *pound cranberry beans*
½ *pound navy beans*
Water
1 *medium-sized onion, cut up*
2 *tablespoons vegetable oil or chicken fat*

Several marrow bones
1 *pound chuck or brisket*
½ *pound barley*
Salt, to taste
1 *teaspoon paprika*
3 *unpeeled potatoes, scrubbed and quartered*

Soak the beans overnight in water. (If you forget to soak them, cover with water, bring to a boil, remove from the heat, and allow to soak for about 1 hour.)

In a large heavy pot, simmer the onion in the oil or fat. Add the bones and meat, the drained beans, the barley, and the seasoning. Cover liberally with water and simmer for 1 hour. Add the potatoes and cook slowly for 30 minutes more. Taste-check for seasoning. Add water to 3 inches above the contents of the pot. Cover tightly and place in a preheated 225-degree F. oven overnight. You'll have a nice hot dish at noon. Serves 6.

ROAST CHICKEN, KASHA, AND ALMONDS

A Shabbos meal would not be complete without roast chicken. And the trio of chicken, kasha, and almonds is marvelous. Kasha (buckwheat groats) is delicious, nutritious, high in fiber, and economical. It is one of the few crops commercially grown without the use of chemicals.

ROAST CHICKEN:

3 *small chickens, halved*

1 *cut lemon or 4 tablespoons lemon juice*

2 *cloves garlic, crushed*

1 *teaspoon ground ginger*

1 *teaspoon crushed dried thyme*

½ *teaspoon crushed sage*

1 *teaspoon dry mustard*

Vegetable oil or chicken fat

Rub the chickens inside and out with the cut lemon or sprinkle on the lemon juice. Rub the chicken with the crushed garlic, then coat with the spices and herbs. Place on a lightly greased (with vegetable oil or chicken fat) baking sheet and bake for about 40 minutes at 350-degrees F., or until tender. A roasted chicken half served on a bed of kasha with almonds to each diner makes an impressive dish. Serves 6.

KASHA AND ALMONDS:

½ *cup chopped onion*

2 *tablespoons chicken fat or vegetable oil*

1 *cup raw kasha*

1 *egg, lightly beaten*

1 *teaspoon salt (optional)*

2 *cups hot chicken broth*

½ *cup whole almonds*

Sauté the onion in the chicken fat or oil in a large (2-quart) saucepan. Combine the kasha, egg, and salt (if desired) with the onion mixture; stir for 2 minutes until the kasha is dry. Add the hot chicken broth, cover, and cook over low heat for about 20 minutes. Roast the almonds for a few minutes in the oven and add them to the kasha mixture.

SABBATH SPONGE CAKE

What goes better with tea and conversation? This very light, bright yellow cake is delightfully versatile. It can be eaten plain or be used as a part of other desserts.

6 *egg yolks*	6 *egg whites*
1 *tablespoon grated orange peel*	1 *teaspoon cream of tartar*
½ *cup orange juice*	2 *tablespoons honey*
½ *cup honey*	
1⅓ *cups whole wheat pastry flour*	

Preheat the oven to 325 degrees F. Using an electric mixer, beat the egg yolks at high speed for about 5 minutes. Add the orange peel and orange juice and beat for another 5 minutes. Gradually beat in the ½ cup of honey, about 1 tablespoonful at a time. Continue to beat until the mixture is very thick and smooth— about 12 to 15 minutes. Sift the flour and fold it into the egg yolk mixture. Set aside.

Beat the egg whites until foamy, then add the cream of tartar and beat until soft peaks form. Gradually add the 2 tablespoons of honey and beat until the mixture is stiff and fine. Using a large rubber spatula, gently fold the egg white mixture into the egg yolk mixture.

Turn at once into an ungreased 10-inch tube pan. Bake for 50 to 60 minutes. Remove from the oven and invert the pan for 1 hour or until the cake is cool. Serves 10 to 12.

SPONGE ROLL:

For a Sponge Roll, place a sheet of parchment paper in a flat pan about 12 x 16 inches. Spread the batter in a thin layer. Bake in a preheated 350-degree F. oven for about 15 minutes. While the cake is still hot, turn it onto a tablecloth spread with powdered unsweetened coconut. Remove the parchment paper. Spread with honey-sweetened jelly, crushed pineapple, unsweetened apple butter, or the filling of your choice and roll up.

SPONGE LAYER CAKE:

Pour the batter into 3 ungreased layer cake pans (about 8 inches in diameter). Bake in a preheated 350-degree F. oven for 20 to 25 minutes, until lightly browned. Spread crushed pineapple or the filling of your choice between layers and on top.

CAROB SPONGE CAKE:
Substitute ¼ cup of carob powder for ¼ cup of the pastry flour. Sift together and proceed as per the basic recipe.

THE HIGH HOLIDAYS

On Rosh Hashanah, the Jewish New Year, we traditionally eat foods that are sweet in taste and round in shape. The sweet foods—the apple dipped in honey, the honey cake, the carrot tsimmes—all imply a wish for a sweet and pleasant New Year. No sour or bitter foods are included on this holiday's menu. The round foods, such as the round challahs, symbolize the wish for health and happiness without end.

For the meal before the Yom Kippur (Day of Atonement) fast, a favorite dish is kreplach. It is said that the meat symbolizes inflexible justice; the soft dough which covers it denotes compassion. Think of that the next time you bite into one of those delicious kreplach and ponder, too, on the many ways in which what we eat is woven into our stream of life.

Other dishes served at the pre-Yom Kippur meal should be bland, without spices, herbs, or salt to lessen the incidence of thirst during the fast.

After Yom Kippur, to break the fast, it is always good to start with something light, perhaps a fruit and yogurt preparation like Ambrosia Cream Dessert (see recipe in Chapter Four) or an omelet with a hot beverage and whole wheat toast, fruit juice, or soup. Pickled herring is much too salty to serve as a fast-breaker. This salt load is dangerous for people with high blood pressure. Recipes for dishes to adorn your Yom Kippur night buffet table can be found throughout the book. You'll find them easily by consulting the Index.

ROUND CHALLAHS

It is traditional to serve a round challah on the High Holidays. It is a silent wish that your joy and good fortune be without end and symbolic of the hope for a well-rounded year.

To make a round challah, follow the instructions for making challah dough in Baking Bread (Chapter Ten). Divide the dough in half. Reserve a chunk of dough about the size of an egg from each half.

Roll out each of the large portions of dough to resemble a rope about 16 inches long, tapering the ends. Coil each rope tightly, tucking the ends under. Place them on a greased cookie sheet or in round cake pans. (Grease with a mixture of lecithin and oil, about a teaspoon of each.)

From the dough you reserved you can make a ladder (symbolic of one's reach up for guidance and the hope that one's prayers may ascend on high). For each ladder, form the dough into 2 thin strips for the sides and 4 thin strips for the rungs. Place one ladder on each challah and brush the ladders and the rest of the challahs with an egg wash (1 egg yolk beaten with 1 teaspoon water). Sprinkle with poppy or sesame seeds.

Cover the challahs with a clean towel and allow to rise for about 2 hours, until double in bulk. Bake for 30 to 35 minutes in a 375-degree F. oven or until a tap on the bottom elicits a hollow sound. *Gut yomtov!*

FARFEL

These are noodle balls no bigger than barley grains. Farfel (not to be confused with matzo farfel, which are tiny pieces of matzo used on Passover, when flour is proscribed) are usually served on Rosh Hashanah because of their rounded form, symbolic of wholeness or perfection. When made from whole wheat flour, they are a health-building food.

1 *egg*
⅞ cup whole wheat
pastry flour

Pinch of salt
(optional)

Combine the ingredients and knead into a hard ball. The dough will be stiff. Grate it on a fine grater and spread it out to dry thoroughly before storing in a jar. Makes about 1½ cups. To cook, add to boiling salted water or drop into boiling soup. Very good in chicken, vegetable, or pea soup. Cook for about 30 minutes. They take longer than most noodles.

POTATO KNISHES
(Soft Top)

A must for holiday meals. Our kids call these knishes "the convertibles" because they don't have hard tops like the knishes that are rolled in dough. These are much easier to make and very delicious.

Nutritionally-speaking, potatoes are high in vitamin C complex, a better vitamin C pattern than is found in citrus fruit because it contains the tyrosinase fraction, the organic copper blood-builder.

6 *potatoes, boiled and mashed*
2 *eggs, beaten (reserve 2 tablespoons) Grieben or sautéed onion (quantities to taste)*
Salt and pepper, to taste
Vegetable oil or chicken fat

Mix together the mashed potatoes, beaten eggs, grieben or sautéed onion, and salt and pepper. Form into patties about ½-inch thick. Place on a cookie sheet greased with oil or chicken fat. Brush the patties with the reserved egg. Bake in a preheated 375-degree F. oven for about 35 minutes, or until brown and fragrant. Makes 12 knishes. Serves 4.

HOT CRANBERRY-HONEY RELISH

This honey-sweetened New Year relish complements chicken or turkey, and it can double as a dessert. Note that cranberries are believed to acidify the urine, thus preventing recurring bladder infections in many cases.

> 3 *cups unpeeled (if unsprayed) apple chunks*
> 2 *cups fresh cranberries*
> ½ *cup honey*
>
> 1 *cup oatmeal*
> 4 *tablespoons vegetable oil*
> 1 *cup walnuts, broken into good-size nuggets*

Place the apple chunks in a 9 x 13-inch baking dish. Add the berries and honey. In a bowl, combine the oatmeal, oil, and walnuts and pour over the berries. Cover the dish tightly with foil and bake in a preheated 350-degree F. oven for 45 minutes. Serves 10 to 12.

CARROT TSIMMES

A carrot tsimmes expresses a wish for a sweet New Year, rich in fulfillment and productivity. The Yiddish word for carrot is *merin,* which also means to increase or multiply.

This tsimmes should do wonders for your complexion and for your health in general. Carrots are loaded with vitamin A (as much as 15,750 international units in a cup of cooked carrots), as are sweet potatoes (15,600 international units per cup).

Our ancestors must have been nutrition-wise to start the year with a good supply of the nutrient (vitamin A) that aids in the growth and repair of body tissues, helps fight infection, and helps maintain smooth, soft, blemish-free skin.

2 *pounds meat (brust,*
flanken, or brisket)
1 *bay leaf*
Water
2 *tablespoons chopped*
onion
1 *carrot*
2 *large or 4 small*
sweet potatoes

1 *tablespoon honey*
¼ *teaspoon ground*
ginger
2 *teaspoons arrowroot*
starch
Cold water
Sea salt, to taste
(optional)

Place the meat and bay leaf in a large pot and cover with water. Bring to a boil on top of the stove; add the onion. Cook over medium heat for 40 minutes. Scrub the carrot and sweet potatoes and dice into fairly large pieces. Place the vegetables over the meat; add the honey and the ginger. Add more water to cover about an inch over all the ingredients. Simmer for 1 hour or until the meat is tender. Mix the arrowroot with a little cold water until smooth; then add a bit of the tsimmes water; add this to the pot. Taste-check for seasoning and add salt if desired. Cook gently for another 10 minutes. Serves 6.

ORANGE-SWEET POTATO CAKE

This sweet cake, enhanced by the flavor of orange (rich in vitamin C), will help you start the year with your heart on the right beat. Sweet potatoes are very rich in vitamin A, and although yams have only a trace of vitamin A, they are very rich in potassium and are sodium-free.

1 *cup honey*
½ *cup vegetable oil*
3 *eggs*
¼ *cup orange juice concentrate, undiluted*
½ *teaspoon vanilla extract*
2½ *cups whole wheat pastry flour*

1 *teaspoon baking soda*
1 *teaspoon baking powder*
1 *teaspoon cinnamon*
½ *teaspoon ground nutmeg*
1 *cup mashed sweet potatoes or yams*
1 *cup chopped walnuts*

In a large bowl, blend together the honey and oil. Beat till fluffy. Beat in the eggs, 1 at a time. Stir in the orange juice concentrate and vanilla. Combine the next 5 ingredients in another bowl. Blend into the liquid mixture alternately with the mashed sweet potatoes. Stir in the chopped walnuts.

Turn the batter into a 10 x 4-inch tube cake pan or a bundt pan. Bake in a preheated 300-degree F. oven for 1 hour, or a little more, until a cake tester or toothpick inserted comes out clean. Cool on a wire rack for 30 minutes before removing from the pan. Serves 10 to 12.

HONEY-APPLE CAKE

It is, of course, customary to eat honey cake on Rosh Hashanah, and this combination honey-apple cake has extra nutritional value and a taste that is superb. Particularly lovely when served at a Rosh Hashanah afternoon tea.

½ cup honey
½ cup vegetable oil
2 eggs
2 cups whole wheat
   pastry flour
1 teaspoon baking
   powder
½ teaspoon baking
   soda

¼ teaspoon grated
   nutmeg
½ cup orange juice
   concentrate,
   undiluted
2½ cups diced unpeeled
   (if unsprayed) apple
1 teaspoon vanilla
   extract

In a large bowl, blend together the honey and oil. Beat in the eggs, 1 at a time. In a smaller bowl, combine all the dry ingredients. Add to the liquid mixture alternately with the orange juice concentrate. Stir in the apple chunks and vanilla. Turn the batter into a 13 x 9 x 2-inch baking pan. Bake in a preheated 350-degree F. oven for 30 to 40 minutes, or until a cake tester or toothpick inserted comes out clean. Cool. Leave whole or cut into squares. Cover and let stand overnight to allow the flavors time to mingle. Serves 8 to 10.

HOLIDAY KREPLACH

Traditionally, kreplach are eaten three times a year: on Purim, the seventh day of Sukkot, and the day before Yom Kippur. Kreplach are tender little squares of dough filled with meat, chicken, or cheese. This recipe calls for chicken or meat.

DOUGH:

2 cups whole wheat
   pastry flour
2 eggs, beaten
1 tablespoon water

½ teaspoon salt
   (optional)
Boiling salted water

Place the flour on a board and make a well in the center. In a bowl, combine the eggs, water, and salt (if desired). Pour the mixture into the well and work the flour in the liquid, kneading until smooth and elastic. Roll the dough out on a floured surface. Cut the dough into 3-inch squares and place a tablespoonful of filling (recipe below) in the center of each. Fold the dough over, forming a triangle. Press the edges together neatly with a fork dipped in flour. Drop each triangle into boiling salted water; cover tightly and cook for 20 minutes or until the kreplach rise to the top. Makes 24 or more, according to how thin the dough has been rolled out.

FILLING:

2 *cups ground cooked* 1 *egg, beaten*
 chicken or meat (or 1 *tablespoon finely*
 1 cup raw and 1 cup *chopped fresh*
 cooked) *parsley*
1 *tablespoon minced*
 onion

Combine all ingredients and the filling is ready to use.

NOTE: Kreplach may also be cooked in boiling soup. Or, after their water bath, they can be sprinkled with a little chicken fat and slipped into the oven for browning. Delicious every way.

VERENIKES

Verenikes are a rounded version of kreplach. They are usually filled with cheese, mashed potato, kasha, or cherries. To make verenikes, follow the same recipe as for the kreplach, but for a real treat fill them with cherries that have been pitted and stewed and thickened with a little arrowroot starch or potato starch. Cook the verenikes in honey-sweetened cherry juice instead of water and serve hot in the juice.

CHANUKAH

Chanukah, the Feast of Lights, is a jolly holiday commemorating the victory of the Hasmoneans over the Syrians. We sing funny songs, play games, tell jokes, give presents, and eat latkes. Why latkes? Because they are fried in oil. Why oil? To commemorate the miracle of the cruse of oil found in the Temple, enough for one day, but it burned for eight days.

There is another association with oil. The Hebrew words for

Hasmoneans *(Hasmonaim)* and for eight *(shemoneh)* contain the Hebrew letters for oil *(shemen)*.

Dairy foods (see Chapter Four, Dairy Specialties) are also served to mark the bravery of Judith, who gained an audience with the enemy General Holofernes and then plied him with cheese to make him thirsty and thus consume lots of wine, which made him sleepy and an easy mark. She slew him; his soldiers took flight, and the besieged Jews were saved.

So, when you eat your dairy foods and your latkes, think of Judith's valor and the Maccabean victory in the first battle ever waged for the principle of religious freedom.

Blender Potato Latkes

They shimmered, they simmered, absorbing the olive oil. You may not guess, but it was the latkes that made the Syrians recoil. Serve these latkes with applesauce.

5 *medium-sized potatoes*	¼ *cup wheat germ*
2 *eggs*	¼ *teaspoon white pepper, or to taste*
1 *teaspoon salt*	⅓ *cup vegetable oil*
1 *small onion, halved*	

Scrub the potatoes well and cut them into cubes. Put 1 egg, a little of the salt, and half the onion in a blender; add 1 cup of the cubed potatoes. Cover and blend for a few seconds. (Do not overblend or you won't get that desirable "grated" consistency.(Pour most of the mixture into a bowl, retaining some to get the blender started again. Repeat the procedure, adding the other egg, more salt, the other onion half, and the remaining potato cubes. When all are grated, add the wheat germ and pepper.

In a large frying pan, heat the oil until it sizzles. Spoon about 2 tablespoons of the mixture into the frying pan to make each latke. Brown well on both sides, then drain on paper towels. If you'd rather not fry them, place the latkes on an oiled cookie sheet and bake at 350 degrees F. until browned. They're not quite so crispy as the fried, but they are good. Makes 30; serves 6 to 8.

CHEESE LATKES

2 eggs, separated
1 cup cottage cheese

1 tablespoon
arrowroot starch
½ teaspoon honey

Beat the egg whites until stiff. Blend together the rest of the ingredients. Fold the egg whites into the cottage cheese mixture. Drop by the tablespoonful onto a hot, buttered skillet. Lower the heat and cook until dry; then brown the flip side. Serve with sour cream or yogurt, applesauce or berries. Serves 2 to 4.

WHOLE WHEAT CHEESE LATKES

To make your cottage cheese go a little farther, try this nutritious version. Cheese contains all the essential amino acids and is therefore a complete protein. Cottage cheese is low in calories and fat, high in phosporous and calcium, and contains some potassium. It is high in sodium, however, unless you make your own and eliminate the salt.

1 cup cottage cheese
2 eggs, well beaten
¼ cup milk or plain
yogurt
1 cup whole wheat
pastry flour

2 tablespoons soy flour
¼ cup vegetable oil or
2 tablespoons butter
and 2 tablespoons oil

Combine the cottage cheese with the beaten eggs. Stir in the milk or yogurt. Combine the flours and salt (if desired), then add to the cottage cheese mixture, stirring gently. Heat the oil or butter and oil in a skillet and drop the mixture by the tablespoonful into the hot fat. Cook till delicately browned on both sides. Serves 4 to 6.

VARIATION: Pour the batter into oiled or buttered muffin tins and bake at 350 degrees F. until browned—about 20 minutes. Makes 12 muffins. Or, of course, you could pour the batter into an oiled or buttered 8 x 4-inch loaf pan and make a kugel. Bake it in a 350-

degree F. oven for 30 to 40 minutes, till brown on top. These are substitutes for the fried latke, which still takes the cake for taste. I don't like to fry but, I figure, once a year is *nisht gefellah*. Any way you make them, be sure to serve with cold applesauce and yogurt.

No-Fry Potato Latkes

The soy grits and soy flour give these latkes many nutrients that contribute to the glow of health. These products are derived from soybeans, considered the most highly concentrated of natural foods. They provide more than twice as much perfect protein as lean beef, 3½ times as much as eggs or cheese, and more than 12 times as much as whole milk.

And soy is no slouch when it comes to providing vitamins and minerals. It is a good source of all the B vitamins, including folic acid, which is necessary to the formation of red blood cells; and it provides 13 important minerals, a good quantity of lecithin combined with phosphorus and choline, which prevents fats from accumulating in the liver and facilitates the movement of fats into body cells. It also plays an important role in the transmission of nerve impulses.

2 *cups grated raw potato*	¼ *cup soy grits*
	¼ *cup milk*
¼ *cup hot milk or water*	2 *eggs, separated*
	2 *tablespoons soy flour*
½ *teaspoon salt*	¼ *teaspoon freshly ground pepper*
1 *tablespoon nutritional yeast*	

In a large bowl, combine the grated potato, hot milk or water, salt, and yeast. Let the mixture cool to lukewarm. In another bowl, soak the grits in the milk. Add the egg yolks, soy flour, soaked soy grits, and the pepper to the potato mixture. Beat the egg whites until stiff; fold into the potato mixture. Heat an ungreased griddle, preferably soapstone. Pour small amounts (about 2 tablespoons' worth at a time) onto the griddle. Let the pancakes cook on the griddle over moderately high heat till browned. Then turn and brown the flip side. As an alternative, drop the batter onto a hot oiled cookie sheet and bake in a 400-degree F. oven for 15 minutes. Serves 4 to 6.

APPLESAUCE FOR LATKES

Sweet—and without sugar.

1½ *pounds tart baking apples (a mixture of different kinds is ideal)*

½ *cup apple juice or apple cider or pineapple juice*
½ *teaspoon cinnamon, or to taste*

Wash the apples but do not peel. If the apples are not organic, give them a vinegar bath. (Let the fruit soak in a bowl of water to which you have added ¼ cup vinegar—any kind, the least expensive. Let it soak for a few minutes, then wash in clear water.) Cut up the washed apples and place in a pot. Add the fruit juice or cider and the cinnamon. If you like a thinner sauce, add a little more fruit juice. Bring to a boil, then reduce heat and let simmer for about 10 minutes. Let cool, then put it through the blender. The best applesauce you ever tasted. Makes 3 cups.

PURIM

Purim is a one-day holiday given over to lighthearted revelry, the playing of pranks, masquerades, and play acting. Even in the synagogue Purim is not a solemn day but an occasion for fun and foolishness, a taste of wine and Purim delicacies.

All the little girls dress up like Queen Esther, the heroine of the day, for it was she who saved the Jews from the gallows prepared for them by Haman, prime minister to King Ahasuerus. When Queen Esther revealed Haman's plot to the king, he ordered that Haman be hung on the gallows prepared for the Jewish people, and on the very date he had chosen for their destruction.

One of the truly lovely customs associated with Purim is a

unique kind of gift-giving called *shalach monos*. Usually the gifts are dishes filled with hamantaschen and such delicacies as rugelah, mandelbrodt, and cookies. You could make up a delicious plate for *shalach monos* using recipes included in this book for carob confections, granola cookies, halvah, etc. See Chapter Eleven (Pastries, Cakes, Pies, and Other Baked Goods) for more ideas.

HAMANTASCHEN

The milk and honey in the raised-dough crust of these pastries are symbolic of the Holy Land. And the soy and wheat flours combine to make a complete protein, which promotes a good feeling that enhances the enjoyment of Purim. So do the delicious fillings.

Note that prunes and apricots are goldmines of vitamin A, which helps build resistance to infection, and contain a healthy portion of the minerals that go to bat for your heart—potassium, calcium, and magnesium. Poppy seeds are a good source of the B vitamins and many minerals, including zinc.

1 *tablespoon dry yeast or 1 yeast cake*	1 *cup scalded milk*
¼ *cup lukewarm milk*	2 *eggs*
¼ *cup honey*	3½ *cups whole wheat pastry flour*
½ *cup butter or ½ cup vegetable oil*	2 *tablespoons soy flour*
½ *teaspoon salt*	1 *egg yolk*
	Water

Dissolve the yeast in the ¼ cup lukewarm milk. Stir in 1 tablespoon of the honey and set aside. In a large mixing bowl, combine the rest of the honey, the butter or oil, salt, and scalded milk. Stir to blend. When this mixture is lukewarm, stir in the yeast. Beat the eggs lightly and add to the mixture with 2 cups of the whole wheat flour. Add the remaining flours to make a soft, pliable dough. Knead for a few minutes, either in the bowl or on a floured board.

Grease a large mixing bowl. Turn the ball of dough so all surfaces are greased. Cover and let rise in a warm place till it doubles in bulk. (This takes 2 hours, sometimes longer.) Knead again for about 1 minute, then roll portions of the dough out about ⅛-inch thick. Cut circles, 3 or 4 inches in diameter, with an inverted glass jar or cookie cutter. Place filling on each (recipes below). Use a heaping tablespoonful's worth of filling for each small hamantasch, 2 tablespoonful's worth for each large one.

To shape, pinch the edges of each circle together over the filling to form triangles. Place on a greased cookie sheet; cover with a dishtowel and let rise again till double in bulk. Mix the egg yolk with a little water and brush the tops. Bake in a preheated 350-degree F. oven for 15 to 20 minutes. Makes 12 large or 24 small hamantaschen.

POPPY SEED (MOHN) FILLING:

2 *cups poppy seeds*
Boiling water
¼ *cup honey*
1 *cup water*
¼ *teaspoon cinnamon*

Pinch of powdered ginger (optional)
1 *egg, well beaten*
1 *tablespoon grated orange peel*
½ *cup raisins (optional)*

Put the poppy seeds in a large bowl. Pour boiling water over them. When the seeds settle to the bottom of the bowl, drain off the water. Grind the seeds fine or pound them in a mortar or wooden bowl. In a large saucepan, combine the ground poppy seeds, honey, cup of water, cinnamon, and ginger; cook over low heat until thick—about 1 hour—stirring frequently. Let the mixture cool, then add the beaten egg, the orange peel, and the raisins. Makes enough filling for 12 large or 24 small hamantaschen.

VARIATIONS: (1) Add ½ cup of finely chopped walnuts, sunflower seeds, or almonds or ¼ cup of fine granola crumbs to the filling. (2) Substitute currants for the raisins. (3) Instead of the orange peel, use 2 teaspoons of frozen orange juice concentrate, thawed but undiluted.

PRUNE FILLING:

1 *pound sweet prunes*
½ *of an orange, cut into*
thin slices, including
the peel
Water
Juice of ½ lemon
Rind of ½ lemon

½ *cup chopped pecans,*
sunflower seeds, or
walnuts
2 *tablespoons honey*
Dash of cinnamon
Dash of grated
nutmeg

Soak the prunes with the orange slices in water to cover for several hours or overnight. Drain and remove the pits. Add the lemon juice and rind and purée in the blender at low speed for about 1 minute. Add the rest of the ingredients. Makes enough filling for 24 small or 12 large hamantaschen.

VARIATIONS: (1) Use half prunes and half dried apricots. (2) Use all apricots. (3) Use apricots, raisins, and prunes. (4) Soak ½ cup almonds along with the dried fruit and blenderize with the soaked fruit. (5) Substitute unsweetened shredded coconut for the nuts. (6) Substitute ½ cup granola for the nuts.

KIPFEL

A very rich pastry dough that can be used for hamantaschen.

DOUGH:

½ *cup butter, softened*
½ *cup cream cheese,*
softened

⅞ *cup whole wheat*
pastry flour
2 *tablespoons soy flour*

FILLING:

½ *cup chopped nuts*
(variety of your
choice)
½ *teaspoon grated*
lemon rind

2 *tablespoons*
unsweetened
coconut flakes,
ground fine
Dash of cinnamon

Combine the butter and cream cheese, blending well. Combine the flours and add to the butter mixture to form a dough. Refrigerate the dough for several hours or overnight. Combine the filling ingredients.

You can handle the dough in either of two methods: Roll it out ⅛-inch thick on a floured surface; cut into squares; put a small amount of the nut mixture on each square; fold over and press the edges together to seal. Or, simply tear off small balls of dough, a piece at a time; press each ball out in your hand; put the filling in, and press to close. (You can use the usual hamantaschen fillings instead of the nut filling. You can also fill them with granola.)

Bake on parchment-lined cookie sheets at 350 degrees F. for 12 to 15 minutes. Makes about 24 kipfel.

PIROGEN
(Yeast-risen Dough)

Pirogen and piroshki are wonderful Purim treats. These pastries can be made extra wholesome by the use of potato water, which contributes both minerals and the water-soluble B vitamins. The whole wheat flour provides fiber and all the goodness of wheat germ. The pirogen can be filled with chopped meat, chicken, liver, heart, or kasha.

½ teaspoon salt	¼ cup lukewarm water
1 cup hot water or potato water (water in which potatoes have been cooked)	2 eggs, beaten
	2 cups whole wheat bread flour
1 teaspoon honey	2 cups whole wheat pastry flour
1 tablespoon vegetable oil	Vegetable oil
1 yeast cake or 1 tablespoon granulated yeast	1 egg yolk
	1 tablespoon water

In a large bowl, dissolve the salt in the hot water; add the honey and oil. Allow to cool to lukewarm. Dissolve the yeast in the ½ cup lukewarm water. Add the dissolved yeast, then the beaten eggs to the first mixture. Add the whole wheat bread flour gradually, stirring well. Add the whole wheat pastry flour gradually, reserving ½ cup for flouring the board on which you will knead the dough. Knead for about 10 minutes, pressing the dough away from you, then folding the dough, moving it around a little and pressing again. Pretend it is a clock and move it 5 minutes on each turn. Continue kneading in this fashion until the dough is no longer sticky. Place the dough in an oiled bowl and brush the top with oil. Cover loosely with a tea towel and put in a warm place. Let it rise until it triples in bulk. Punch the dough down. Divide into 2 portions. Roll each portion out to ¼-inch thickness.

Cut into 5-inch squares or rounds. Place 2 tablespoons of filling (see recipe below) in the center of each. Bring the edges together to form triangles from the squares, or half moons from the rounds. Brush with an egg yolk diluted with 1 tablespoon of water. Place the filled pirogen on a cookie sheet lined with parchment paper or greased with a mixture of ½ teaspoon oil and ½ teaspoon liquid lecithin. Put in a warm place to rise for 1 hour. Bake in a preheated 375-degree F. oven for 25 to 30 minutes, until golden brown. Makes about 36 pirogen.

FILLING (MEAT OR CHICKEN):

1 onion, finely chopped
1 tablespoon chicken fat
2 cups chopped meat or chicken
¼ teaspoon black pepper
¼ teaspoon paprika
1 egg, beaten

To make a tasty filling, sauté the onion in the 1 tablespoon of chicken fat. Add the meat or chicken, seasonings, and the egg; mix lightly. The filling is now ready to use.

PIROSHKI

A piroshki is a small version of a pirogen. These filled pastries can be made with a pastry dough or yeast-risen bread dough. This recipe calls for a pastry dough. Use the filling recipe given for the pirogen (above), or create a tasty filling of your own.

½ teaspoon salt
1½ cups whole wheat
    pastry flour
½ cup chicken fat
1 egg, beaten

¼ cup water,
    approximately
Egg yolk or melted
    chicken fat

To make the pastry dough, combine the salt with the flour. Cut in the ½ cup of chicken fat until the flour is crumbly. Add the beaten egg and only enough water to make a dough that can be rolled. Roll the dough out on a floured board until quite thin—about ⅛-inch thick. Cut into 3-inch rounds.

Make a filling (see pirogen recipe above) and place a tablespoonful of the filling in the middle of each pastry round. Close the circle, making a half moon; crimp the edges together. (If you were using yeast dough, you would let them rise at this point for about 1½ hours.) When ready for the oven, brush with egg yolk or melted chicken fat and bake for 20 minutes in a preheated 375-degree F. oven. Makes about 30 piroshki.

8

Passover Specialties:
The Natural Way

With what joy do we recall the Passovers of our childhood: the fun of the nuts-against-the-wall game and the heavenly aromas from the kitchen, which made our taste buds do a *hora!*

The whole house was scrubbed from top to bottom; freshly-starched white curtains framed the windows like bridal veils. Our venerable ancestors were smiling out of picture frames that shone with a new coat of golden luster; us kids freshly bathed and dressed in brand new clothes; everybody's eyes twinkling, reflecting all the sparkling surfaces of polished wood, stove, and samovar. Everything was *freilach.*

I remember feeling very sorry for my gentile friends because they didn't have the joy and excitement of Passover. They thought we were deprived because we couldn't have bread. Can you imagine? Who needs bread when there are knaidlach in the soup; charoses, kugels, bitter herbs, and sweet wine on the table; and memories, hopes, and family togetherness?

For, in spite of the restrictions against bread, flour, legumes, yeast, and anything which would with the addition of water begin to ferment, the foods of Passover have a very special *Pesachdik tam.*

However, since regular whole wheat flour, wheat germ, and bran are proscribed, we know, now that we are nutritionally aware, that we must seek other sources for the nutrients and fiber which these foods provide or we'd feel like one of my friends who once confided, "I love Pesach but my digestion doesn't."

Here are some suggestions for enjoying the holiday without digestive *tsouris:*

- Use kosher for Passover whole wheat matzo at the table and in baked kugels, matzo brei, and fried matzo. Whole wheat matzo contains wheat germ and bran. If your family balks, try a mix of white and wheat. Encourage them to try the whole wheat.
- Serve baked potatoes in their jackets. The skin provides valuable fiber and nutrients.
- Serve lots of salads and fresh fruits.
- Make your own matzo meal from whole wheat matzo. Use it for knaidlach, latkes, and wherever you use matzo meal. Until your family accepts it, use a blend of both.
- Make your own cake meal from whole wheat matzo. Use the blender or a rolling pin to pulverize it to a floury consistency.

The specialties in this chapter are ones you will surely want to add to your Passover repertoire. Because they are prepared the natural way, you won't find them in standard kosher cookbooks. They will round out your menus beautifully by adding extra nutritional values as well as exciting new tastes.

White Horseradish

Horseradish, one of the bitter herbs used on Passover, has a good reputation as a healing herb. It is believed to be a potent diuretic and is used to treat kidney conditions. Horseradish is used to alleviate symptoms of coughs, colds, and bronchitis. It also relieves nasal congestion—as you probably know if you've ever taken a whiff of it.

1 *large horseradish*	*Apple cider vinegar*
Cold water	*or lemon juice*

Soak the horseradish in cold water for a few hours. Peel it and cut it into chunks. Blenderize the chunks with a dash of vinegar or lemon juice; put it in a jar; add more vinegar of lemon juice to cover. Keep tightly covered under refrigeration. This is strong enough to clear your sinuses, so take it easy. Makes 1 pint or more, depending upon the size of the horseradish used.

RED HORSERADISH

Add 2 grated raw beets to the horseradish recipe above, or cut the beets into chunks and place them in the blender with the horseradish. You may use cooked or canned beets instead, but raw provides more nutritional value.

CHAROSES

This delicious sweet-tart mixture is used at the Seder as a symbol of the brick and mortar that Jews were forced to make during their enslavement in Egypt.

2 *peeled red apples, preferably tart*	*Grated rind of ½ lemon*
½ *cup chopped walnuts*	1 *teaspoon cinnamon*
1 *teaspoon honey*	2 *tablespoons sweet red wine (approximately)*

Chop or grate the apples into a bowl. Add the rest of the ingredients, but only enough wine to bind the mixture. Place in a bowl and refrigerate until ready to use. Taste-check for a good blend of sweet, sour, and crunch. Serves 4 to 6.

BEET BORSCHT

This borscht—kosher for Passover but excellent throughout the year—should make your eyes sparkle and enrich your blood. Beet greens are loaded with vitamin A (more than 5,000 international units in 3½ ounces) and are an excellent source of iron. Borscht has a robust, refreshing flavor whether served hot or cold.

2 *bunches of beets*	1 *teaspoon salt*
(approximately 8	*(optional)*
beets in all)	2 *eggs*
Cold water	2 *tablespoons honey*
1 *onion*	¼ *cup lemon juice*
2 *quarts boiling water*	

Cut the tops off about 2 inches above the beets. Reserve the tops for later use. (Be sure to do this before scrubbing them.) After scrubbing carefully, place the beets in a pot, cover with cold water, and cook for 15 minutes or until fork-tender.

Meanwhile, wash the beet leaves very carefully and chop them fine. Be sure to include the stems: they have good nutrients that shouldn't be wasted.

When the beets are cooked, drain the liquid into a soup pot. Slip the skins from the beets and discard; then grate the beets into a bowl. Grate the onion into the grated beets. Add this to the liquid in which the beets were cooked. Add the chopped beet tops and the boiling water. Add salt if you wish, and bring to a boil; then reduce and simmer for 5 minutes.

Beat the eggs in a bowl. Add the honey and lemon juice. Stir a little of the hot liquid from the borscht into the eggs. Mix it up quickly so the egg doesn't cook. Pour this mixture into the soup pot and— you've got borscht. Serve cold with a spoonful of sour cream or yogurt, or hot with a boiled potato. Serves 6 to 8.

LOW-FAT, LOW-CALORIE
PASSOVER KISHKE

Seconds on the kishke? Why not! It's wholesome, low in fat and calories, and tastes just like the real thing but without the heart-burn.

2 *stalks celery, with*
   leaves
1 *large carrot, cut into*
   pieces
1 *large onion,*
   quartered
1 *egg*
¼ *cup peanut oil*

½ *teaspoon salt*
   (optional)
¼ *cup poppy seeds*
1¼ *cups whole wheat*
   cake meal
1 *teaspoon paprika*

Whiz the vegetables, egg, oil, salt, and poppy seeds in a blender. Combine this mixture with the cake meal and paprika. Spoon half of this mixture onto a sheet of parchment paper. Shape into a roll similar to a traditional kishke. Roll it securely, then twist the ends of the paper. Repeat with the other half of the mixture. Put the rolls on a cookie sheet or in a baking dish and bake in a preheated 350-degree F. oven for 1 hour. This kishke can be frozen before or after baking. Serves 8 to 10.

KNAIDLACH
(Matzo Balls)

These taste like Mom's—light and fluffy—but have the added nutritional values and the important fiber provided by the wheat germ in the whole wheat matzo.

4 *eggs, separated*
½ *cup white matzo*
   meal and ½ cup
   whole wheat matzo
   meal
1 *teaspoon salt*
   (optional)

Dash of ground
ginger
Dash of cinnamon
Boiling soup or
salted water

Beat the egg whites until stiff. Continue beating while you gradually add the yolks, the matzo meal, and the seasonings. Refrigerate for at least 15 minutes. Wet your hands, then form the mixture into balls, handling very lightly. Drop into boiling soup or salted water. Cover and cook until the matzo balls rise to the top—about 20 minutes. Makes 12 to 16 knaidlach.

POTATO KNAIDLACH

The creative culinary genius of our grandmothers was really put to the test on Passover, when they had to forego the old standbys—cereals and beans—as filler-uppers. So they made knaidlach from whatever they had on hand: liver, vegetable, bone marrow, nuts, fruits, and potatoes. Using this basic recipe for potato knaidlach, go creative and use what you've got.

2 *cups mashed potatoes*
2 *eggs, lightly beaten*
½ *teaspoon salt, or to taste*
Dash of pepper

2 *tablespoons chicken fat (optional)*
⅔ *cup whole wheat matzo meal, approximately*
Boiling soup or salted water

Place the mashed potatoes in a bowl; add the eggs and seasonings. Add the chicken fat if desired and enough matzo meal to hold the mixture together. Form into balls with wet hands and drop into boiling salted water or soup. Cover and cook for about 20 minutes. These may be served in soup or may be browned in a hot oven and be served plain or with gravy. Serves 4 to 6.

PASSOVER NOODLES

Fortunately for us, potato flour is kosher for Passover. It is far more wholesome than cornstarch, which is ultra-refined and contributes lots of calories and hardly any nutrients. Potato starch, on the other hand, contributes lots of potassium—as much as 1,588 milligrams in 3½ ounces. It is also a fairly good source of iron and calcium and provides vitamin C and some of the B vitamins, particularly niacin, which according to recent research from Hoffman-LaRoche has qualities similar to those of some tranquilizers and barbiturates but without the side effects. So, enjoy noodles and a good night's sleep.

6 *eggs*
¼ *teaspoon salt*

¾ *cup potato flour*
Peanut oil for frying

Place the eggs in a bowl. Add the salt and beat lightly. Stir in the potato flour, mixing well. Into a lightly greased preheated frying pan pour a small amount of the mixture and immediately pour off excess batter. Fry lightly on both sides but do not brown. Remove and let cool. When all batter has been used up, roll each pancake individually and slice thinly into noodles. Allow to dry out and store in tightly-sealed containers until ready to use. Nice in chicken soup. Makes approximately 8 ounces.

NOTE: You can also use the pancakes, cooked on 1 side only, to make blintzes.

FARFEL CHICKEN CASSEROLE

Chicken is high in protein, low in fat, low in calories, and is easily digested. It is also an excellent source of iron, potassium, calcium, vitamin A, and the B vitamins—especially niacin, which has been shown to dilate small blood vessels and lower cholesterol. Chicken provides no carbohydrate and no fiber, both of which are amply supplied in the whole wheat matzo farfel and the vegetables called for in the recipe. This casserole is so tasty, it's nice to know your body is enjoying it as much as your palate.

2 *tablespoons chicken fat*
1 *large onion, diced*
1 *cup chicken soup*
1 *cup vegetable juice, stock, or water*
2 *cups cooked chicken, cut cup*

2 *cups cooked sliced carrots, or other cooked vegetables*
1 *cup diced celery*
1½ *cups matzo farfel (whole wheat matzo, broken into farfel)*
Pepper and paprika

In a large saucepan, melt the chicken fat. Add the onion and sauté until transparent but not yet browned. Add the chicken soup and vegetable juice, stock, or water to make a sauce. Arrange the chicken, vegetables, matzo farfel, and the sauce in alternate layers in a 2-quart casserole. Season to taste with a bit of pepper and paprika. Cover and bake in a preheated 350-degree F. oven for 30 minutes. Serves 6 to 8.

PASSOVER PUFFS

These puffs made with eggs and whole wheat matzo provide a high-protein nutrient-rich "overcoat" for many delicious fillings. Use the filling recipes below, or experiment and create fillings to suit your taste.

1 *cup boiling water*	1 *cup cake meal*
⅓ *cup peanut oil*	*(whole wheat matzo*
½ *teaspoon salt*	*ground fine in*
	blender)
	4 *eggs*

Combine the boiling water, oil, and salt in a saucepan. Bring to a slow boil and reduce the heat. Add the cake meal all at once. Stir vigorously over low heat until the mixture forms a ball and leaves the sides of the pan. Remove from the heat. Add the unbeaten eggs, 1 at a time, beating very thoroughly after each addition until the dough is smooth and thick.

Drop by the heaping tablespoonful onto an oiled or parchment-lined cookie sheet, about 2 inches apart. Bake in a preheated 400-degree F. oven for about 40 minutes, until puffed and golden brown. (Do not open the oven door during the early part of the baking period.) When the puffs are cool, cut off the tops and fill with chicken, tuna, mixed vegetables, or a dessert filling. Makes 12 to 16 puffs.

CHICKEN SALAD FILLING FOR PUFFS:

1 *cup diced cooked chicken*	½ *cup slivered almonds or chopped cashews*
½ *cup chopped celery*	3 *tablespoons mayonnaise*
½ *cup presoaked raisins, chopped apple, or pineapple cubes*	

In a medium-sized bowl, combine the chicken, celery, fruit of your choice, and nuts. Add the mayonnaise and mix to blend. Makes 1½ cups, enough to fill 6 large or 12 small puffs quite generously.

TUNA SALAD FILLING FOR PUFFS:

1 *can (7 ounces) tuna, drained*
1 *stalk celery, chopped*
3 *tablespoons mayonnaise*
2½ *tablespoons lemon juice*

1 *medium-sized carrot, grated*
Pinch of paprika
Pinch of dill weed
Pinch of oregano

In a medium-sized bowl, combine all the ingredients. Makes a little over a cup, enough for 6 large or 12 small puffs.

CUSTARD FILLING FOR PUFFS (CREAM PUFFS):

⅓ *cup potato starch*
1¼ *cups milk*
2 *egg yolks*

2 *tablespoons honey*
1 *teaspoon vanilla extract*

In a small bowl, dissolve the potato starch in ⅓ cup of the milk. In the top part of a double boiler, heat the remaining cup of milk to simmer. Stir the dissolved potato starch in the simmering milk and cook until thickened, stirring constantly—about 1 minute.

Beat the egg yolks with the honey. Add a little of the hot mixture to the egg mixture, then stir this into the remaining hot milk mixture. Cook for about 1 minute, stirring constantly to prevent lumps from forming. Add the vanilla extract. Pour into a bowl and chill. Makes 1½ cups, enough to fill 6 large or 12 small puffs.

CARROT PUFF

A hint of orange brings out the sweetness of the carrots in this lovely puff. Will the carrots make your hair curl? That was the gimmick used to induce us to eat carrots in the days when every little girl aspired to a head full of Mary Pickford curls. Maybe the carrots never fulfilled their curly promise, but they sure contributed a luster to our locks and good nighttime vision to our eyes. One cup of carrots gives us 15,750 international units of vitamin A, which is needed to make visual purple, the pigment that enables the retina of the eye to see better in the dim light of twilight and in the dark.

1 *pound carrots (4 to 6)*

2 *tablespoons orange juice*

1 *egg*

¼ *teaspoon honey*

⅛ *teaspoon ground ginger*

2 *tablespoons butter, chicken fat, or peanut oil*

⅓ *cup finely chopped onion*

3 *tablespoons finely chopped parsley*

Steam the carrots till fork-tender—about 15 minutes. Place them in a mixing bowl or blender with the orange juice. Add the egg, honey, and ginger. Melt the butter or chicken fat or pour the oil into a small skillet; sauté the onion and parsley until just tender. Add this to the carrot mixture. Turn into an oiled 1-quart casserole and bake in a preheated 350-degree F. oven for 20 minutes. Serves 4.

APPLE-MATZO KUGEL

A cinnamony apple flavor is present in every bite of this moist kugel, which is equally compatible with meat or dairy.

4 *whole wheat matzos*
Water
3 *eggs, well beaten*
⅓ *cup honey*
2 *tablespoons peanut*
oil or melted chicken
fat or butter
1 *teaspoon cinnamon*
Pinch of nutmeg
½ *cup chopped*
walnuts or pecans

2 *large unpeeled*
apples, chopped
(Before chopping,
wash in a solution of
¼ *cup vinegar to a*
dishpan of tepid
water; soak for a
few minutes and
rinse under clear
water.)
½ *cup raisins*

Break the matzos into ½-inch pieces. Place in a bowl and soak them in water until soft. Drain, but do not squeeze dry. In a separate bowl, beat the eggs with the honey; add the oil, melted fat, or melted butter and the spices. Stir in the chopped nuts, chopped apple, and the raisins. Dot with additional fat. Bake in a preheated 350-degree F. oven for 45 minutes or until lightly browned. Serves 6 to 8.

VARIATION: Soak the matzos in apple juice instead of water, just enough to soften them. Don't drain. Use only 2 tablespoons of honey because the apple juice is naturally sweet. For a pineapple kugel, drain a can (20 ounces) of unsweetened crushed pineapple. Soak the matzos in the juice. Substitute the pineapple for the apple in the recipe above.

BANANA-NUT KUGEL

A lovely marriage of flavors and textures. This kugel, which is rich in potassium, can double as dessert.

3 *cups whole wheat*
matzo farfel (whole
wheat matzo broken
into ½-inch bits)
Cold water
4 *eggs*
4 *tablespoons honey*

¼ *cup butter, melted,*
or peanut oil
2 *medium-sized*
bananas, peeled
and sliced
½ *cup chopped walnuts*
Cinnamon

Place the farfel in a bowl and pour cold water over it; drain immediately so that the farfel is moist but not soggy. In a separate bowl, beat the eggs with the honey and melted butter or oil. Add to the farfel.

In a 1½-quart baking dish greased with butter or peanut oil, place half of the farfel mixture. Arrange the sliced banana on top and sprinkle with nuts. Top with balance of the farfel mixture. Add a dusting of cinnamon. Bake in a preheated 350-degree F. oven for 45 minutes or until lightly browned. Serves 6.

LARGE MATZO BREI

A great breakfast—on Passover or the year 'round. Eggs are an excellent source of protein and vitamins A, B, E, and K. Eggs also provide many essential minerals, including iron, calcium, phosphorus, potassium, and selenium. The egg is one of the few foods that provides vitamin D, so essential to the proper utilization of calcium. The wheat germ in the whole wheat matzo provides a good supply of pantothenic acid, the antistress substance that helps us cope. Wheat germ is also rich in B complex vitamins, vitamin E, and fiber—all of which are in relatively short supply in the Passover diet.

8 *whole wheat matzos*	*Salt and pepper, to*
3 *to 4 cups boiling*	*taste*
water	*Butter for frying*
4 *eggs, lightly beaten*	*(about 4 tablespoons)*

Break the matzos into 2-inch squares. Place in a large bowl or pot. Pour boiling water over the matzo pieces and drain immediately through a colander. (The pieces should be only slightly moistened, so they will absorb the egg.) Return the matzo to the bowl or large pot. Add the beaten eggs and seasoning. Toss with a fork until all pieces are coated.

Heat the butter in a heavy 10- to 12-inch skillet until bubbly but not browned. Pour the matzo mixture into the butter and fry over medium heat. When the underside begins to brown, turn the entire matzo brei with a spatula. If it breaks, turn in sections. Turn until all sides are golden. It doesn't matter if it crumbles. Those little morsels add an extra dimension to the dish. Taste-check and adjust the seasoning. It will take about 10 minutes to complete the frying. This matzo brei is excellent with cottage cheese or yogurt. Serves 4 to 6.

SCRAMBLED MATZO BREI

3 *whole wheat matzos*	2 *tablespoons water or*
Water	*milk*
2 *tablespoons butter*	¼ *teaspoon salt*
2 *eggs*	

Break the matzos into bite-sized pieces. Place in a bowl and cover with water for a few seconds; pour the water off quickly. Press excess water out of the matzo pieces. Melt the butter in a skillet, add the matzo pieces, and fry lightly. In a bowl, beat the eggs; add the water or milk and salt. Pour this over the pieces of matzo and fry, stirring constantly until the eggs are set. Serves 2 or 3.

ORANGE PASSOVER CAKE

Orange concentrate, carrots, coconut, and nuts meld their nutritional virtues to make a deliciously different featherlight cake. This cake freezes well and slices better when only partially defrosted.

9 *eggs, separated*	1 *tablespoon grated*
¾ *cup honey*	*orange peel*
¾ *cup flour made from*	1 *cup shredded carrot*
whole wheat matzo	½ *cup finely chopped*
(takes about 4	*walnuts*
matzos)	½ *cup raisins*
¾ *cup potato starch*	
2 *teaspoons cinnamon*	
½ *can (6 ounces) orange*	
juice concentrate,	
undiluted	

In a large bowl, beat the egg whites until stiff; set aside. In another bowl, beat the egg yolks until thick; gradually beat in the honey. Combine the dry ingredients and add to the egg yolk-honey mixture alternately with the orange juice concentrate. Stir in the orange peel, carrot, nuts, and raisins. Fold the egg yolk mixture gently into the beaten whites. Turn into an ungreased 10-inch tube pan. Bake in a preheated 325-degree F. oven for 55 to 60 minutes, until the cake is golden brown. Invert the pan on a wire rack; let the cake cool completely. This cake is delicious just as is, but if you want to enhance it, try this yummy cream cheese icing suggested by Jean Farmer, who used it on her daughter's wedding cake. Serves 12 to 16.

CREAM CHEESE ICING:
> ½ *pound cream cheese*
> *Juice of ½ lemon*
> ½ *teaspoon vanilla*
> *extract*
> ¼ *cup honey*
> *Orange sections for*
> *garnish*

Combine all ingredients except the orange sections until smooth. Spread on the top and sides of the cake. Garnish with orange sections. (Put some candles in it and you have a spectacular birthday cake!)

SHOSHANA'S APPLE CRISP

Ground nuts add extra nutrients to this easy-to-prepare dessert reminiscent of Grandma's apple pie.

4 *tart unpeeled apples*	⅓ *cup potato starch*
⅓ *cup whole wheat*	¼ *cup honey*
matzo meal	¼ *cup peanut oil*
⅓ *cup ground nuts or*	
seeds	

Wash the apples (if they have been sprayed, wash in a solution of ¼ cup vinegar to a dishpan of tepid water; soak for a few minutes, then rinse) and cut them into bite-sized chunks. Cover the bottom of a 9 x 9-inch baking dish with the apple chunks. Combine the rest of the ingredients and distribute over the apples. Bake in a preheated 350-degree F. oven for 30 minutes. Serves 4 to 6.

CARROT COCONUT CAKE

Moist, kosher for Passover, and rich in vitamin A, magnesium, potassium, and fiber. What more could you ask?

1 *cup grated raw carrot*	6 *eggs, separated*
¾ *cup coconut crumbs*	1 *cup ground raw cashews*
¾ *cup honey or maple syrup*	3 *teaspoons potato starch*
1 *teaspoon vanilla extract*	

In a large bowl, blend the carrot, coconut crumbs, and honey or syrup. Add the vanilla and blend. In a separate bowl, beat the egg yolks to a creamy consistency. Fold the egg yolks into the carrot-coconut mixture and let it stand in the refrigerator for 1 hour, or until it has soaked up the moisture. Add the ground cashews and blend.

In another bowl, beat the egg whites until stiff. Sprinkle the potato starch over them and mix it in. Fold the egg white mixture into the carrot-coconut mixture. Make two 9-inch layers or pour the mixture into a bundt pan. Bake in a preheated 400-degree F. oven for 10 minutes, then reduce the temperature to 350 degrees F. and bake for an additional 20 to 30 minutes or until the cake shows signs of leaving the sides of the pan. Cool on a wire rack. Serves 4 to 6.

MOCK OATMEAL COOKIES

These crunchy cookies, loaded with nuts and raisins, fill a real need for a nutritious Passover snack food.

⅓ cup peanut oil
¾ cup honey
4 eggs
2 cups whole wheat
    matzo meal

2 cups matzo farfel
1 cup raisins
1 cup chopped
    walnuts
1 teaspoon cinnamon

In a large mixing bowl, combine the oil and honey; beat well. Beat in the eggs. Add the rest of the ingredients. Mix well. Drop by the teaspoonful onto a cookie sheet greased with peanut oil or butter or lined with parchment paper. Bake in a preheated 325-degree F. oven for 20 to 25 minutes. Makes about 48 cookies.

LEMONY CARROT-NUT PUDDING

Carrots lend moistness to this nut-studded pudding, which with a fresh vegetable salad and a beverage would make a complete, satisfying meal. A nice change from the usual heavy fare of Passover.

8 eggs
Juice of 1 lemon
½ cup honey
2 cups grated carrot
2 cups finely chopped
    almonds, walnuts,
    pecans, or sunflower
    seeds, or a
    combination

6 tablespoons whole
    wheat matzo meal or
    potato flour

Preheat the oven to 350 degrees F. In a large bowl, beat the eggs. Add the lemon juice and honey and continue beating until fluffy. Add the grated carrot and chopped nuts or seeds. Mix in the matzo meal or potato flour. Pour the mixture into an oiled 8 x 10-inch baking dish or bundt pan. Bake for 50 minutes. Serves 8 to 10.

Passover Granola

Tasty, crunchy, and nutritious, this breakfast dish is a welcome change from fried matzo. It can also be used as a topping for desserts and in place of unbaked pie crusts.

6 *whole wheat matzos, broken into ½-inch pieces*
2 *cups unsweetened shredded coconut*
1 *cup sunflower seeds*
½ *cup pumpkin seeds (optional)*
¼ *cup cashew nuts (optional)*

⅓ *teaspoon cinnamon*
½ *cup honey*
2 *tablespoons peanut oil*
1 *cup cold water*
½ *cup slivered almonds*
Raisins, dates, prunes, figs, or grated apple

In a large bowl, combine matzo pieces with the rest of the dry ingredients except the almonds and fruit. Mix well. In a small bowl, combine the honey and oil. Add this mixture to the dry ingredients. Drizzle the water over all, a little at a time, mixing it through.

Preheat the oven to 225 degrees F. Spread this mixture onto 2 cookie sheets lined with parchment paper or lightly greased with oil. Bake for 2 hours, stirring every 15 minutes. Add the almonds and bake for another 15 minutes or until the mixture is dry and toasty brown in color. Turn off the oven and let the mixture cool in the oven. You can add the fruit at this point or at serving time.

Store in tightly-covered containers (mason jars are good) in the refrigerator or freezer. Good with either cold or hot milk or with yogurt. Makes 2 quarts; serves 16 to 20.

9

Entertaining Kosher
& Naturally

Bar Mitzvah, Bat Mitzvah, and confirmation ceremonies are highlights on my calendar. That magic, electrifying moment when the child is called to the Torah is like a trumpet that signals another link being forged in the lifeline of the Jewish people. That young voice, sometimes childlike, sometimes hoarse with emotion and a hint of the inevitable farewell to childhood, plays a poignant tune on one's heartstrings.

The mother of the boy or girl is on cloud nine. She wants everything super-lovely. She has spent lots of time, thought, and money to provide festive refreshments.

And, *oi vei*, what refreshments! Kugels laced with sugar—even the chopped herring is full of sugar. Not a piece of pastry that isn't drowned in confectioners' sugar.

Is it possible to have a lavish party that does not represent a fast trip to cavity corners and coronary precipice? Sure it is.

Nobody missed the white sugar, white flour concoctions at the all-natural Bar Mitzvah celebration for Joshua Susser, son of Dr. and Mrs. Buzz Susser of Pittsburgh. Dr. Susser practices preventive medicine, and everything on the menu was calculated to keep the doctor away. A big beautiful salad bowl with lots of sprouts was the centerpiece for the lavish spread enjoyed outdoors in a natural setting.

Dr. and Mrs. Michael Lerner of Lexington, Kentucky, for their son's Bar Mitzvah, commissioned the baker to prepare whole wheat and rye bagels. They asked the caterer to use only whole wheat flour for baked goods and only honey as a sweetener. The menu included three kinds of fruit-and-nut bread, three kinds of quiche, noodle kugels, whole wheat pita bread with sprouts and cherry tomatoes, several kinds of salads, and gefilte fish. "It was a huge success and we're still on cloud nine," Mrs. Lerner told me.

An all-natural celebration does not mean you have to forego the lovely dishes associated with a *simcha*. You can have your kugels. But, you don't have to load those kugels with sugar to make them scrumptious. Follow the recipes in the kugel chapter (Chapter Two) and fulfill your wish for good health with every portion.

Another special time for me is Friday evening, Oneg Shabbat, the joy of the Sabbath. A lovely time to greet your friends, to forget your worries of the week and to refresh your spirit.

Here again we have an opportunity to prepare a natural smorgasbord featuring confections that please the palate, delight the eye, nourish the body, and bring the true unblemished spirit of joy to the occasion.

Whenever you entertain, provide a dish of mixed dried fruits and watch how your guests will flock toward it. Dried fruits—raisins, dates, prunes, peaches, apricots—are all good sources of iron, potassium, calcium, phosphorus, and fiber. Prunes are also an excellent source of vitamin A. This dish requires no baking, no mixing, no freezing.

Hummous With Tahina and Baba Ghanouj are always popular and bring the flavor of Israel to your party. Whole Wheat Pizza will win over the younger set. See the recipes in this chapter.

Mixed seeds and nuts make another delicious and nutritious dish. Combine sunflower seeds, pumpkin seeds, sesame seeds, walnuts, cashews, soy nuts, raisins, chopped apricots or dates, and unsweetened coconut flakes in several small attractive bowls and place them in strategic places. This kind of wholesome food adds special joy to any occasion.

Fresh fruit, when available, makes a beautiful and refreshing platter, a delight to behold and to nosh—pineapples, quartered, sliced, and arranged on a platter with cut-up melons, strawberries, tangerine and orange sections. You'll always find the nicest people around the fruit platter.

A bowl of apples and pears makes a nice centerpeice, but very few people will pick up uncut fruit. To encourage fruit-eating and to make the fruit go farther, cut up a few apples in uniform slices, sprinkle with lemon or pineapple juice, and arrange them around a little dish of honey. This is good any time of year but is especially welcome when the snow is on the ground and the fruit in the marketplace is scarce and expensive.

Tea and coffee are standard beverages at every social function, so they should be offered. But, also offer a nice assortment of herb teas. Peppermint, rose hip, red zinger, and roastaroma are all popular with our guests. These teas have no caffein or tannic acid and will encourage rather than disturb one's slumber pattern. We also make available coffee substitutes that are free of chemical manipulation. These are available at specialty shops and health food stores and are cheerful substitutes for that "other" cup that gives you a caffein kick and an acid stomach.

Provide honey for those who like their beverages sweetened, instead of white sugar.

Everyone enjoys a delicious cookie to munch on while sipping tea. Provide heavenly Granola Delights, Polynesian Fruit Squares, Cheesecake Squares, or any of the recipes in this chapter. All are designed to build health and taste sinfully good.

You can use other chapters in this book to stimulate creative culinary management of festive events in your own life. Get your friends together for a Blintz Brunch. Offer an interesting variety— cheese, potato, fruit mixtures, etc. Make them ahead and store in the freezer. Defrost slightly before heating in the oven.

Many of the dishes in Chapter Five, To Be Kosher and Vegetarian, lend themselves beautifully to a buffet party, and your friends will be delighted to learn about the many great dishes that can lessen one's dependence on meat.

If you're involved with an organizational luncheon or a large festive occasion of any kind, like a fiftieth anniversary, try the Rainbow Salad for 50 and the Pineapple Lukshen Kugel for 50, both included in this chapter. Include a few Pistachio Cheese Balls and you'll have a sure winner.

HUMMOUS WITH TAHINA

Introduce a touch of Israel with a dish of hummous surrounded by whole wheat pita cut into small triangles for dipping and a large tray of fresh raw vegetables. Your waist-watching friends will bless you.

2 *cups dried chickpeas (garbanzo beans)*
Water
1 *teaspoon salt*
4 *medium-sized or 3 large cloves garlic*

⅓ *cup fresh lemon juice*
1 *cup tahina (sesame butter)*
Paprika and parsley sprigs

Wash the chickpeas under cold water. Remove any that are broken or discolored. Place them in a large bowl and add water to a level 2 inches above the beans. Soak for 12 hours, or overnight; the beans will triple in size. If the weather is warm, allow them to soak in the refrigerator. Transfer the peas and the soak water to a large pot, adding the salt and enough fresh water to cover completely. Bring to a boil, then reduce the heat; simmer, partially covered, for about 2 hours, until the peas are tender. If necessary, add more boiling water to keep them immersed during the cooking period. When the chickpeas are tender, drain but do not discard the liquid. Reserve about ½ cup of the chickpeas for garnish and blenderize the rest with ½ cup or a bit more (depending on the consistency desired) of the reserved liquid, the garlic, and lemon juice. (If you don't have a blender, use a sieve. Chop the garlic very fine or crush it with a garlic press.)

When the chickpea mixture is smooth, add the tahina and mix it in with a wooden spoon. Add more of the cooking liquid if necessary to achieve a consistency that will spread easily. Taste-check for seasoning. (Some like to add a dash of ground cumin and freshly ground pepper.)

Spread the hummous on plates or in flat-bottomed bowls. Garnish with paprika, parsley, and a ring of cooked chickpeas. Dip and enjoy! Serves 16 as a dip.

NOTE: Whole wheat pita is available at some health food stores and delicatessens. To locate a distributor in your area, write or call Toufayan Bakery, 9255 Kennedy Boulevard, North Bergen, New Jersey 07047; telephone (201) 861-4131. Their pita and pitettes (hamburger-size) are marked pareve and kosher.

PISTACHIO CHEESE BALL

If you want to enlarge the scope of your refreshment table and serve someting rather substantial, try a nut-coated cheese ball, a sophisticated snack that is always received well.

The pistachio is the seed found inside a small fruit indigenous to the Middle East and has been cultivated for thousands of years in Israel, Turkey, Syria, Greece, and Italy. The pistachio's superb flavor alone makes it irresistible, but it provides more than good taste. Two ounces of pistachio nuts provide as much as 10 grams of protein, 5 milligrams of iron, 58 milligrams of calcium, 612 milligrams of potassium, 130 international units of vitamin A, and some of the B vitamins—all at a cost of 328 calories, less than half the calories you get from an equal amount of peanuts.

The blue cheese in the cheese ball, besides providing many essential nutrients, contains a ferment conducive to a healthy bacterial climate in the intestines.

1 *pound cream cheese, softened*
¾ *cup (about 4 ounces) crumbled blue cheese*
1 *cup (about 4 ounces) shredded sharp Cheddar cheese*
¼ *cup minced onion*
1 *tablespoon Worcestershire sauce*
2 *cups shelled and chopped pistachio nuts*

Combine the cheeses in a bowl and let stand at room temperature until soft enough to mold. Add the onion and Worcestershire sauce. Blend, using an electric mixer at low speed; then beat at medium speed until fluffy. Cover and chill for 8 hours. Then shape the mixture into 2 large balls and roll each in the chopped pistachio nuts. Serve surrounded by beautiful crisp raw vegetables, crisp whole wheat additive-free crackers, whole wheat matzo, or whole wheat pita cut into small triangles.

You can also shape this mixture into 1-inch bite-size balls; roll in pistachio nuts and serve with a pick in each. This makes 30 one-inch balls.

BABA GHANOUJ
(Eggplant and Tahina)

Another party dip with an Israeli flavor is this eggplant and tahina delicacy. It has a cool, refreshing taste. Eggplant is one of the foods which, it has been found, tends to lower cholesterol levels. I like to serve it at festive functions that feature rich foods.

2 *medium-sized eggplants*
½ *cup lemon juice*
4 *tablespoons tahina (sesame butter)*
3 *medium-sized cloves garlic, finely minced*
1 *teaspoon salt (optional)*

1 *hard-cooked egg*
2 *tablespoons oil (olive oil is very good)*
2 *tablespoons chopped fresh parsley*
¼ *cup chopped green onions*

Bake the eggplants until the skins dry out—about 1 hour. Remove from the oven and let cool. When cool enough to handle, peel and mash into a bowl. Add the lemon juice and tahina, then the finely minced garlic. Taste-check for seasoning. Add salt if necessary. Spread the mixture on a flat plate or serve it in a pretty glass bowl. Sieve the hard-cooked egg over all; sprinkle with the oil and garnish with the parsley and green onions. Serve with whole wheat pita or fresh vegetables. Serves 20 as a dip.

HORSERADISH-EGG DIP

The zip of horseradish and the touch of lemon give this protein-rich creamy dip a pleasantly sharp flavor that will entice your guests into consuming lots of crisp raw vegetables. The yogurt provides lactic acid, which contributes to better digestion and creates an environment that inhibits the growth of harmful bacteria.

6 *hard-cooked eggs*
½ *cup mung bean sprouts*
½ *cup sour cream*
½ *cup plain yogurt*
½ *cup white horseradish*
4 *teaspoons prepared mustard*

4 *teaspoons lemon juice*
1 *teaspoon honey*
½ *teaspoon kelp*
Paprika
Chopped fresh parsley

In a bowl, mash or chop the eggs fine. Add the sprouts. Combine the rest of the ingredients and add to the egg mixture. Sprinkle with paprika. Garnish with parsley. Makes 2½ cups. Can also be used as a salad dressing.

MOCK SALMON SALAD

Made from tuna but it looks and tastes like salmon. Delightful when served with a green salad and a kugel or cheesecake dessert.

Tuna provides more good protein than an equal amount of porterhouse steak and is much kinder to your budget. Water-packed tuna is practically fat-free. Tuna is an excellent source of niacin, which recent research indicates may be a factor in preventing cancer and helping to prevent mental confusion in the elderly.

1 *can (7 ounces) tuna,*
    drained
1 *hard-cooked egg,*
    mashed
1 *tablespoon lemon*
    juice
2 *tablespoons*
    mayonnaise
1 *large carrot, grated*
2 *stalks celery, finely*
    chopped
    Parsley sprigs

In a bowl, mash the tuna with a fork. Add the egg, lemon juice, and mayonnaise; combine well. Add the grated carrot and chopped celery to the tuna mixture. Mix all ingredients well. (Doesn't it look like salmon?) Now taste for seasoning and consistency. Garnish with parsley sprigs and serve some of the garnish with each portion. (Parsley is very healthful, so don't let it go to waste.) Serves 4 to 6.

Mock Crabmeat Salad

2 *cups raw parsnips,*
    grated
2 *ribs celery, finely*
    chopped
2 *tablespoons finely*
    chopped red pepper
½ *small onion, finely*
    chopped
½ *cup sunflower seeds*
¼ *cup mayonnaise, or*
    enough to moisten
1 *tablespoon lemon*
    juice
½ *teaspoon kelp*

Combine the parsnips, celery, pepper, onion, and sunflower seeds. Mix the mayonnaise with the lemon juice and kelp. Combine the mixtures. Serve on salad greens. Serves 6 to 8 or more.

Sillisalaati

For the old folks, this herring salad brings back memories of the shtetl.

SALAD:

1 *matjes herring*
Cold water
1 *cup diced cooked*
beets
1 *cup diced cooked*
potato

1 *cup diced cooked*
carrot
1 *cup diced apple*
½ *cucumber, diced*
2 *small onions, diced*
Dark green lettuce
leaves

DRESSING:

1 *cup sour cream or*
plain yogurt

¼ *cup vinegar*
A little beet juice

Soak the herring briefly in cold water. Remove the bone and cut into bite-size pieces. Add the rest of the ingredients and toss. Serve on lettuce leaves in a large glass bowl or on individual salad plates. Combine the dressing ingredients and serve separately. Serves 12 on the smorgasbord or 6 as a salad.

CHOPPED HERRING

4 *matjes herrings*
½ *cup finely chopped*
tart apple
2 *hard-cooked eggs,*
finely chopped
2 *tablespoons finely*
chopped onion
3 *tablespoons apple*
cider vinegar

2 *tablespoons*
vegetable oil
1 *teaspoon honey*
2 *slices challah*
Cayenne pepper, to
taste
1 *hard-cooked egg*
yolk, sieved

Soak the herring for 12 hours, changing the water twice. Drain, then chop the herring. Combine the chopped herring with the apple, eggs, and onion.

Combine the vinegar, oil, and honey. Pour this mixture over the challah and let it soak for a few minutes. Add the soaked challah to the herring mixture and chop together. Add seasoning to taste and chill. When ready to serve, garnish with the sieved yolk of a hard-cooked egg. Serves 6 to 8 or more.

Rainbow Salad for 50

The alfalfa sprouts bring a quality of "aliveness" to this colorful vitamin-rich salad. The chickpeas and sunflower seeds lend a pleasant contrast in texture as well as complementary protein values.

Salad:

2 *heads red leaf lettuce, torn into pieces*

2 *heads romaine lettuce, torn into pieces*

2 *pounds spinach, torn into pieces*

1 *gallon jar of alfalfa sprouts*

2 *cups cooked chickpeas (garbanzo beans)*

2 *cups sunflower seeds*

2 *cups fresh green beans, cut into 1-inch pieces*

2 *cups grated carrot*

1 *cup chopped green onions with tops (approximately 1½ bunches)*

1 *cup chopped fresh parsley*

2 *cups sliced fresh mushrooms*

4 *cups tomatoes, cut into chunks*

Combine all ingredients and serve in 2 large salad bowls. Serve the dressing on the side.

Dressing:

3 *cups homemade mayonnaise (see Index for recipe)*

¾ *cup chili sauce*

½ *cup homemade catsup (see Index for recipe)*

3 *tablespoons tarragon vinegar*

1 *tablespoon paprika*

3 *tablespoons chopped fresh parsley*

6 *hard-cooked eggs, cut up*

Combine all ingredients well and the dressing is ready to use.

NEVER-FAIL CHEESE SOUFFLÉ

Great for a party brunch. You do all the preparation the night before, leaving you free to accept the compliments of your guests while you tell them how healthful this dish truly is. The lecithin in the soufflé helps to emulsify fat. The selenium in the eggs may turn out to be the most important trace mineral discovery of the century. Selenium has already been shown to play a role in delaying the aging process, in fertility, and in the prevention of some chronic diseases, including cancer.

Butter	*2½ cups milk*
6 *slices fresh whole wheat bread*	1 *teaspoon dry mustard*
1½ *cups grated Cheddar cheese*	1 *tablespoon lecithin granules*
5 *eggs*	

Spread a thin layer of butter on 1 side of each slice of the bread. Place each slice buttered-side-up in a buttered casserole. Cover with the grated cheese. (If your casserole does not accommodate the 6 slices of bread, layer the bread and the cheese to fit.) In a bowl, beat the eggs. Add the remaining ingredients. Pour over the bread-and-cheese layers. Cover the casserole and place it in the refrigerator overnight. Next morning, remove it and place it in a preheated 325-degree F. oven for 45 minutes or until set. Makes about 12 servings.

BAR MITZVAH KUGEL

In the olden days, before caterers took over the feeding of the Bar Mitzvah guests, we would get together with a few good friends, go to the temple kitchen, swap stories and recipes, recall the "good ole days," share our hopes for our children, laugh and weep and sing as we made kugels—huge kugels—all different. This was my favorite.

Butter for the baking
dish
1 pound cream cheese
¼ cup honey
8 eggs, beaten
1½ cups plain yogurt or
sour cream
2 tablespoons butter,
melted

1½ cups milk
2 teaspoons vanilla
extract
¼ cup wheat germ
2 tablespoons lecithin
granules
8 ounces medium
noodles, cooked
and drained

Butter a 9 x 13-inch baking dish. In a mixing bowl, blend the cheese with the honey. Add the eggs and the rest of the ingredients, adding the cooked noodles last; mix well. Bake in a preheated 350-degree F. oven for 1 hour or until browned. Serves 20.

PINEAPPLE LUKSHEN KUGELS
FOR 50

2½ pounds medium
noodles, cooked
5 pounds cottage
cheese, drained
5 cups sour cream
5 cups milk
5 cups crushed
pineapple
15 eggs, beaten

¾ cup honey
1¼ cups butter, melted
1½ cups raisins
5 teaspoons vanilla
extract
1¼ teaspoons salt
(optional)
3 teaspoons cinnamon

Combine all the ingredients in a huge bowl. Grease 5 pans about 10 x 8 inches each. Pour the mixture in equal amounts into each of the pans and bake in a preheated 350-degree F. oven for 1 hour. If making these kugels in advance, bake them for 30 minutes and refrigerate or freeze. When ready to use, bring to room temperature and bake for at least 30 minutes before serving. As a delicious accompaniment, serve bowls of strawberries in yogurt. Serves 50.

Mamaligge With Rozhinkes and Mandlin

1 teaspoon vegetable
oil
1 teaspoon sea salt
2 cups boiling water
1 cup yellow cornmeal
½ cup raisins
½ cup chopped
almonds, pecans, or
pistachios

3 tablespoons butter
2 eggs, lightly beaten
Dry whole grain
bread crumbs or
wheat germ or
sesame seeds
Sour cream or plain
yogurt, applesauce
or berries

Add the oil and salt to the boiling water, then gradually add the cornmeal, stirring constantly. Continue to heat and stir until the mixture thickens—about 5 minutes. Add the raisins and nuts and continue cooking for 15 minutes, stirring occasionally. Add a little more water if necessary.

Serve as is with sour cream or yogurt, or pour the mixture into a buttered cake dish and refrigerate. When it is cold, cut it into squares. Dip the squares in the beaten eggs, then into bread crumbs, wheat germ, or sesame seeds (try a mixture of all 3). Fry the squares in butter or dot them with butter and heat them in the oven. Serve with sour cream, yogurt, applesauce, berries, or maple syrup. Makes a terrific dish for a company brunch. Everything can be prepared in advance. Just put the squares in the oven when the first guest arrives.

Whole Wheat Pizza

A pizza with a whole wheat crust. It's just as delicious and much more nutritious than the traditional kind.

1 tablespoon dry yeast
2 cups warm-to-hot
   water
¾ teaspoon honey
2 tablespoons
   vegetable oil
5 cups whole wheat
   pastry flour
1 can (6 ounces)
   tomato paste
1 cup water
1 onion, chopped
½ teaspoon dried
   crushed basil

½ teaspoon crushed
   oregano
⅓ teaspoon garlic
   powder
¼ teaspoon sea salt or
   kelp
2 to 4 cups grated
   mozzarella cheese
Sliced green pepper,
   freshly sliced
   mushrooms, and
   sliced onion for
   topping

In a large bowl, dissolve the yeast in the water. Add the honey and oil. Stir in the flour. Knead for 5 minutes. Let rise in a warm place for 1 hour. Divide the dough in half and pat into 2 large pizza pans or cookie sheets. Bake in a preheated 350-degree F. oven for 20 to 25 minutes. Now prepare the sauce.

In a saucepan, simmer the tomato paste, water, onion, and seasonings until the sauce thickens. The sauce is now ready to use.

Remove the crusts from the oven and cover each with a layer—about 1 cup for each—of grated cheese. Spread the tomato sauce on top. Add additional toppings, such as green pepper, mushrooms, onions, and lots more grated cheese and bake for 30 minutes at 350 degrees F. Makes 2 large pizza pies. Serves approximately 16.

ADELE'S CHEESECAKE TARTS

These tarts will add a lovely decorative touch to your confection platter. They give everybody, even weight-watchers, the joy of cheesecake without eating a whole big piece. The wheat germ provides vitamin E and the B vitamins, which boost one's morale.

¾ cup graham cracker
   crumbs or your own
   natural cookie or
   cake crumbs
¼ cup wheat germ
3 tablespoons butter,
   melted

1 egg
8 ounces cream cheese
¼ cup honey
1 teaspoon vanilla
   extract

Combine the first 3 ingredients. Line muffin tins with 12 cupcake or 24 candy-size paper cups. Line the cups with the crumb mixture.

Blend the remaining ingredients, then half fill the paper cups with the mixture. Bake for 15 minutes in a preheated 350-degree F. oven. Allow to cool, then spoon some cherry or blueberry topping over each. Makes 12 cupcake-size or 24 candy-size tarts.

TOPPINGS:

2 cups pitted sour
   cherries or
   blueberries
   Scant ¼ cup honey

2 teaspoons arrowroot
   starch
¼ cup water

In a small saucepan, combine the fruit and honey. Stir over low heat until just below the boiling point. In a bowl, combine the arrowroot and the water; add it to the fruit. Cook slowly until the mixture thickens. Cool and keep refrigerated until ready to use.

DRIED FRUIT CONFECTION

It is said that King David accepted solar-dried grapes or raisins in payment of taxes. Why not? Besides providing a fantastic symphony of flavors, dried fruits are a good source of protein as well as vitamin A, which recent research points to as a cancer inhibitor. They also provide all-purpose vitamin C and many minerals, including potassium, magnesium, iron, and calcium.

There is no cooking involved in the preparation of these naturally sweet confections.

½ cup pitted dates
½ cup pitted prunes
1 cup raisins
1 cup dried apricots
1 cup figs, some black
   and some white
2 tablespoons honey
1 cup unsweetened
   shredded coconut

½ cup sunflower seeds
1 cup homemade or
   natural peanut butter
Unsweetened shred-
   ded coconut, sesame
   seeds, and chopped
   nuts

Grind the dried fruit in a food grinder, using a fine blade. Add the rest of the ingredients. Mix well, then form into small balls and roll in the coconut, sesame seeds, and/or chopped nuts. Makes 36 confections.

BETTY'S TOFFEE BARS

Makes the graham cracker a party dessert.

15 sugar-free graham
   crackers (available at
   health food stores)
½ cup honey

½ cup butter
1 cup chopped
   walnuts, pecans, or
   peanuts

Lay the graham crackers out flat in an 8 x 12-inch baking dish. Combine the honey and butter in a small saucepan and bring to a boil. Lower the heat and cook for 2 minutes. Add the chopped nuts. Pour over the graham crackers, spreading the mixture to cover all crackers. Bake in a preheated 350-degree F. oven for 10 minutes. Let cool. Makes 15 portions.

POLYNESIAN FRUIT SQUARES

We flipped for these when we dined at the Yes! restaurant in Washington, D.C. The wheat and soy in this recipe provide complementary protein augmented in value by the coconut and cashews, which also contribute iron, potassium, and B vitamins. The fruit sugar provided by the pineapple is quickly absorbed by the blood and carried into the muscle cells, where it plays an energy-giving role.

2 *tablespoons butter or vegetable oil*
2 *eggs*
¼ *cup honey*
1 *tablespoon orange juice concentrate, undiluted*
1 *teaspoon vanilla extract*

1 *cup whole wheat pastry flour*
¼ *cup soy flour*
1 *cup unsweetened coconut flakes*
¾ *cup chopped roasted cashews*
1 *can (20 ounces) crushed pineapple with juice*

With an electric mixer or in a blender, combine the butter or oil, eggs, honey, orange juice concentrate, and vanilla. Add the whole wheat and soy flours gradually, until well mixed. Using a wooden spoon, mix in the coconut, cashews, and pineapple with juice. Spread in a greased or parchment-lined 13 x 9 x 2-inch pan. Bake in a preheated 350-degree F. oven for 45 minutes or until nicely browned. Cool before cutting into 1½-inch squares. Makes approximately 75 squares.

GRANOLA DELIGHTS

Granola is not just for breakfast. Not when you can so easily bake oats, nuts, and raisins into crunchy confections that are high in protein and very rich in blood-building iron, magnesium, potassium, and the anti-fatigue B vitamins.

3½ *cups rolled oats (not the instant)*
1 *cup raisins*
1 *cup chopped walnuts or sunflower seeds*
½ *cup melted butter or vegetable oil*

¼ *cup honey and ¼ cup blackstrap molasses*
1 *egg, beaten*
1 *teaspoon vanilla extract*

Toast the oats on an ungreased cookie sheet in a 300-degree F. oven for 15 minutes. In a large bowl, combine the rest of the ingredients with the toasted oats. Mix well. Line a 10 x 15-inch baking dish or jelly roll pan with parchment paper or brush it with butter, oil, or a mixture of liquid lecithin and oil (½ teaspoon of each). Press the mixture firmly into the pan and bake in a preheated 350-degree F. oven for about 20 minutes. Let cool, then cut it into bars or squares. Makes about 36 one-inch squares or 18 two-inch bars.

CHEESECAKE SQUARES

Sinfully good! They'll be the highlight of your confection tray.

1 *cup minus 2 tablespoons whole wheat pastry flour*
2 *tablespoons soy flour*
¼ *cup finely ground unsweetened coconut*
¼ *cup butter, softened*
½ *cup chopped walnuts*
8 *ounces cream cheese, softened*

¼ *cup honey*
1 *egg*
2 *tablespoons milk*
1 *tablespoon lemon juice*
1 *teaspoon vanilla extract*
1 *teaspoon grated lemon rind*
Few gratings of nutmeg

Combine the flours and the ground coconut. Using a pastry blender or 2 knives, cut this mixture into the butter. Add the nuts. Reserve ¾ cup of this crumb mixture for topping, and spread the remaining mixture over the bottom of an 8 x 8-inch baking dish. Bake for 15 minutes in a preheated 350-degree F. oven. Place the cream cheese and the rest of the ingredients in a blender jar and blend until smooth (or beat with an electric mixer). Pour the cream cheese mixture over the baked crust, top with the rest of the crumb mixture, and bake for another 30 minutes. Let cool slightly, then cut into squares. Makes 16 two-inch squares.

10

Baking Bread

"Where there is no bread,
There is no Torah."

—The Ethics of the Fathers

In that one pithy sentence, the early Jewish sages expressed the philosophy of a brand new concept in health care: holistic medicine, which maintains that to be healthy one must enjoy a harmonious balance of body, mind, and spirit.

If the body is not well nourished, the mind cannot concentrate and the spirit will droop. Therefore, where there is no bread (sustenance) there can be no energy for learning, wisdom, and spiritual insights (Torah).

To the sages of old, bread was the generic term for food and sustenance, since in those days flour was not refined and doused with chemicals. Bread was indeed the staff of life.

I love to bake bread. Nothing gives me more pleasure than watching my family enjoy a loaf of bread that I have magically conjured up, with the help of my oven, from a little yeast, flour, eggs, and maybe a little oil.

Bread baking, at one time, was a routine household procedure incumbent upon every *eshet chayil*. Today it is considered a hobby for men and women alike. I agree with Betty Iams, who says in her booklet "Bread Baking from A to Z" (Clef House Publications, Temecula, California), "There is no other hobby in the world as rewarding as bread baking. When one is happy, it is a joy to breeze through the kneading process. . . . When you are sad, frustrated, unhappy, you can unleash all your hostilities on the helpless dough as you knead away. Whatever your state of mind, the bread-making process is sure to have an uplifting effect."

And, in case you don't have any aggressions, it's still great exercise, and a good slimmer for the upper arms.

Bread baking is also a boon to your budget. You can enjoy two beautiful nutritious loaves for what it would cost for one mediocre loaf (with additives) at supermarket prices.

I used to love to watch my mother bake challah. There was a special glow about her, her cheeks pink and her eyes full of stars. She would sing as she mixed and kneaded and braided. I considered her a miracle-maker—to fill the house with such a tantalizing, yeasty, appetite-awakening fragrance, and then produce those beautifully braided, shiny challahs dotted with poppy seeds, sesame seeds, or black caraway ("karnitchka," she called it). She always made a few small challahs for the eager little mouths that couldn't wait till after Friday night candle-lighting for a heavenly taste.

Today I make my own challah and I still consider the results a miracle. Even more than eating the challah, baking it gives wings to the spirit, especially when one observes the practice of "taking challah." This is the age-old practice of taking a small piece of dough (about as large as a walnut), which may be wrapped in tinfoil, and casting it into the oven while whispering a prayer for the welfare of your loved ones and for peace in the world. This tradition dates to the time when loaves were carried to the priests in the Temple in Jerusalem.

Challah is usually made from white flour because white bread, once the food of the aristocrats, was considered a luxury, something special to be savored on the Sabbath and holidays.

Now that white bread is an everyday empty-calorie commodity more available than a good, tasty, wholesome whole-grain bread, challahs made from whole wheat flour, or a mixture of whole wheat and unbleached white, are gracing many Sabbath tables. And they are simply delicious!

If your family is still accustomed to white flour challah, use only one cup of whole wheat flour in your first batch. Gradually replace more of the white with the whole wheat flour. You may never get them to accept a 100 percent whole wheat challah. Don't despair. For every cup of unbleached white flour you use, take away one heaping tablespoon and add one heaping tablespoon of wheat germ. Put the wheat germ with the flour in the blender and whiz it fine. This will give the wheat germ a finer texture and will, in effect, sift the flour. Remeasure the flour after blending.

No matter what kind of bread you are baking, the option is yours to add sprouts (wheat, rye, alfalfa, sunflower seeds) to the bread dough to make a superior, moist, delicious loaf. At the same time, you are increasing the nutrient values of the bread. The sprouts can be chopped, blended, or used whole. Work them into the dough during the last kneading. Limit the sprouts to one cup for every two cups of liquid in the recipe.

Make sure the yeast you use in bread baking does not contain BHA. Health food stores carry baker's yeast in bulk. It has excellent keeping qualities. One tablespoon equals one yeast cake or one package of "active dry yeast."

Make sure the baking powder you buy is aluminum-free. Better yet, make your own (see recipe in Chapter Fifteen, Don't Buy It— Make It Yourself).

Wheat and Soy Challah

A high-protein, highly-nutritious Sabbath twist. Two loaves of challah are placed on the Sabbath table to recall the double portion of manna that fell in the desert every Friday.

2 *tablespoons dry*
yeast or 2 yeast
cakes
½ *cup lukewarm water*
or use vegetable
cooking water or the
water in which you
have soaked seeds
for sprouting)
4 *eggs*
3 *tablespoons*
vegetable oil
1 *tablespoon honey*
2 *teaspoons salt*
(optional)
2 *cups hot water*
4 *cups whole wheat*
bread flour

½ *cup soy flour*
3½ *cups unbleached*
white or 3 cups
whole wheat pastry
flour
1 *cup unbleached*
white or popcorn
flour (To make
popcorn flour, pop
the corn, blenderize,
then strain. Popcorn
adds lightness to
whole wheat flour.)
Poppy, sesame, or
caraway seeds

Dissolve the yeast in the ½ cup lukewarm water. Beat the eggs and reserve 2 tablespoons to be used for brushing the loaves later. In a large bowl, combine the oil, honey, salt (if desired), beaten eggs, and hot water. When the mixture cools to a bit hotter than lukewarm, add the yeast mixture. Mix well with a wooden spoon. Gradually add the 4 cups of whole wheat bread flour, reserving some for the kneading board; mix well.

Combine the rest of the flours. Add this mixture of flours and work it in. Let the dough rest for 10 minutes. Knead the dough on a floured board for about 10 minutes. Add more flour if the dough is too sticky. Put a little oil on your hands for smoother handling.

Form the dough into a ball. Place the ball in an oiled bowl, and turn to grease all sides. Cover with a damp dishtowel and set it in a warm place (on a radiator or the back of the stove) for about 2 hours—until it doubles in bulk.

Punch the dough down and knead it again for a few minutes. Divide the dough in half and shape each half into a braided loaf. You braid a challah the same way you do a pigtail. For each loaf, divide the dough into 3 equal sections. Roll them out just a bit longer than the pan in which you will bake the challah. Pinch the strands together at one end. Then take the piece on the outer right; cross it over the middle one; then take the piece on the outer left and also cross it over the middle. Repeat this procedure until you have completed shaping the bread. Pinch the strands together at the other end.

To make the challah extra fancy, divide the dough into 4 equal portions and make a thin braid out of the fourth section. Place this down the center of the large braid. Braids can be made in infinite variety, depending upon your skill. My mother-in-law can handle 16 strands.

After shaping the loaves, place both on a greased baking sheet or in greased bread pans and let them rise till double in bulk—for an hour or so—in a warm, not hot, place. Add a teaspoonful of cold water to the remaining 2 tablespoons of egg and brush the surface of both loaves. Sprinkle on poppy or sesame or caraway seeds. When the loaves have risen, bake them in a preheated 400-degree F. oven for 15 minutes. Then reduce the temperature to 350 degrees F. and continue baking for 45 minutes. Makes 2 large loaves.

MINIATURE CHALLAHS
(For the Kinder)

After dividing the dough, pinch off a small portion from each section. Braid and shape these the same way as described for the large loaves. Let them rise till double in bulk, brush with egg and sprinkle with seeds, the same as for large loaves. Bake on a greased cookie sheet in a 375-degree F. oven for 20 to 30 minutes, depending on size.

You can make just 1 large challah and 12 small ones if you have many children to delight. For the Sabbath, you need 2 unbroken loaves. One of the 2 can be a miniature challah. Incidentally, they freeze very well.

BULKALACH

Challah dough is very versatile. You can make many delicious things with it. Try shaping some of it into small round balls. Let them rise till double in bulk, then bake on a greased baking sheet in a 375-degree F. oven for about 20 minutes. My mother called these bulkalach. Use them as hamburger buns. Make them long and narrow and you have hot dog, or karnatzlach, rolls.

PULTABULCHAS

The very name of these fragrant, slightly sweet buns brings back memories of the lovely aromas in my Auntie Nina's kitchen and her loving urging to "Eat, eat, you need your strength!" Believe me, nobody needed any urging to eat the warm cinnamony pultabulchas.

Pultabulchas can be made from coffee-cake dough or from challah dough. Since you already have your challah dough, remove ⅓ of it after the first rising. Make a well in the center and add this mixture: 3 tablespoons softened butter, ¼ cup honey, 1 teaspoon cinnamon, a little grated orange peel (optional), ½ cup raisins or currants, and ½ cup chopped pecans or walnuts. Knead these ingredients into the dough; then form into small rolls or shape into a loaf or flatten out egg-size pieces; then fold 2 sides towards the center. Brush with egg wash (1 egg yolk beaten with 1 teaspoon cold water) and top with cinnamon and crushed nuts. Let rise again till they double in bulk. Bake in a 350-degree F. oven for 25 to 35 minutes, depending upon the size. Makes approximately 12 pultabulchas.

ZEMMEL

Who doesn't remember with nostalgia these crisp-on-the-outside, soft-on-the-inside rolls? Make some from the challah dough.

When the challah dough is ready to shape, pinch off pieces no bigger than a small apple. Knead each piece and form into flat cakes. Press each piece lightly down the middle with the edge of your hand or the back of a knife. This tends to give the zemmel their characteristic shape. Let rise in a warm place until they double in bulk. Brush with egg wash (1 egg yolk beaten with 1 teaspoon cold water). Sprinkle on poppy seeds, sesame seeds, or chopped onion. Press down the centers with your fingertips. Bake at 350 degrees F. for 15 to 20 minutes, until the crusts are firm and light brown. Makes about 36 zemmel.

Sweet Challah

Add a few raisins and nuts and it's a cake!

2 tablespoons dry yeast
1 tablespoon honey
2 cups warm water (about 110 degrees F.)
¼ cup vegetable oil
2 tablespoons honey
1 teaspoon sea salt (optional)

½ cup unsweetened apple butter
5½ to 6 cups whole wheat pastry flour
Raisins, nuts, and cinnamon (optional)
Egg wash (1 egg beaten with 1 teaspoon cold water)

In a large bowl, dissolve the yeast with the 1 tablespoon of honey in ½ cup of the warm water. Let stand for a few minutes, until it bubbles. In the meantime, combine the remaining water, oil, 2 tablespoons of honey, sea salt (if desired), and apple butter. Add this mixture to the yeast mixture. Beat in the flour, 1 cup at a time. Add only enough to make a stiff but pliable dough. Turn onto a floured surface and knead, adding a little more flour if necessary. Shape into a ball and place in an oiled bowl, turning the dough to coat with oil all sides. Cover and let rise in a warm place till double in bulk—about 2 hours. Punch the dough down.

If you wish to make a large challah, divide the dough into 4 strands and braid. If you wish to make 2 regular-size challahs, divide the dough in half, then divide each half into 3 or 4 strands and braid. Or make 1 regular-size challah, and to the rest of the dough add raisins, nuts, and cinnamon and make miniature challahs. Or use this dough to make pultabulchas (see recipe earlier in this chapter).

After shaping, place on a greased baking sheet and let rise till double in bulk—about 1 hour. When the loaves or pultabulchas have risen, brush with the egg wash and bake in a preheated 375-degree F. oven for 15 minutes. Then reduce the temperature to 350 degrees F. and continue baking for 35 to 45 minutes. Makes 2 medium-sized or 1 large sweet challah, or 1 medium-sized sweet challah and 12 pultabulchas.

CORN BREAD

A marvelous sourdough rye.

I searched volumes for a recipe that would satisfy my longing for the unique hearty flavor of this crusty loaf and, Eureka, I found it in Sue Gross's marvelous booklet called "Old World Breads" (Kitchen Harvest Press, 3N681 Bittersweet Drive, St. Charles, Illinois 60174).

A funny thing about corn bread, Sue explains, is the absence of corn from the ingredients. It does have cornmeal on the bottom, and thus it took its name.

You must plan ahead when you make this bread, but it's worth it. The bread itself is made in two stages, but first you must prepare a rye sourdough starter.

RYE SOURDOUGH STARTER:

1 *package dry yeast*
2 *cups warm water*
2 *cups rye flour*

1 *small onion, peeled and speared through several times with a fork*

Dissolve the yeast in the warm water. Add the flour and stir. Add the onion. Place the mixture in a large (2 quarts or more) glass or crockery pot with a lid and cover loosely. Let stand at room temperature overnight. In the morning, remove the onion. Continue to let the mixture stand at room temperature for a day or 2, until it develops a nice "fermented" smell. Then it is ready to use. If the mixture separates, that is normal; just stir before using.

To keep the sourdough starter going, just add water and rye flour in equal parts (1 cup of each) to bring the pot back to its original level. If the yeast in a sourdough starter is to remain active, it occasionally has to be "fed" with new flour. So, use your pot at least once a week, preferably twice, which isn't hard to do. In between, keep the pot covered and refrigerated.

If you haven't used your sourdough pot for a while and the starter doesn't bubble up within a reasonable period of time (several hours) after adding new flour and water to it, you can help it along by adding a little yeast—about 1 tablespoon.

Now, to make the actual bread.

STAGE ONE: THE NIGHT BEFORE:

1 *cup rye sourdough*
   starter
1½ *cups warm water*
3 *cups medium rye*
   flour

1 *small onion, peeled*
   and speared through
   several times with a
   fork (optional)

Stir these ingredients together in a bowl; cover, and let sit overnight. The onion is optional, but it gives added acidity and a certain subtle flavor to the bread.

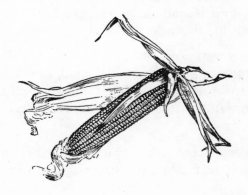

STAGE TWO: THE NEXT MORNING:

1 *package dry yeast*	*Cornmeal*
½ *cup warm water*	*Egg glaze (1 egg*
1 *tablespoon salt*	*yolk beaten with 1*
1 *tablespoon caraway*	*teaspoon cold water)*
seeds	
1½ *teaspoons poppy*	
seeds	
1 *cup 41 percent*	
unsifted gluten	
flour plus*	
2½ *cups unsifted all-*	
purpose flour, or	
½ *cup 76 percent*	
unsifted gluten flour	
plus 3 cups unsifted	
all-purpose flour	

If you used the onion in Stage One, fish it out of the sourdough mixture and discard. Dissolve the yeast in the warm water. Add the salt, caraway and poppy seeds, and yeast/water to last night's mixture. Stir. Add the gluten and all-purpose flour and stir to mix.

Knead the dough until smooth, either by hand on a floured board or with a dough hook. Put the kneaded dough in an ungreased bowl, cover, and let rise in a warm place until doubled in bulk— about 2 hours. Punch down and divide into 2 pieces.

Take each piece and form into a round loaf. Place the dough on a floured board, flatten it, and fold it into thirds, first from 1 direction and then the other. Pinch the dough to seal it and pat into a round shape.

Place the loaves on a greased baking sheet that has been sprinkled with cornmeal. Cover, and let rise in a warm place for about 30 minutes, until the dough is light-looking but not quite doubled in bulk.

---

*Gluten flour is available at health food stores; it generally comes in one of two strengths, either 41 percent gluten or 76 percent. Either type will do.

Just before baking, brush the tops of the loaves with the egg glaze. Bake the loaves in a preheated 425-degree F. oven for 40 to 50 minutes, or until the loaves are browned and sound hollow when tapped on the bottom. Do not hurry the baking; this rye bread takes a long time to cook thoroughly. If the loaves have a tendency to burn on the bottom, double up on the baking sheets. When the bread is cool enough to slice, butter a slice, rub the crust with garlic, and savor the taste of Heaven. Makes 2 loaves.

DARK RYE AND CORNMEAL BREAD

Whole rye flour gives this bread a distinctive, earthy, satisfying flavor. The rye, which is low in gluten, gets a rising assist and some complementary nutrients from the whole wheat flour and the cornmeal. The trio makes a highly nutritious loaf that's practically a meal in every slice.

½ *cup cornmeal*
1 *cup cold water*
1 *cup boiling water*
1 *tablespoon vegetable oil*
2 *teaspoons salt*
2 *tablespoons blackstrap molasses*
2 *teaspoons caraway seeds*
1 *tablespoon carob powder*
2 *tablespoons dry yeast*

¼ *cup warm water (110 to 115 degrees F.)*
2½ *cups sifted dark rye flour (warmed to room temperature)*
2 *cups sifted whole wheat bread flour (warmed to room temperature)*
½ *cup wheat germ*
Cornmeal
Egg wash (1 egg white beaten with 2 tablespoons water)
Caraway seeds

Combine the cornmeal and the cold water. Add this mixture to the boiling water and stir until thickened. Stir in the oil, salt, molasses, caraway seeds, and carob powder. Dissolve the yeast in the warm water and add to the mixture. Stir well.

Blend in the flours and the wheat germ. Add a bit more warm water if necessary, but the dough should be a little sticky. Turn out onto a floured surface and knead well for 10 minutes, adding more flour if necessary.

Form the dough into a ball and place in a greased bowl, turning to coat the ball on all sides. Cover and place in a warm spot until it doubles in bulk—about 1 hour.

Punch the dough down and knead for a few minutes more. Form into 2 balls. Place on a greased cookie sheet sprinkled with cornmeal and allow to rise again until almost doubled in bulk— about 30 minutes. Brush with the egg wash, sprinkle with more caraway, and bake in a preheated 375-degree F. oven for 1 hour or until the loaf bottoms make a hollow sound when tapped. Makes 2 loaves.

SUNFLOWER PUMPERNICKEL

Once you've tasted this bread, you'll never be satisfied with the store-bought variety. The sunflower seeds add a delicious nutty crunch and provide a good source of zinc, magnesium, pectin, the B vitamins, and hard-to-get vitamin D.

- ½ cup sunflower seeds, preferably sprouted
- 2⅔ cups lukewarm water
- 2 teaspoons honey
- 1 tablespoon plus 1 teaspoon dry yeast
- 2 cups whole wheat bread flour
- 2½ cups whole rye flour
- ½ cup soy flour
- 2 tablespoons wheat germ
- 2 tablespoons bran
- 1 teaspoon salt (optional)
- 3 tablespoons blackstrap molasses
- 3 tablespoons caraway or sesame seeds

The night before you want to bake the bread, put the ½ cup of sunflower seeds in a jar and add 1 cup of tepid water. This is an optional procedure, but very good. Use the water in which the seeds were soaked as part of the 2⅔ cups water allotment.

In a large bowl, pour 1 cup of the lukewarm water over the honey. Sprinkle the yeast over the honey-water mixture and set in a warm place for about 10 minutes.

Warm the flours: the whole wheat in 1 bowl; the rye mixed with the soy, wheat germ, bran, and salt (if desired) in another bowl. Place the flours in a warm oven (250 degrees F.) for 15 to 20 minutes.

When the flours are warm, add the whole wheat portion to the activated yeast mixture; mix well. Add the molasses to ½ cup of the lukewarm water. Add to the yeast mixture, then add the combined flour mixture and the rest of the water. Work in the caraway or sesame and drained sunflower seeds.

Grease a large loaf pan (9 x 5 x 3 inches) with a mixture of oil and liquid lecithin (½ teaspoon of each), or line with parchment paper. Turn the dough, which will be slightly sticky, into the greased pan. No need to knead this particular dough. Sprinkle the top with more caraway or sesame seed or karnitchka (black caraway). Leave in a warm place to rise to ⅓ more its size—about 45 minutes to an hour.

Preheat the oven to 375 degrees F. Bake for 50 minutes to 1 hour. Give it the toothpick test. Sometimes it requires a little more baking. When nice and brown and crusty, remove from the oven and cool on a rack for 10 minutes. Then, turn it out of the pan onto the rack and let it cool completely. If you used parchment paper, lift the bread out of the pan, holding the ends of the parchment. Peel the parchment from the bread to permit thorough cooling. Makes 1 two-pound loaf.

Wheat Germ Braided Herb Bread

If you are easing your family step by step into acceptance of 100 percent whole grain bread, here is a recipe for a wholesome in-between loaf that is irresistible.

2 *tablespoons dry yeast*
1 *to 1½ cups unbleached white flour*
1 *cup wheat germ*
3 *tablespoons bran*
½ *teaspoon salt*
½ *teaspoon oregano*
½ *teaspoon marjoram*
½ *teaspoon caraway seeds (optional)*
½ *cup milk*

¼ *cup butter or vegetable oil*
2 *tablespoons honey*
½ *cup water*
2 *eggs*
1½ *cups whole wheat bread flour*
Egg wash (1 egg beaten with 1 teaspoon cold water)
Sesame or poppy seeds

In a large bowl, combine the undissolved yeast, 1 cup of the unbleached white flour, the wheat germ, bran, salt, herbs, and seeds. In a saucepan, combine the milk, butter or oil, honey, and water. Heat until warm—125 degrees F. Add the liquid mixture to the yeast mixture. Add the eggs and beat at low speed with a mixer for about 2 minutes. Now add the whole wheat flour and enough of the remaining white to make a firm dough. Turn out onto a floured board and knead for about 2 minutes. Place the dough in a greased bowl and turn to grease all sides. Cover and let rise in a warm place for about 1½ hours, until double in bulk.

Cut off ¼ of the dough. Divide this into 3 equal parts. Shape each part into a 10-inch strand and braid the strands together the same as for challah (see Wheat and Soy Challah recipe above for braiding instructions). Shape the remaining dough into a loaf. Place in a baking dish approximately 8 x 4 x 2 inches. Place the braid on top. Brush with the egg wash. Sprinkle with sesame or poppy seeds.

Cover and let rise again for about 45 minutes. Bake in a preheated 350-degree F. oven for 30 minutes. Remove from the pan and cool on a wire rack. This is a great bread for cheese, tuna fish, or peanut butter sandwiches. Makes 1 loaf.

QUICK BRAN BREAD

Spices enhance the flavor of this moist bread with a crunchy crust. Rich in essential fiber, each slice provides one's daily quota of bran.

1½ cups whole wheat pastry flour
1½ cups coarse bran
1 tablespoon baking powder
1 teaspoon kelp powder
½ teaspoon powdered cinnamon
¼ teaspoon powdered ginger
¼ teaspoon grated nutmeg

½ teaspoon grated orange peel
1 cup plain yogurt or milk
2 tablespoons vegetable oil or butter, softened
1 egg
¼ cup honey or blackstrap molasses
½ teaspoon vegetable oil blended with ½ teaspoon liquid lecithin

Combine the dry ingredients in a large bowl. Combine the yogurt or milk, oil or butter, egg, and honey or molasses in a small bowl. Pour the liquid ingredients over the dry mixture and stir just until moistened. Turn into an 8 x 4-inch loaf pan greased with the oil-lecithin mixture. Bake in a preheated 350-degree F. oven for 40 to 45 minutes, until a toothpick inserted in the center comes out clean. Cool in the pan for 10 minutes. Then, invert on a wire rack to cool. Delicious with cream cheese. Makes 1 loaf; 12 half-inch slices.

VARIATIONS: (1) Add ½ cup raisins or currants and ½ cup sunflower seeds or walnuts to the dry ingredients before combining with the liquid ingredients. (2) This batter can also be baked as muffins. Bake for 20 to 25 minutes. Makes 12.

GRANOLA BREAD

When you want something more than bread, but not so sweet as cake, this one fills the bill. The oats and seeds of the granola combined with the milk, eggs, and whole wheat flour make each slice a perfect protein food that is rich in vitamins, minerals, and the kind of complex carbohydrates that provide energy.

2 *packages dry yeast*
½ *cup warm water*
1 *egg*
¼ *cup honey*
¼ *cup butter, melted*
1 *cup milk, scalded*
2½ *cups granola*
1 *tablespoon grated lemon rind or orange peel*

4 *cups whole wheat pastry flour*
Egg wash (1 egg yolk beaten with 1 teaspoon cold water)
Chopped nuts and cinnamon, mixed (quantities to taste)

Dissolve the yeast in the warm water. Let stand till it bubbles—about 5 minutes. In a large mixer bowl, combine the egg, honey, butter, and milk. Stir in the granola, lemon rind or orange peel, and the yeast mixture. Add the flour gradually. Combine well to form the dough.

Knead the dough on a lightly floured surface for about 10 minutes. Place in a greased bowl; turn the dough greased side up. Cover and place in a warm place to rise until it doubles in bulk—about 1 hour. Punch the dough down, knead lightly, then divide in half. Shape each half into a loaf and place each in a greased loaf pan 8½ x 4½ x 2½ inches. Or you can braid the whole dough into 1 bread, like a challah. This is very festive. After shaping, let the dough rise again—about 30 minutes—till double in bulk.

Heat the oven to 350 degrees F. Brush the loaves with the egg wash and sprinkle with a mixture of chopped nuts and cinnamon. Makes 1 large or 2 small loaves.

BUTTERMILK BREAD WITH SESAME SEEDS

An old-fashioned sourdough taste in a high-fiber loaf.

¾ cup warm water or
vegetable cooking
water

2 tablespoons dry
yeast

1¼ cups buttermilk

4 cups whole wheat
flour

¼ cup soy flour

2 tablespoons butter,
softened

2 tablespoons molasses
(blackstrap or
unsulphured)

1 teaspoon salt

2 teaspoons baking
powder

2 tablespoons wheat
germ

2 tablespoons coarse
bran

Cornmeal

Melted butter

Sesame seeds

Pour the water into a bowl. Add the yeast; stir and let stand for 5 minutes. In a separate bowl, bring the buttermilk to room temperature (about 70 degrees F.). Warm the flours to room temperature (place in a 250-degree F. oven for about 10 minutes or until warm).

Add the butter and molasses to the buttermilk. In another bowl, combine 2½ cups of the whole wheat flour with the salt and baking powder. Add both mixtures to the yeast mixture and mix at low speed with an electric mixer, or beat by hand until the ingredients are well blended. Increase the mixer speed and beat for 2 minutes more.

Combine the warmed soy flour, wheat germ, and bran and add to the remaining whole wheat flour; add this mixture to the other, by hand, to make a stiff dough. Let the dough rest for 5 minutes, then give it a good kneading. If it is too sticky, add a little more flour. Prepare the pans. If you want 1 large loaf, grease (using ½ teaspoon liquid lecithin mixed with ½ teaspoon vegetable oil) or line with parchment paper a 9 x 5 x 3-inch loaf pan. If you want 2 smaller loaves, prepare 2 pans about 8½ x 4½ inches. In either case, sprinkle cornmeal on the bottom of the prepared pan(s). (For 2 loaves, divide the dough in half. Roll each half into a rectangle. Roll up tightly and tuck in the ends.) Put the dough into the prepared pan(s) and brush with some melted butter and sprinkle with sesame seeds. Cover and let rise until double in bulk—about 40 minutes. Bake in a preheated 375-degree F. oven for 40 to 50 minutes. Give it the tap test: if it sounds hollow, it's done. Makes 1 large or 2 small loaves.

High-Protein Bread

A few slices a day insure your protein and fiber requirements. This bread contains many nutrients, but few calories. It is coarse in texture, chewy, and satisfying.

2 *tablespoons blackstrap molasses*	4 *tablespoons powdered skim milk (spray dried)*
1 *cup lukewarm water*	
2 *tablespoons dry yeast*	1½ *teaspoons vegetable salt*
2½ *cups whole wheat bread flour*	¼ *cup millet*
	¼ *cup nutritional yeast*
3 *tablespoons wheat germ*	¼ *cup coarse bran soaked in ½ cup warm water*
3 *tablespoons soy flour*	

In a bowl, combine the molasses with the lukewarm water. Dissolve the yeast in this mixture. Combine the dry ingredients; add them to the yeast mixture, then add the soaked bran with its liquid. Add more flour if necessary to make a soft dough. Knead for a few minutes, mixing well.

Place the dough in an oiled bowl. Cover and place in a warm spot, to rise, for 1½ hours. Punch the dough down; let rise again for 20 minutes. Form into 2 small loaves and let rise in a warm place until double in bulk. Bake in a preheated 400-degree F. oven for 10 minutes, then lower the heat to 350 degrees F. and bake for 50 minutes or until a thump elicits a hollow sound. Makes 2 loaves.

ZUCCHINI, RAISIN, AND NUT BREAD

Great for brunch, lunch, or snacks. Especially delicious when spread with cream cheese and apple butter. Zucchini is rich in vitamin A and potassium and incredibly low in calories—your waistline will love it.

½ cup raisins
2 cups grated unpeeled zucchini
3 eggs, beaten
½ cup vegetable oil
½ cup plus 2 tablespoons honey
2 teaspoons grated orange peel
1 teaspoon vanilla extract
2 cups whole wheat pastry flour

½ cup soy flour
½ cup oatmeal
3 tablespoons wheat germ
2 tablespoons nutritional yeast
2 teaspoons baking powder
1 teaspoon baking soda
1 teaspoon cinnamon
½ cup chopped walnuts or pecans

Mix the raisins with the grated zucchini. In a separate bowl, combine the eggs, oil, and honey; beat well; add the orange peel and vanilla. Add to the zucchini mixture. In a large bowl, combine the flours, oatmeal, wheat germ, yeast, baking powder, baking soda, cinnamon, and nuts. Add the zucchini mixture and mix well.

Line 2 one-pound coffee cans with parchment paper or grease them with a mixture of 1 teaspoon liquid lecithin and 1 teaspoon vegetable oil. Divide the batter between the 2 cans and bake for about 1¼ hours in a preheated 325-degree F. oven. Each loaf makes 10 to 12 slices.

NOTE: Make several of these loaves when zucchini is abundant in the gardens and marketplace. Store in the freezer and you'll be way ahead of the game when company drops in at holiday time or when you're packing lunches for school and office. The Zucchini, Raisin, and Nut Bread also makes a delicious hostess gift. This is a high-protein, very nutritious bread, so don't despair if the children make a meal of it.

BAGELS

Who doesn't like bagels? So, instead of buying the commercial variety made from white flour, bake a batch yourself and enjoy the difference: you get more flavor, more nutrients, more fiber. Believe me, it's not difficult, and they do fill the house with a lovely "welcome home" fragrance.

These bagels made with whole wheat and soy flours are excellent nutritionally and taste superb.

1 *cup milk*
¼ *cup butter, softened (use vegetable oil for pareve)*
1 *tablespoon honey*
¼ *teaspoon salt*
1 *yeast cake or 1 tablespoon dry yeast*
1 *egg, separated*
3¼ *cups sifted whole wheat bread flour*
¼ *cup sifted soy flour*
½ *cup wheat sprouts (optional, but very nice)*

Butter (use vegetable oil for pareve)
Egg wash (1 egg yolk beaten with 1 teaspoon cold water)
Sesame seeds, poppy seeds, black caraway seeds, coarse bran, wheat germ, or chopped sunflower seeds

Combine the milk, ¼ cup of butter or oil, honey, and salt in a saucepan. Heat to lukewarm and add the yeast. Beat the egg white until frothy and add it to the saucepan. Combine the whole wheat and soy flours. In a large bowl, place half the flour. Make a well in the center and pour in the yeast mixture. Stir together till well mixed; then add the wheat sprouts (if desired) and more flour to make a soft dough. It isn't necessary to use up all the flour; the amount you need to make a soft dough depends on the humidity. Use some to flour a board for kneading. Work the dough on the floured board until it is smooth. Place it in a buttered or oiled bowl and grease the top of the dough. Cover the bowl with a towel and set in a warm (not hot) place, to rise, till double in bulk—about 1 hour. Knead it again on the floured board.

Divide the dough into 4 pieces. Roll each piece into long strips the width of your middle finger. Cut each strip into 6-inch pieces. Shape each piece into a ring and press the ends together. Let them stand on the board for about 10 minutes.

Fill a large shallow pan with water and heat until very hot but not boiling. Drop the bagels in to cook, 2 at a time. When they rise to the surface, turn them over for a few more minutes. Grease a baking sheet, or line it with parchment paper. (Or use ½ teaspoon liquid lecithin mixed with ½ teaspoon oil; it makes a non-stick surface and is pareve.) Remove the bagels with a slotted spatula and place on the baking sheet. Brush the top of each bagel with the egg wash. Sprinkle the tops with your choice of sesame seeds, poppy seeds, black caraway seeds, coarse bran, wheat germ, or chopped sunflower seeds. Bake in a preheated hot oven—400 degrees F.—for about 15 minutes or until browned. They look so appetizing you'll have a hard time waiting till they cool. Makes 12.

PUMPERNICKEL BAGELS

The commercial so-called "pumpernickel" bagels are made with sugary caramel syrup to color the dough, lots of white flour, and a little rye flour. Try this wholesome flavorful version, which calls for whole rye flour, whole wheat flour, and blackstrap molasses to provide a rich dark color and hearty flavor.

2 tablespoons dry
yeast
2 cups warm water or
warm potato water
(water in which a
potato has been
boiled)
1 tablespoon
blackstrap molasses
3 cups whole wheat
bread flour (warmed
to room temperature)
2 teaspoons kelp
powder
1 whole egg

1 egg white
1 teaspoon Tamari soy
sauce
¼ cup vegetable oil
2½ cups whole rye flour
(warmed to room
temperature)
Vegetable oil
4 quarts water
Egg wash (1 egg
yolk mixed with 1
teaspoon cold water)
Poppy, sesame, or
caraway seeds or
finely chopped
sauteed onion

Dissolve the yeast in ½ cup of the warm water or warm potato water with ½ teaspoon of the blackstrap molasses. Sift the whole wheat flour into a large bowl. Add the kelp. Stir the yeast mixture into the whole wheat flour. Add the whole egg and the egg white. Add the rest of the warm water or warm potato water, the rest of the molasses, the Tamari, and the ¼ cup of oil. Beat vigorously—100 strokes by hand or 3 minutes by machine. Work in the rye flour by hand.

Turn the dough out onto a floured board and knead for 10 minutes. Place the dough in an oiled bowl; turn to cover all sides with oil. Cover the bowl with a towel and place it in a warm, draft-free area. Let it rise until doubled in bulk—1½ to 2 hours. The dough is ready if after you stick your finger in it the indentation remains.

Preheat the oven to 375 degrees F. In a large pot, boil the 4 quarts of water. Punch down the dough and knead for a few minutes. Divide the dough into 18 pieces the size and shape of golf balls. If you want miniature bagels, divide each of the 18 pieces in half. To form these balls into bagels, you have a choice of method:

Method #1:
Roll each ball into a rope about 6 inches long and 1 inch in diameter. Coil each rope into a ring, pinching the ends together firmly (a little water on each end will make this easy).

Method #2:
Make a hole through the center of each ball by poking your index finger through it. Then shape each into a ring. When you use this method, they can't come apart in the water bath which follows.

Let the bagels rest for about 10 minutes. Using a slotted spoon, slip about 5 bagels at a time into the pot of boiling water, and cook for 2 minutes on each side. Remove with the slotted spoon to an oiled cookie sheet. Repeat until all bagels have had their bath.

Brush each bagel with the egg wash. Sprinkle with poppy, sesame, or caraway seeds or with finely chopped sauteed onion. For variety, make a few of each. Bake for 25 to 30 minutes. Place on a wire rack to cool. Makes 18 average-size bagels or 36 miniatures.

BIALYS

This recipe for bialys, which are named for Bialystock, Poland, where they originated, is based on one included in a little booklet called "The Roll Basket," by Sue Gross (Kitchen Harvest Press, 3N681 Bittersweet Drive, St. Charles, Illinois 60174). Sue includes detailed directions for making unusual breads, such as onion boards (pletzels), hamburger buns, and pita in this and in her other booklets. One that might interest you is "Bagels, Bagels, Bagels." Another is "Danish to Donuts."

1 *package dry yeast*
2¼ *cups warm water*
1 *tablespoon honey*
1 *tablespoon salt*
1½ *cups 41 percent unsifted gluten flour (El Molino brand, available at natural food stores)*

3¼ *cups whole wheat pastry flour*
Egg wash (1 egg beaten with 1 teaspoon cold water)

Dissolve the yeast in 1 cup of the warm water; set aside. Mix the honey and salt with the rest of the water. Add the gluten flour and stir. Add the yeast water and stir. Add the whole wheat flour and mix until well combined. Knead (preferably by machine; the dough is slack) until smooth (10 minutes by machine).

Place the ball of dough in an ungreased bowl. Cover and let rise until very light—about 1½ hours. Punch the dough down, turn the dough over, and let rise a second time until very light. Punch again.

Divide the dough into 16 or 20 pieces, depending on the size bialys you desire. Shape the rolls as if you were making hamburger buns, thicker in the middle than at the edges, which should be about ⅜ of an inch thick. A baked bialy is about 1¼ inches thick.

Place the shaped bialys on lightly floured wooden boards to rise; cover with a moist towel so they won't dry out. Let the dough rise part way—about 20 minutes—then indent a circle about 1 inch in diameter in the center of each bialy roll. Use either your thumb or the top of a spice jar as a press. Brush with the egg wash. Spread (see below) onion-garlic topping in the indentations and sprinkle the tops of the bialys with topping as well. Let the bialys rise again—about 20 minutes—until light (not quite double in volume).

ONION-GARLIC TOPPING:

¼ cup dried minced onions, soaked in water and squeezed dry

1 tablespoon vegetable oil

½ teaspoon poppy seeds

Pinch salt (optional)

½ teaspoon garlic powder (or to taste)

Combine all the ingredients (for plain onion topping, omit the garlic powder) and the topping is ready to use.

BAKING THE BIALYS:

Authentic bialys should be baked on a baker's stone. If you have a stone (they are now available from Barth's, in Valley Stream, Long Island), place the risen bialy rolls on a dry sptula and slide them onto the hot stone. If you don't have a baker's stone, bake the bialys on ungreased baking sheets. Bake at 450 degrees F. for 12 to

15 minutes, until brown. They are delicious with cream cheese, tuna fish, lox, and white fish. Also delicious split and toasted and spread with a little butter. Makes 16 to 20 bialys.

NOTE: If you would rather not use gluten flour, substitute an equal amount of unbleached white or whole wheat bread flour for the gluten flour. They won't have the distinctive chewy bialy texture, but they will be delicious in their own right.

PITA

Pita is the pocket bread so popular in Arab countries and in Israel, where it is filled with hummous or falafel and vegetables.

1 *teaspoon honey*	½ *teaspoon kelp*
½ *cup lukewarm water*	6 *cups whole wheat*
4 *teaspoons dry yeast*	*bread flour*
2 *cups lukewarm*	1 *egg white, beaten*
water	*Sesame, poppy, or*
2 *tablespoons*	*caraway seeds*
vegetable oil	

Combine the honey with the ½ cup lukewarm water; add the yeast and set aside to proof for about 10 minutes. Combine the 2 cups of lukewarm water with the oil and kelp. Make a well in the center of the flour and add the liquid mixture. Stir in the proofed yeast. Knead the dough until it pulls away from the sides of the bowl— about 5 minutes. Place in an oiled bowl; turn the dough so that all sides are oiled. Cover and set in a warm place to rise till double in bulk—about 1 hour.

Punch the dough down. You can shape the pita by hand by taking a piece of dough about the size of a small egg and patting it to a round shape—like a hamburger bun. Or you can roll the dough out on a floured surface till it is ¼ inch thick. Cut circles with a cookie cutter or the edge of a glass. Place 2 circles together, 1 on top of the other, and press the edges together. This way you will get a puffier pita. Brush with the beaten egg white and sprinkle with the seeds of your choice (try some of each). Let rise again for 1 hour. Preheat the oven to 500 degrees F. Bake in the lower third of the oven for 10 minutes or until golden brown. Makes about 24 pita.

11

Pastries, Pies, Cakes
& Other Baked Goods

Bite into a piece of Grandma's crunchy strudel and you want to dance a *hora*. Cakes, cookies, all kinds of baked goods are lovingly intertwined with our heritage. We celebrate holidays and happy occasions with tea and honey cake, or a platter of mondelbrodt gently toasted to a golden brown.

When the children come home from school, we greet them with love and rugelah, crisply delicious oatmeal cookies, or slices of banana bread. When friends drop in, we offer assorted baked goods surrounding a pumpkin cream cheese roll, which has been hidden in the freezer for just such an occasion, and rejoice to see how our culinary achievements can bring a few moments of sweet respite to others.

At every stage of life and on every occasion desserts can play a joyful part, if they are not nutritional disasters. And the nice part is, they need not be. The baked goods in this section are delectable and nutritious. But don't limit your dessert selections to this chapter. You'll find many desserts designed to build good health throughout the book—in Chapter Seven, Sabbath and Festival Specialties; in Chapter Four, Dairy Specialties, where you'll find lovely cheesecake and other dairy delights; and in the chapter on tofu (Chapter Six), where you'll find a luscious cream pie and a cheesecake that are pareve.

MONDELBRODT
(Almond Bread)

Whenever we kids were under the weather, my mother would serve us mondelbrodt and hot milk. This pareve recipe was adapted with the help of my daughter, who is also a kosher cook—the natural way.

1¾ cups whole wheat
    pastry flour
3 tablespoons soy flour
1½ teaspoons baking
    powder
4 eggs
½ cup honey
3 tablespoons
    vegetable oil

1 teaspoon vanilla
    extract
¼ teaspoon almond
    extract
1 tablespoon cinnamon
1 cup chopped
    almonds

In a bowl, combine the flours and baking powder; set aside. In a separate bowl, beat the eggs until lemon-colored; add the honey, oil, and extracts. Gradually add the flour mixture, then the cinnamon and nuts. Turn the dough out onto floured wax paper. With floured hands, shape into 2 loaves about 3 inches wide and 1 inch high.

Grease (with a mixture of ½ teaspoon vegetable oil and ½ teaspoon liquid lecithin) or line with parchment paper 2 nine-inch loaf pans. Place a loaf in each and bake in a preheated 350-degree F. oven for about 30 minutes, until a cake tester inserted comes out clean. While still warm, but not hot, cut into slices about ⅜ of an inch thick. Place the slices on a cookie sheet and brown them lightly in a hot oven. Watch them carefully lest they burn. Makes 40 to 45 slices.

VARIATION: Before you shape the loaves, remove ¼ of the dough and add 3 teaspoons of carob powder to it. Form this piece into a ½-inch roll. Wrap the white dough around it, shape into 2 rolls, and bake.

KICHLACH
(Plain or Poppy Seed)

These light-as-air baked snacks are delicious plain, but remember that poppy seeds are little dynamos of vitality: a source of the B vitamins and many minerals, including zinc. So, try these kichlach both ways. The eggs in the recipe contribute high-quality protein and selenium, the mineral that has been shown to help prevent cancer.

1 cup plus 2 tablespoons whole wheat pastry flour
2 tablespoons soy flour
¼ teaspoon salt
½ cup poppy seeds (optional)
3 eggs
1 tablespoon honey (optional)

Combine the dry ingredients. (For mohn kichlach, include the poppy seeds.) Make a well in the center. Add the eggs and the honey (if desired). Beat with a fork until blended into a smooth, paste-like dough. It will be a slack dough. Drop by the teaspoonful onto a greased cookie sheet, allowing room for expansion—about 2 inches. Bake for 20 minutes in a preheated 325-degree F. oven, or until lightly browned and the edges puffed. Makes 30 to 36.

HIGH-PROTEIN NUT-OATMEAL COOKIES

Put a few in your husband's pocket so he can pass up the danish at coffee break.

⅓ cup butter or
vegetable oil
¼ cup honey
2 tablespoons
blackstrap molasses
1 egg
1 teaspoon vanilla
extract
1 cup whole wheat
pastry flour
¼ teaspoon baking
powder

¼ teaspoon baking
soda
½ teaspoon kelp
1 cup rolled oats
¼ cup powdered milk
(spray dried)
¼ cup water
¾ cup chopped walnuts
or sunflower seeds
(preferably sprouted)

In a large bowl, cream together the butter or oil, honey, molasses, egg, and vanilla. Beat till light and fluffy.

Combine all the dry ingredients except the powdered milk and nuts or seeds. Blend well. Dissolve the powdered milk in the water and add to the creamed mixture alternately with the dry ingredients. Stir in the nuts or seeds.

Drop by rounded tablespoonfuls onto prepared cookie sheets lined with parchment paper or brushed with a blend of equal parts liquid lecithin and oil. As a variation, top each cookie with a walnut or pecan half. Bake in a preheated 350-degree F. oven for 10 to 12 minutes, until lightly browned. Makes approximately 36 cookies.

NOTE: For pareve cookies, omit the powdered milk and add 2 tablespoons of soy flour to the dry ingredients.

RUGELAH

These old-country rugelah taste like love.

2 tablespoons dry
yeast or 2 yeast
cakes
¼ cup warm, almost
hot, milk
3½ cups whole wheat
pastry flour
½ cup soy flour
¾ cup butter, softened
3 eggs, beaten (hold
back some of the
white for topping)
½ cup plus 2
tablespoons sour
cream or plain
yogurt
3 tablespoons honey
Grated rind of 1
lemon or peel of 1
small orange

3 tablespoons butter,
melted
2 tablespoons honey or
date sugar
½ cup chopped
walnuts
½ cup raisins
2 tablespoons light
cream, milk, or
fruit juice
¾ teaspoon vanilla
extract
Grated rind of ½
lemon or peel of
½ small orange
½ cup crushed walnuts
mixed with 1
teaspoon cinnamon

Dissolve the yeast in the milk and set aside. Combine the flours and whiz in the blender. Remeasure to 4 cups and place in a large mixing bowl. Cut in the ¾ cup of butter, as for a pie crust. Add the beaten eggs, sour cream or yogurt, the honey, the grated rind or peel, and the dissolved yeast. Knead until the dough comes away from the bowl. Cover and set in the refrigerator overnight.

Next morning, divide the dough into 8 parts; return all but 1 part to the refrigerator. (Work with 1 part of dough at a time, leaving the rest refrigerated: the dough handles better when cold.) Roll out each piece of dough to form a 9-inch round. Brush with the melted butter.

Combine the rest of the ingredients except the walnut-cinnamon mixture for filling, and sprinkle in equal amounts over each piece of buttered dough. Cut each of the 8 rounds into 6 wedge-shaped pieces, the same as you would cut a pie. Roll each wedge from the outer rim of the circle to the center, then curve it to form a crescent. (Are they beginning to look like rugelah?) Dip 1 end of each crescent into the reserved beaten egg white (if you didn't hold out enough egg white, beat up some more) and then into the mixture of crushed nuts and cinnamon. Let rise for 2 hours. Bake in a preheated 325-degree F. oven for 30 to 40 minutes, until golden brown. Makes 48.

Bobke

A more nutritious, high-protein version of Grandma's coffee cake.

2 tablespoons dry yeast	2 teaspoons grated lemon rind
1 cup warm water or milk	3 cups whole wheat pastry flour
½ cup honey	½ cup soy flour
1 cup whole wheat bread flour	1 cup raisins
½ cup butter, softened	1¼ cups coarsely chopped walnuts
3 eggs	½ teaspoon cinnamon Butter

Dissolve the yeast in the warm water or milk. Add ½ teaspoon of the honey and let it proof for 10 minutes. Stir in the 1 cup of whole wheat bread flour and let it rise till double in bulk—about 1 hour. Keep it covered in a warm place. This is called the sponge.

In the meantime, cream the butter. Add the remaining honey and beat until smooth. Add the eggs, 1 at a time; add the lemon rind. Beat in the risen sponge. Combine the whole wheat pastry and soy flours. Add the mixed flours gradually, beating with an electric mixer until it gets too heavy for the beaters. Incorporate the rest of the flour by hand. Add the raisins and 1 cup of the nuts. Place the dough in a buttered bowl; turn it over. Cover and let rise in a warm place for at least 2 hours or until double in bulk.

Preheat the oven to 350 degrees F. Grease the bottom of a 10-inch tube pan. Take pieces of the dough about the size of a small orange and place the balls side by side in the tube pan. Brush with butter and sprinkle with the remaining chopped nuts and the cinnamon. Let it rise for ½ hour. Bake for about 40 minutes. The house will be filled with a special fragrance. Makes 1 large cake, about 24 slices.

Sour Cream Breakfast Cake

This is the recipe you've been looking for: a sour cream cake that tastes like bobke.

BATTER:

1 *pint sour cream or plain yogurt*
2 *teaspoons baking soda*
½ *cup butter, softened*
⅞ *cup honey*
4 *eggs*
3½ *cups whole wheat pastry flour*
¼ *cup soy flour*

2 *tablespoons lecithin granules*
2 *tablespoons wheat germ*
2 *tablespoons bran flakes*
2 *teaspoons baking powder*
1 *teaspoon vanilla extract*

TOPPING:

½ *cup unsweetened ground coconut*
1 *teaspoon cinnamon*

½ *cup chopped nuts (variety of your choice)*

Combine the sour cream or yogurt and the baking soda; set aside. Cream the butter with the honey, then add the eggs. Combine the rest of the dry ingredients (not the topping ingredients). Add the butter mixture to the dry mixture alternately with the sour cream mixture. Stir in the vanilla. Grease the bottom of an angel food cake pan. Combine the topping ingredients. Pour half the batter into the pan; add half the topping mixture. Pour in the rest of the batter and top with the rest of the topping mixture. Bake at 350 degrees F. for 1 hour. Makes 1 large cake.

Braided Coffee Cake

Lovely to look at, delightful to nibble from, the combination of soy and wheat flours makes this a high-protein cake you can eat in good conscience. The raisins and nuts bring a good measure of vitamins, minerals, and flavor to every bite.

5¾ cups whole wheat pastry flour	2 large eggs, well beaten
¼ cup soy flour	½ cup chopped walnuts
1½ cups milk	½ cup raisins
½ cup butter	3 teaspoons cinnamon
½ cup honey	½ teaspoon grated nutmeg
2 tablespoons dry yeast	Handful of chopped walnuts
¼ cup warm water	

Combine and warm the flours in a 250-degree F. oven for 10 minutes. In a saucepan, scald the milk; stir in ¼ cup of the butter and ¼ cup of the honey. Let cool to lukewarm. Meanwhile, dissolve the yeast in the warm water. Add the eggs to the milk mixture. Combine the milk mixture and the yeast mixture. Add the warmed flours, and mix to a soft dough. Knead lightly on a floured surface until smooth and elastic.

Place the dough in a greased bowl, and turn to grease all sides. Cover and let rise until double in bulk—about 30 minutes. Punch the dough down and let it rise again—about 20 minutes. Divide the dough in half. Divide each half into 3 equal parts. Roll each part into a 7 x 12-inch rectangle.

Melt the remaining ¼ cup butter in a saucepan; add the remaining ¼ cup of honey. Brush each rectangle with some of the honey-butter mixture. Combine the nuts, raisins, cinnamon, and nutmeg. Sprinkle this mixture over the honey-butter on each rectangle. Roll each rectangle up tightly lengthwise. Braid 3 of these rolls and place on a greased or parchment-lined baking sheet. Repeat the procedure with the other 3 rolls. Brush the tops with the remaining honey-butter; sprinkle on some additional chopped nuts. Let rise until double in bulk—about 30 minutes. Bake at 350 degrees F. for 30 minutes. Makes 2 big beautiful coffee cakes.

STRUDEL

Whenever we had front-parlor company, my mother would whip out a plate of scrumptious strudel. Where she hid it was a big mystery to us kids who climbed to the highest cupboard in search of a heavenly morsel. Strudel was always prepared for great occasions, especially Bar Mitzvahs. A month before our three Bar Mitzvahs, I would start on the strudel. I would make a batch every time I had access to the kitchen. I made them while conducting committee meetings and play rehearsals till I had 250 pieces salted away. After all, every guest has to sample the strudel!

You can make strudel dough with whole wheat pastry flour. It will have a good taste, but it will not be quite so tender or "stretchy" as with the unbleached white flour. If you choose to use the unbleached, compensate for its deficiencies by adding wheat germ to the filling, 1 tablespoon per cup of flour. Sprinkle it on the stretched dough.

You'll notice that the filling in the recipe below calls for a grated orange and a grated lemon. That means the *whole* thing: skin, pulp, and all. If you can't find unsprayed fruit, soak the orange and lemon in a solution of ¼ cup vinegar to 2 cups water for 10 minutes before grating.

APRICOT FILLING:

2 *cups dried apricots*	1 *whole lemon, grated*
Hot water	*(pits removed)*
¼ *cup honey*	1 *whole orange, grated*
	(pits removed)

NUT MIXTURE:

1 *cup crushed walnuts*	1 *tablespoon vegetable*
½ *teaspoon cinnamon*	*oil*
1 *cup raisins*	1 *cup unsweetened*
½ *cup cake crumbs*	*grated coconut*
½ *cup finely ground*	
wheat germ	

STRUDEL DOUGH:

1 *egg*
¼ *cup vegetable oil*
6 *tablespoons warm*
   water

2 *cups whole wheat*
pastry or unbleached
white flour
Vegetable oil
Ground walnuts
(optional)

To prepare the filling, wash the apricots, then cover with hot water. Let soak for a few hours or overnight. Drain off the water (save it for use in homemade fruit juice). Chop the apricots fine; place in a bowl and add the honey. Add half of the grated lemon and orange to the chopped fruit and honey. Reserve the other half for use with the nut mixture. Although the apricot mixture makes a great filling, you may substitute any honey-sweetened fruit preserve.

To make the nut mixture, combine all the ingredients, adding the reserved grated lemon and orange from the filling.

To make the dough, beat the egg in a bowl. Add the oil and water, then the flour. Knead lightly until the dough is soft. Cover and set in a warm place for 1 hour. It is easier to roll out half the dough at a time, so divide the dough in half. Place 1 of the halves of dough on a floured tablecloth and roll it out. Stretch and pull gently until it is as thin as tissue paper, or as thin as possible without tearing.

After the dough has been stretched as thin as possible, spread the nut mixture over the entire sheet. Drizzle a little oil over all. Spread ¼ of the fruit mixture in a thin line across 1 end of the sheet about 3 inches from the edge. Fold this edge over the fruit mixture, raise the tablecloth and let it roll halfway down the sheet of dough. Follow the same procedure with the other side of the sheet. Roll out the second piece of dough and fill in the same manner. Place the rolls in well-greased pans. Brush with oil and dust with extra ground nuts, if desired. Let stand for about 15 minutes. Slice the strudel into 1-inch pieces, but do not cut all the way through. Bake in a preheated 350-degree F. oven for about 45 minutes. When cool, cut all the way through. Makes 20 pieces.

HONEY-OATMEAL CAKE

Besides contributing a nutlike flavor to this cake, the rolled oats provide potassium, calcium, iron, magnesium, and zinc, the mineral essential to a lovely complexion, to healing, and to the entire reproductive system.

1 *cup rolled oats*	1 *teaspoon baking soda*
½ *cup butter or vegetable oil*	½ *teaspoon sea salt*
1¼ *cups boiling water*	1 *teaspoon cinnamon*
1 *cup honey*	¼ *teaspoon grated nutmeg*
1 *teaspoon vanilla extract*	¼ *teaspoon ground ginger*
2 *eggs, lightly beaten*	*Almonds for garnish*
1¾ *cups whole wheat pastry flour*	

Combine the oats, butter or oil, and boiling water in a large bowl and let set for 20 minutes. Then add the honey, vanilla, and beaten eggs. Combine the dry ingredients and add to this mixture. Pour into a greased 8 x 4-inch bread pan. Garnish with a few almonds. Bake for 30 to 40 minutes in a preheated 350-degree F. oven, or until a toothpick inserted in the center comes out clean. Delicious plain or with a cream cheese icing (see Index). Makes 16 half-inch slices.

ORANGE-DATE-NUT CAKE

This is the nutritious cake Joanie Huggins served at her daughter's wedding. Everybody wanted seconds—and the recipe. It's in her book, *Out of the Sugar Rut* (HAH Publications, Colorado Springs, Colorado, 1978).

The baker quadrupled the recipe to make enough batter for four tiers, which he decorated with fancy flowerets and curlicues made from a whipped orange-cream cheese frosting.

¾ cup butter, softened
¾ cup honey
4 eggs, separated (beat the yolks, reserve the whites)
2 tablespoons vanilla extract
3 tablespoons unsweetened applesauce

2½ cups sifted whole wheat pastry flour
1 tablespoon baking soda
¾ cup buttermilk
1½ cups finely chopped dates
1 cup chopped pecans
Grated peel of 2 oranges

In a large bowl, cream the butter with the honey. Add the beaten egg yolks, vanilla, and applesauce; mix well. Add 2 cups of the sifted flour and the baking soda alternately with the buttermilk; mix. Mix the chopped dates with the other half cup of sifted flour and mix till well coated and separated. Stir the coated dates, the nuts, and grated peel into the batter. Beat the egg whites until stiff, then carefully fold them in as well.

Grease and generously flour a 10-inch tube or angel food cake pan. Pour the cake batter into the pan. Bake in a preheated 350-degree F. oven for 1 hour. Serve with fresh whipped cream or lemon sauce. Serves 12.

LEMON SAUCE:

⅓ cup honey
4 teaspoons arrowroot starch
1 cup hot water
2 egg yolks, beaten

2 teaspoons grated lemon rind
4 tablespoons lemon juice
3 tablespoons butter

Mix the honey and arrowroot in a saucepan. Gradually add the hot water and blend until smooth. Cook over high heat, stirring until thick. Reduce the heat and cook for 5 to 7 minutes, until clear. Remove from the heat. Quickly blend in the beaten egg yolks to which a little of the hot mixture has been added. Cook for 2 minutes. Add the lemon rind, lemon juice, and butter. Drizzle over the cooled cake.

NOTE: This cake has a lovely texture and is better when served cold. Do not try to slice while still warm. It will stay fresh for a least a week if kept in an airtight container in the refrigerator. Also freezes well.

COMPLETE-PROTEIN BANANA BREAD/CAKE

Each slice has about 4 grams of usable protein—that's without the nuts and raisins! An ideal bread/cake for the vegetarian.

¼ *cup butter*
⅔ *cup honey*
3 *eggs, beaten*
1 *cup mashed banana pulp*
⅓ *cup water*
1 *teaspoon vanilla extract*
¼ *cup noninstant powdered milk (spray dried)*
1 *teaspoon kelp*

2 *teaspoons baking powder*
1 *teaspoon baking soda*
2 *cups minus 2 tablespoons whole wheat flour*
2 *tablespoons soy flour*
1 *cup each chopped walnuts and raisins (optional)*

In a bowl, cream the butter and honey until light. Beat in the eggs, banana pulp, water, and vanilla. In a separate bowl, combine the dry ingredients; stir them into the first mixture, blending with a few strokes. If you want to fancy it up and further increase the nutrient values, stir in 1 cup of chopped walnuts and 1 cup raisins. Turn the batter into a greased 5 x 9-inch pan. Bake in a preheated 325-degree F. oven for about 1 hour, until well browned and a cake tester inserted comes out clean. Makes 12 slices.

COMPLETE-PROTEIN PUMPKIN CAKE

The eggs, nuts, and whole wheat flour make this a complete-protein cake. The pumpkin provides calcium, phosphorous, and more than 2,000 international units of vitamin A—very important for resistance to disease—in each of 12 portions. In all, this spicy, spongy cake is a powerhouse of wholesome nutrients.

6 *or 7 eggs, separated*
⅞ *cup honey*
¾ *cup vegetable oil*
2 *teaspoons lemon juice*
2 *cups mashed pumpkin or butternut squash, well drained*

1 *cup chopped walnuts*
2 *cups whole wheat pastry flour*
1 *teaspoon pumpkin pie spice (cinnamon, ginger, nutmeg)*
4 *teaspoons baking powder*

Beat the egg yolks and honey well. Add the oil and lemon juice, beating until smooth. Add the pumpkin or squash and the nuts, mixing thoroughly. Gradually blend in the flour, spice, and baking powder. Beat the egg whites until stiff and fold into the mixture. Pour into a 10-inch tube pan greased only on the bottom and bake in a preheated 350-degree F. oven for 1 hour or until a toothpick inserted in the center comes out clean. Serves 12 to 16.

Pumpkin Cream Cheese Roll

Spices enhance the flavor of this pumpkin cake wrapped around a cream cheese filling—with just enough lemon juice to heighten its flavor. A weight-watcher's delight that tastes like a zillion calories, this cake is rich in vitamin A and essential minerals.

BATTER:

3 *eggs*
¾ *cup fresh pumpkin, cooked and mashed, or canned*
⅔ *cup honey*
1 *teaspoon lemon juice*
¾ *cup whole wheat pastry flour*
1 *teaspoon baking powder*

2 *teaspoons cinnamon*
1 *teaspoon ground ginger*
½ *teaspoon ground or freshly grated nutmeg*
1 *cup finely chopped nuts (optional)*

FILLING:

6 *ounces cream*
cheese, or 3 ounces
cottage and 3 ounces
cream cheese
¼ *cup honey*
½ *teaspoon vanilla*
extract

½ *teaspoon lemon juice*
Unsweetened
coconut flakes
(optional)
Chopped nuts
(optional)

To make the batter, beat the eggs at high speed for 5 minutes. Beat in the pumpkin, honey, and lemon juice. Combine the dry ingredients; fold into the pumpkin mixture.

Spread the batter on a greased or parchment-lined cookie sheet. Top with chopped nuts (if desired). Bake in a preheated 350-degree F. oven for 15 minutes. Roll up with the parchment paper or, if you didn't use paper, turn onto a dish towel sprinkled with a little whole wheat flour or dry powdered milk. Roll up and let cool.

Make the filling by combining all the filling ingredients in a blender. When the roll is cool, unroll it and spread with the filling. Roll up again, enclosing the filling. At this point you can serve it, refrigerate it, or freeze it. Remove from the freezer 30 minutes before serving. Makes 1 roll, which can be sliced into 10 portions.

Orange-Coconut Pie

Toasted coconut on a meringue topping makes this pie a visual treat.

¾ cup orange juice
Juice of ½ lemon
1½ cups water
½ cup honey
3 tablespoons whole wheat pastry flour
3 tablespoons arrowroot starch
3 egg yolks, beaten
Grated peel of 1 orange

½ cup unsweetened coconut flakes
1 prebaked pie shell (9½ inches)
3 egg whites
2 tablespoons honey
¼ cup unsweetened coconut flakes for topping

Combine the orange juice, lemon juice, 1 cup of the water, and the ½ cup of honey in the top part of a double boiler and heat. Combine the flour and arrowroot. Gradually add the remaining ½ cup of water, stirring to dissolve. Add this mixture to the orange juice mixture. Cook for 10 minutes, stirring all the while. Add the beaten egg yolks and cook for another minute. Add the orange peel and the ½ cup of coconut flakes. Cool. Pour into the prebaked pie shell.

Beat the egg whites until stiff to form a meringue. Add the 2 tablespoons of honey to the meringue very, very slowly; mix. Pour over the pie. Bake in a 350-degree F. oven for 15 minutes. Sprinkle the coconut flakes over the meringue and bake for 2 more minutes, until the coconut turns golden brown. Serves 8.

VARIATION: Use a crust made from granola or cookie crumbs—or make the pie without a crust.

BRANDY ALEXANDER PIE

A creamy pie, like a heady blend of mousse and ice cream. The wheat germ provides you with the B vitamins needed to handle its delightfully intoxicating effects.

1½ cups finely crushed graham cracker crumbs or natural cookie and cake crumbs or granola
¼ cup wheat germ
2 tablespoons butter, melted

2 teaspoons kosher gelatin
⅓ cup heavy cream
4 egg yolks
¼ cup honey
⅓ cup brandy
⅓ cup Kahlua or Crème de Cocoa
1 cup whipped cream

Combine the crumbs or granola, wheat germ, and melted butter. Press the mixture to cover the bottom and sides of a 9-inch pie plate and bake in a preheated 350-degree F. oven for 5 minutes. Let cool.

In a small bowl, sprinkle the gelatin over the ½ cup of heavy cream. Let stand for 5 minutes. Stir the gelatin mixture over hot water in a double boiler until it is dissolved. Let it cool, but do not let it set.

In another bowl, beat the 4 egg yolks until frothy. Gradually beat in the honey. Stir in the liqueurs and the gelatin mixture. Chill until slightly thickened. Then fold in the whipped cream and pour the mixture into the pie shell. Put the pie in the freezer. Remove 10 minutes before serving to delighted guests. Serves 8.

NOTE: The alcohol content makes this pie unsuitable for children.

PIE CRUST

An excellent crust for any dessert pie.

1 *cup sunflower seeds, ground to a meal*
¼ *cup unsweetened coconut, ground to a meal*
2 *tablespoons ground bran*

2 *tablespoons ground wheat germ*
2 *tablespoons lecithin granules*
1 *tablespoon vegetable oil*
1 *tablespoon sorghum or honey*

Combine all ingredients. Grease a 9-inch pie plate. Spread the mixture on the plate and up the sides. Bake for 5 minutes in a 325-degree F. oven.

12

Carob Instead of Chocolate

Carob has the taste of chocolate without the oxalic acid, the-obromine, and fat. It is kind to your heart—high in potassium, low in sodium, rich in minerals. So, let it not be said of you that you failed to enjoy the many delightful dishes that can be made with carob, the flour of the long, flat brown seed pod of the honey locust tree, which originated in the Mediterranean area.

Many faiths claim a carob connection. It is known as Saint John's bread because, legend has it, it sustained John the Baptist in the wilderness. Mohammed's armies called it "kharub" and they, too, relied on it as a survival food. The Romans called it "carobi." In the British Isles, the children call it "locust bread," and Jews call it "boeksur" and put the spotlight on it one day a year, on TuB'Shevat, Jewish arbor day.

In ancient times, the seed of the carob was used as a standard by which to measure a carat of gold. As a food which pleases the palate and promotes health, carob is indeed worth its weight in gold. Consider what you can do with it and what it can do for you.

Use carob in any recipe that calls for chocolate or cocoa and you will eliminate negative ingredients and accentuate the positive.

WHAT'S WRONG WITH CHOCOLATE?

Many people—especially children—suffer from nasal congestion, stomachache, headache, skin disorders, or bronchial asthma and don't realize that the chocolate they crave is the source of their problems.

This is so because cocoa contains 2 percent theobromine, a stimulant related to caffein. It also contains 0.1 percent caffein, enough to establish an addictive need. In many children these drugs trigger hyperactivity, which seriously impairs their ability to learn.

As if that weren't enough to sever your cocoa connection, consider that chocolate delivers a dose of oxalic acid, which latches onto calcium and takes it right out of your system. It also binds calcium into stones that can cause more mischief, such as blocking the urinary passage.

Since oxalic acid makes calcium less available to the body, children who drink chocolate milk are not getting the full use of this mineral so important to their growth and well-being. Carob, on the other hand, contains no theobromine, no caffein, no oxalic acid, and has a very low allergenic potential.

Consider, too, that chocolate is high in calories and in fat, and low in fiber. According to U.S. Department of Agriculture Handbook No. 8 (Composition of Foods), you get 477 calories, 39.7 grams of fat, and only 1.8 grams of fiber in 100 grams or 3½ ounces of bittersweet chocolate.

Now, let's take a look at the scorecard for carob. The same amount (3½ ounces) of carob provides 180 calories, 1.4 grams of fat, and a whopping 7.7 grams of roughage. This makes carob a close runner-up to the all-time champ, wheat bran, in the fiber department.

Besides being high in calories and fat, chocolate has a bitter flavor which demands more sweetness, and therefore more calories, to counteract it. Carob, with one-third of the calories and practically no fat, has a natural sweetness that comes with its own package of vitamins to metabolize it and turn it into energy instead of fat. Furthermore, an independent laboratory report on carob reveals that it is loaded with minerals: calcium, magnesium, potassium, phosphorous, silicon, iron, aluminum, strontium, manganese, barium, boron, chromium, copper and nickel, and a little sodium.

Learn how to use carob instead of cocoa and chocolate and you will be taking a giant step on the road to better nutrition and more vibrant health.

HOW TO CONVERT TO CAROB

If carob is new to your family, take two heaping tablespoons of cocoa and mix it with a cup of carob flour. This will give them the old familiar aroma and taste. As carob acceptance grows, gradually reduce the amount of cocoa.

If your favorite chocolate cake calls for cocoa, simply use an equal amount of carob powder. If it calls for chocolate, use three tablespoons of carob powder plus one tablespoon of water as a substitute for one square of chocolate.

Since carob is high in natural sugars, use less sweetener when you substitute it for cocoa in candies, cakes, cookies, and pies. In the following recipes, the conversion has already been adjusted.

This chapter includes some beverages featuring carob. For others, see Chapter Fourteen, Beverages for "L'Chaim!"

Carob Mousse

Every creamy spooonful of this mousse is filled with body-building protein; vitamin A; vitamin B2 (riboflavin), which is helpful to your eyes; vitamin D, the sunshine vitamin, which is so rarely found in foodstuffs; and vitamin E, which has been shown to retard the aging process, strengthen the capillary walls, and protect the red blood cells from destruction by poisons.

The cream in the recipe provides lots of vitamin A, calcium, magnesium, potassium, phosphorus, and some zinc. Of course, it is high in calories (about 200 in a quarter cup of heavy cream). That's why we use it sparingly.

4 *large eggs, separated*
1 *cup carob chips*
¼ *cup heavy cream*

1 *teaspoon vanilla extract (or brandy or rum)*
2 *tablespoons honey*

Beat the egg yolks lightly with a whisk or fork. Heat the carob chips in the top part of a double boiler over hot (not boiling) water until just about melted; remove the top of the double boiler and stir the chips rapidly until they are completely melted. Add the egg yolks. Add the cream and vanilla and stir vigorously. In a bowl, beat the egg whites until foamy, adding the honey a little bit at a time. Fold the egg whites into the carob mixture until blended. Spoon into individual custard or sherbet cups; cover with plastic wrap and refrigerate. This is what you serve to the *kinder*. Now, for the adults, instead of the vanilla, use a tablespoon of brandy or rum. Serves 6 to 8. It's quite rich, so make the portions small.

CAROB MINT PUDDING OR PIE

The refreshing, minty flavor makes this a superb ending for a dairy meal. The pectin-rich carob helps rid the body of lead and other toxic chemicals.

2 *cups milk*
½ *cup carob powder*
3 *tablespoons lecithin granules*
3 *eggs*

½ *teaspoon mint extract*
Cookie crumbs or granola (for a pie)

Place the first 5 ingredients in a blender and mix at low speed until well combined—about 2 minutes. Place in the top part of a double boiler over simmering water. Stir the mixture occasionally until it thickens. Pour into pudding dishes. Makes 4 large or 6 small servings. For a pie, line a 9-inch pie plate with cookie crumbs or granola, pour in the pudding mixture and refrigerate.

Carob-Poppy Seed Cake

The chocolaty flavor of the carob and the pleasant crunch of the tiny poppy seeds make an unusual but very happy partnership that is rich in body-purifying pectin and blood-building iron.

½ cup butter, softened
½ cup honey
6 eggs, separated
¾ cup carob syrup (see recipe later in this chapter) or ¾ cup carob chips, melted
¾ cup ground poppy seeds

Pinch of cream of tartar
2 tablespoons wheat germ
Apricot jam or apple butter
Finely ground unsweetened coconut (optional)

In a bowl, cream the butter and honey. Add the egg yolks, 1 at a time, beating well after each addition. Stir in the carob syrup or melted chips and the ground poppy seeds. Beat the egg whites with a pinch of cream of tartar until stiff peaks form. Fold them into the batter alternately with the wheat germ. Grease the bottom of a 10-inch spring-form pan (use ½ teaspoon liquid lecithin mixed with ½ teaspoon vegetable oil). Pour in the batter and bake for 1 hour in a preheated 350-degree F. oven.

Allow the cake to cool in the pan for at least 30 minutes. Then remove the cake from the pan and cut into 2 layers. Place the bottom layer on a plate, cut side up. Brush with the jam or apple butter and top with the other cake layer, cut side down. (To fancy it up, place a perforated paper doily on the cake and sprinkle with finely ground coconut. Remove the doily. The doily design will remain.) Serves 8.

CAROB TOLL HOUSE COOKIES

Unlike the store-bought variety or the homemade variety that contains sugar and chocolate bits, every bite of these carob chip cookies contributes to health. So, every mother and grandmother should have a supply on hand.

2 *cups whole wheat*
pastry flour
2 *tablespoons soy flour*
½ *cup carob powder*
2 *tablespoons*
powdered milk
½ *teaspoon baking*
soda
½ *teaspoon sea salt*
½ *cup butter, softened*

½ *cup honey*
1 *egg*
1 *cup sour cream*
1 *teaspoon vanilla*
extract
½ *cup carob bits*
¼ *cup chopped*
walnuts or sunflower
seeds

Mix the flours, carob powder, powdered milk, baking soda, and salt in a medium-sized bowl. In a large bowl, cream the butter and honey; add the egg; then add the sour cream and vanilla. Add the flour mixture gradually, then stir in the carob bits and nuts or seeds. Drop by the teaspoonful on a greased or parchment-lined baking sheet. Bake in a preheated 350-degree F. oven for 8 to 10 minutes. Do not overbake. These cookies will harden as they cool. Makes about 48 two-inch cookies.

ORANGE-CAROB CAKE

A high-protein fudgy cake that is festive enough for a celebration. Place a few candles on it and your wishes for a happy birthday will light up someone's life with health as well as good cheer.

½ cup butter
1 cup honey
2 cups whole wheat
  pastry flour
½ cup soy flour
1 teaspoon baking
  powder

½ teaspoon baking
  soda
½ cup carob powder
2 eggs
⅔ cup orange juice
1 teaspoon grated
  orange peel

In a large bowl, cream the butter with the honey until thick. Combine the dry ingredients (a good way to combine and sift at the same time is to put all in the blender and whiz for a few seconds). Add ¼ of the flour mixture to the creamed mixture and mix until smooth. Add the eggs, 1 at a time, beating well. Add the rest of the flour mixture alternately with the orange juice, beating well after each addition. Add the orange peel.

Preheat the oven to 350 degrees F. Lightly grease (use a mixture of ½ teaspoon oil and ½ teaspoon liquid lecithin) or line with parchment paper a 12 x 7½-inch baking dish. Pour the batter into the baking dish and bake for 45 minutes or until a toothpick inserted comes out clean. Makes 18 portions (2½-inch squares).

This cake is delicious as is, but as an alternative for special occasions freeze it, then top with Carob Fudge Icing (recipe below) and freeze again.

VARIATION: Slice the cake horizontally into 2 layers. Spread 1 layer with apricot preserves. Top with the second layer, then cover with the Carob Fudge Icing.

CAROB FUDGE ICING

This icing tastes like chocolate fudge but provides many more nutrients and has fewer calories. Nevertheless, spread it thinly.

¼ cup butter
¼ cup honey
1 tablespoon vanilla
  extract
⅓ cup carob powder

2 tablespoons
  powdered milk
  (spray dried)
2 tablespoons
  arrowroot starch

Cream together the butter, honey, and vanilla. Combine the dry ingredients and add to the creamed mixture. This makes an easy-to-spread icing that is sufficient to ice two 12 x 7½-inch cakes or 1 cake and a dozen cupcakes.

"High I.Q." Carob Fudge Brownies

Rich in the B vitamins that encourage clear thinking and an upbeat attitude, these moist and nutty brownies get their strength and character from superfoods: wheat germ, soy, and carob.

½ cup honey
⅓ cup vegetable oil
2 tablespoons lecithin granules
2 eggs, beaten
1½ cups whole wheat pastry flour
¼ cup soy flour

¼ cup wheat germ
½ cup carob powder
½ teaspoon cinnamon
⅓ cup chopped walnuts
1 teaspoon vanilla extract

Blend the honey, oil, and lecithin granules. Add the eggs. Combine the flours and wheat germ. Gradually add the combined flours, carob, and cinnamon to the honey mixture. Lastly, add the nuts and vanilla. Turn into a greased 8-inch pan. Bake in a preheated 350-degree F. oven for 25 minutes. Remove from the oven and cut into squares while warm. Makes about 16 brownies.

WALNUT-CAROB COOKIES

These cookies are crunchy, nutty, full of that ole time "sweet shop" flavor plus good bone-building nutrients.

5 *tablespoons carob
  powder*
½ *cup whole wheat
  pastry flour*
¼ *cup honey*
¼ *cup butter, softened
  (use oil for pareve)*

1 *egg*
1½ *teaspoons vanilla
   extract*
1½ *cups coarsely broken
   walnuts*

Combine all the ingredients except the walnuts in a large bowl and mix well. Then stir in the walnuts. Line 2 cookie sheets with parchment paper, or brush them with a mixture of oil and liquid lecithin (1 teaspoon of each). Drop the cookie mixture by the tablespoonful onto the cookie sheets. Leave about 1 inch of space between each spoonful. Bake at 325 degrees F. in a preheated oven for 15 minutes. Cool; store in a tightly-covered container. Makes about 18 luscious cookies.

WALNUT-CAROB HALVAH

A delicious Turkish confection rich in calcium and potassium—minerals needed to keep your heart muscle strong.

¼ *cup tahina (sesame
  butter)*
¼ *cup honey*
½ *cup unsweetened
  coconut flakes*
½ *cup wheat germ*

½ *cup sunflower seeds*
2 *tablespoons carob
  powder*
½ *teaspoon cinnamon
  Crushed walnuts*

Combine the tahina and honey in a medium-sized bowl. Put the coconut, wheat germ, and sunflower seeds in the blender and purée to a powder. Combine with the tahina and honey. Add the carob and cinnamon and knead it till it resembles a ball of dough.

Separate into 4 portions. Roll each portion into a 1-inch thick roll. Roll each in crushed walnuts. Wrap each roll in wax paper and refrigerate. Cut into ¼-inch slices as needed. Makes a lovely edging on a platter of goodies. Makes 4 rolls, each 6 inches long. Each roll yields 24 slices.

VARIATION: For plain halvah, omit the carob and cinnamon and add 1 teaspoon vanilla extract.

PEANUT-CAROB CLUSTERS

Remember how we used to drool over those crunchy chocolate peanut clusters? Well, here they are, without the sugar, oxalic acid, or fat. These are easy to make, and every bite contributes protein, vitamins, and minerals essential to soma and psyche.

3 *egg whites*	½ *cup carob powder*
¼ *cup honey*	1 *cup whole or halved*
½ *cup homemade or*	*peanuts*
natural (additive-	
free) peanut butter	

Beat the egg whites until stiff. Add the honey, peanut butter, and carob powder until well mixed. Add the peanuts. Drop by spoonfuls onto a greased (use a mixture of equal amounts oil and lecithin) or parchment-lined cookie sheet and bake in a preheated oven for 10 to 12 minutes at 300 degrees F. Makes 32 Peanut-Carob Clusters, each 1½ inches in diameter.

CAROB FUDGE BALLS I

Better than ordinary chocolate fudge—and there's no cooking involved, so children will enjoy participating in the preparation as well. These Carob Fudge Balls are rich in vitamin E, calcium, magnesium, zinc, and potassium, which contribute to strength and endurance.

½ cup honey
½ cup homemade or
natural peanut butter
2 tablespoons hot
water
½ cup walnuts, broken
into pieces
½ cup carob powder
½ cup sesame seeds

½ cup ground
sunflower seeds
2 tablespoons lecithin
granules
1 teaspoon vanilla
extract
⅓ cup unsweetened
shredded coconut

Combine the honey and peanut butter in a large bowl. Add the rest of the ingredients except the coconut. Shape into 1-inch balls and roll in the coconut. Makes approximately 30 balls.

CAROB FUDGE BALLS II

½ cup homemade or
natural peanut butter
½ cup honey
½ cup sunflower meal
½ cup wheat germ

¼ cup carob powder
Wheat germ or
Wheat germ or
sunflower meal

Mix the first 5 ingredients well. Roll into 1-inch balls. Roll the balls in more wheat germ or sunflower meal. These confections have a delicate chocolate flavor, and they freeze well. Makes 18 balls.

BANANA-CAROB CRUNCHY GRANOLA

You won't have any "breakfast skippers" when you have this tasty blend of nutritious ingredients on hand. The high protein content helps keep blood sugar levels on an even keel.

3 *cups uncooked*
rolled oats
1½ *cups unsweetened*
dry coconut flakes
1 *cup wheat germ*
½ *cup bran*
½ *cup carob powder*
½ *cup sunflower seeds*

½ *cup sesame seeds*
¼ *cup honey*
2 *tablespoons*
vegetable oil
½ *cup cold water*
½ *to 1 cup banana*
chips (recipe below)

In a large mixing bowl, combine all dry ingredients except the banana chips. Combine the honey and oil in a small bowl. Add to the dry ingredients and stir; mix well. Add the cold water gradually and stir till the mixture is crumbly.

Spread this mixture on a cookie sheet lined with parchment paper or brushed with an oil and lecithin mixture (1 teaspoon of each). Place in a preheated low oven—about 200 degrees F.—and bake for 2 hours, stirring the mixture every 30 minutes. When it is dry and toasty, add the banana chips. Makes 2 quarts.

Banana Chips:
Line a cookie sheet with parchment paper. Slice a few ripe bananas very thin, spreading the slices out so they don't touch. Place in a warm oven until dry. If using a gas range, the pilot light is all the heat you need. It may take 24 to 36 hours.

Banana-Carob Popsicles

Carob desserts can be plain or fancy, crunchy with nuts, chewy with raisins, velvety with whipped cream or tofu, or frozen over fruit. Try this recipe for frozen bananas on a stick.

3 *tablespoons orange*
juice or water
⅓ *cup carob powder*

3 *bananas, peeled*
Chopped nuts

Prepare a paste by gradually adding the orange juice or water to the carob powder. It should not be too thin or too "fudgy." Cut each banana in half. Dip each banana half into the carob paste, coating well on all sides. Use tongs or a fork to turn. Roll each coated piece in the chopped nuts. Place them on a cookie sheet lined with wax paper and freeze. When partially frozen, insert a popsicle stick into each banana half and place in an appropriate container, or pack separately in plastic bags. Makes 6 popsicles.

Carob Popsicles

Ideal in summer. Cool, refreshing, and velvety smooth, these popsicles are rich in magnesium and potassium, minerals needed to help us cope with the heat.

1 *cup milk*
½ *cup whipping cream*
2 *tablespoons carob syrup (recipe below)*
2 *tablespoons powdered milk*
2 *teaspoons lecithin granules*
2 *tablespoons tahina (sesame butter)*
½ *teaspoon vanilla extract*
½ *teaspoon cinnamon*

Whiz all ingredients in a blender for 1 minute. Pour into popsicle molds, ice cube trays, or paper cups, then freeze. When partially frozen, insert popsicle sticks. Makes 8 popsicles.

Carob Syrup

Use this syrup as you would chocolate syrup: 2 teaspoons to a glass of milk, hot or cold.

½ *cup honey*
½ *cup carob powder*
1 *teaspoon arrowroot starch*
1 *cup water*
1 *teaspoon vanilla extract*

Combine all ingredients in a saucepan and bring to a boil, stirring all the while. Let simmer for 5 minutes. Let cool. Chill and store in the refrigerator. Makes 1 cup.

TAHINA-CAROB DRINK

2 *cups cold milk*
½ *cup carob powder*

¼ *cup tahina (sesame butter)*

Combine all ingredients in a blender. Whiz until frothy—just a few seconds. A delicious, nutritious drink for 2.

BANANA-CAROB MILKSHAKE

Some historians claim that the apple Eve used to tempt Adam was actually a banana. There's no doubt that a yellow banana speckled with sugar spots can be very tempting. Bananas are also highly nutritious and, contrary to common conception, low in calories and practically fat-free.

One medium-sized banana provides about 100 calories, a feeling of satiety, and lots of nutrients, particularly vitamin B6 (pyridoxine), which has recently been found to play an important role in the prevention and cure of atherosclerosis and arteriosclerosis. It is also a natural diuretic and together with magnesium, also present in significant amounts in bananas, helps prevent kidney stone formation.

This milkshake is a great beverage for mornings when you want to drink your breakfast.

1 *cup milk*
1 *egg*
1 *teaspoon vanilla extract*
1 *tablespoon lecithin granules*

1 *tablespoon carob powder*
1 *tablespoon honey or blackstrap molasses*
1 *banana*

Whiz everything in the blender and drink in good health. This recipe will fill up 2 average-size kids and keep their blood sugar on an even keel till lunch.

Hot Banana-Carob Drink

A heart-warming beverage. Serve in mugs before an open fire or for breakfast.

2½ *cups milk*
1 *large banana, peeled*

3 *tablespoons carob powder*
2 *tablespoons honey*

Blend all the ingredients together until smooth. Place over medium heat and stir till it simmers, but do not let it boil. Takes about 5 minutes. Serves 3.

Hot Carob Drink

Often served as a treatment for upset stomachs. Because carob is a good source of pectin, it helps rid the body of lead and other toxins.

2 *cups milk*
½ *cup heavy cream*
6 *tablespoons carob powder*

¼ *cup honey*
½ *teaspoon vanilla extract*

Heat the milk until tiny bubbles form around the edge. Do not allow it to boil. Meanwhile, in a small bowl whip the cream. Add the carob and honey gradually. Add the vanilla; combine well. Pour the milk into a warmed pitcher. Spoon the whipped cream mixture into 4 cups. Fill the cups with the hot milk. Serve to 4 delighted children while you regale them with stories of "when I was a child." Double the recipe and count the adults in. They love it, too.

13

Especially for the Children

If you, like increasing numbers of thoughtful concerned parents, are disturbed about the quality of the food served at your child's school, then why not do something about it? In many school systems throughout the country, parents have been the prime movers in upgrading the nutritional quality of the food served in school cafeterias and in getting rid of the junk from the vending machines.

What can you do? Take a good hard look at what your children are eating for lunch. Are they being fed devitalized white bread loaded with additives, polished white rice devoid of its B vitamins, canned fruit cocktail sweetened with sugar and topped with an embalmed maraschino cherry, hot dogs preserved with nitrites, peanut butter preserved with BHA and BHT, fruit punches made from artificially colored and flavored mixes, canned vegetables with salt and sugar added?

Not only can these foods transport your children very quickly to Cavity Corners, Acne Alley, and climb-the-walls hyperactivity, they can also undo much of the good work parents have been doing in the campaign to promote good nutritional habits. Children, especially the little ones, tend to accept the authority of the school as if it were brought down from Mount Sinai.

When school systems have upgraded their nutrition, they have observed noticeable improvement in many areas—better discipline, longer attention span, less absenteeism, fewer injuries on the playground and athletic fields, better complexions, and sunnier dispositions. These were some of the results noted by Gena Larsen when she used her initiative and nutritional knowledge to improve the nutrition at a California high school.

Here are some of the helpful suggestions she and other school dieticians very graciously shared with me:

1. In general, it is well to convert from starches and sugar foods to protein foods whenever possible. For example, substitute soy macaroni, noodles, and spaghetti for the usual white flour pasta. Use eggs to extend the meat in the sauce.
2. If you're using commodity flour, request whole wheat.
3. Arrowroot, with its high mineral content, can replace cornstarch in all recipes. In sauces and gravies, use ⅓ cup of arrowroot for each 1 cup of cornstarch called for. In puddings sweetened with honey or molasses you will need ¾ cup of arrowroot for each 1 cup of cornstarch called for. The lesser quantity needed makes the cost comparable, or even less.
4. Fruits, raw and unsweetened, are the ideal dessert. If your school system cannot afford a whole fruit, serve half an apple, not peeled or cored, dipped in pineapple juice and placed cut side down on a baking liner. Or serve a few orange segments mixed with coconut flakes or nuts. Small bananas, served whole, fresh melon, and grapes or berries in season are also favorites.
5. Buy unsweetened (waterpacked) fruits in No. 10 cans. Pour off the juice, sweeten with a little honey (¼ to ½ cup), and return to fruits.
6. If you're using commodity rice, ask for brown rice. It is now made available in the school commodity program.
7. For an elegant nutritious dessert, roll half a banana in yogurt or lemon juice, then in chopped nuts.
8. Use honey to sweeten cakes and cookies. Use ⅓ to ½ cup for each cup of sugar called for in your recipe. Blend with shortening. Date sugar or date butter can also replace white sugar— cup for cup. Try half honey and half date sugar. Grind up dried dates to make date sugar.

9. To add protein to potato salad, be generous with hard-cooked eggs. Also, beat cottage cheese (4½ pounds for each 100 servings) with an electric beater till light and fluffy. Add required mayonnaise slowly, then add other dressing ingredients. Delicious! Higher in protein and lower in calories and fat than the usual dressing.

10. For whipping cream, to make it go farther and increase its protein content, beat 1 quart whole milk, ⅓ cup honey, and 1 tablespoon vanilla. When well blended, begin adding powdered milk till the cream holds its shape. Beat well after each addition of the dry milk. This cream holds its shape well on desserts.

11. For a delicious icing, blend cream cheese with fruit or berry juice to soften. Add powdered milk and a tiny bit of honey. Beat, then add more dry milk till it is as thick as you want it.

12. Ask your meat supplier to make chopped meat of ¼ ground heart and ¾ ground beef or lamb. Use the mixture for meat loaf, meatballs, meat sauce, stuffed cabbage, kreplach, or whatever.

13. Sprouts are very popular on salads and inexpensive. Use them liberally.

14. Sunflower and pumpkin seeds are delicious, nutritious snacks. Serve in small soufflé cups as an extra once in a while. Provide them as an optional ingredient to be added to salads, applesauce, or other fruits.

For some sound guidelines on how to make the switch to more wholesome food, where to shop for whole grains, how to use the government commodities to good advantage, how to train staff, how to win over the students, and some good quantity recipes, send for *A Guide for Nutra Lunches and Natural Foods,* available from Sara Sloan, Fulton County Schools Food Service Program, 786 Cleveland Avenue S.W., Atlanta, Georgia 30315.

Another excellent guide for improving not only school nutrition but all institutional food is *Better Food for Public Places,* by Anne Moyer (Rodale Press, Emmaus, Pennsylvania, 1977). This book not only suggests how to integrate natural foods into quantity food service, it relates institutional experiences where the changeover has been successful and so gives you the courage to "Go fight city hall."

A charming filmstrip series on nutrition for kindergarten through grade school and for high school children is available from Nutrition Encounter, Route 25A, Cold Spring Harbor, Long Island, New York 11724; (516) 692-5243. Excellent for PTA programs as well as for classroom viewing.

More information is available from the *Center for Science in the Public Interest,* 1755 S Street, N.W., Washington DC 20009. Send for the School Food Action Packet or for the condensed version, School Lunch Action Guide.

Until your school provides good food why not let your child brown bag it nutritionally?

It's not only schools that need nutritional guidelines. So do grandparents.

Grandparents find it very hard to refuse anything to those tiny tots they love so much. But, when they hand out sugary *nosherai,* they are not expressing love for the child. They are trying to buy the child's affection—but at what a price!

A friend of mine stocks up on soda whenever her six-year-old grandson comes to visit. "I know it's not the best thing in the world for him," she admits, "but he asks for it. How can I refuse?"

Grandparents should take a course in how to say "no" with love, and how to provide nourishing snacks that taste good, look good, help build beautiful teeth, lovely complexions, pleasant dispositions and the ability to cope. This is a sincere way to express love.

Try the recipes in this chapter. Every one is designed to taste appetizing to young folk. There are many more recipes throughout the book that will appeal to children. Refer to Chapter Twelve for suggestions on how to use carob, to Chapter Eleven for delicious baked goods, and to Chapter One for innovative ways to use raw foods.

Here's what I like to stock up on when our grandchildren are due for a visit:

1. Sprouts, especially mung bean. Even the toothless babies love to gum them. Older children love to observe the sprouting process and grow their own.

2. Natural cheeses—especially Muenster. It's a good nosh.
3. Fruit juices, unsweetened, preferably from unsprayed fruit.
4. Frozen pops made from unsweetened fruit juices or yogurt and fruit combinations. (See recipe for Pineapple-Banana Pops in this chapter.)
5. Fresh fruit—gobs of it. Melons in season, tangerines, apples, grapes, oranges, grapefruit. First thing in the morning while they're waiting for PopPop to scramble the eggs, we share some kind of citrus fruit.
6. Yogurt, homemade. We add fruit, nuts, and seeds to order.
7. Granola, homemade. Jodi loves hers with sweet cream. We use raw milk which we get from a nearby dairy. The children love to go with us to get it and see the cows that provide it. Jodi's cream is the top milk.
8. Hard-cooked eggs sieved into Russian dressing. They love to dip raw vegetables in it.
9. Raw string beans, preferably fresh from the garden. I keep a dish of them in the fridge and they help themselves.
10. Carob fudge balls, carob toll house cookies, cookie jar hermits, and nut breads.

These are their special treats. Keep this kind of *nosherai* available and they'll never miss the junk food.

SANDWICHES THAT NOURISH
AND DELIGHT

PEANUT BUTTER COMBOS:
Kids love peanut butter, and it is a good high-protein, nutritious food. Use the brands that have no additives, no hydrogenated fats, and no sugar. Natural food stores and some supermarkets carry them. But the best peanut butter is the kind you make yourself. Put lightly roasted peanuts in the blender with a little bit of peanut oil and whiz. If you want chunky peanut butter, turn off the power before the peanuts are completely mashed. (For other nut butter recipes see Chapter Fifteen, Don't Buy It—Make It Yourself.)

Here are some good peanut butter combinations. Be sure to use a good whole grain bread.

- ½ cup grated carrots plus 1 teaspoon seedless raisins
- wheat germ and banana slices
- sunflower seeds and raw jam
- unsweetened apple butter and coconut flakes
- wheat sprouts and chopped apricots
- wheat sprouts and unsweetened apple butter or raw fruit jam
- cream cheese and walnuts on whole wheat raisin bread

MORE SANDWICH IDEAS:

- date-nut bread with cream cheese (see Index for date-nut bread recipe)
- date-nut bread with apple butter and wheat sprouts or sunflower seeds
- date-nut bread with cream cheese and crushed pineapple
- Go creative. As a change from peanut butter, try tahina or some other nut butter.

BANANA-PEANUT BUTTER SANDWICHES AND SNACKS

Slice unpeeled bananas lengthwise right through the skin. Spread one half with peanut butter. Sprinkle with sesame or sunflower seeds and top with the other half. Wrap in foil and send it to school to delight your youngster at lunchtime.

Using the same technique, peel the banana before spreading and then slice into chunks and serve as an afterschool nosh or on a bed of watercress as a side dish.

VARIATION: Spread with tahina and a bit of honey and you'll pleasure your palate with the nostalgic taste of halvah.

HONEY-ALMOND GRANOLA

If your kids are hooked on dry cereals in psychedelic boxes with BHA and BHT, artificial colors, and three different kinds of sugar, don't despair. Make your own granola—and make it so good they can't refuse it.

3 cups uncooked
rolled oats
1 cup shredded
unsweetened
coconut
½ cup sesame seeds
½ cup shelled
sunflower seeds
½ cup soy grits or soy
flakes
¼ cup powdered milk
(spray dried)
1 teaspoon cinnamon

½ cup sliced or
chopped almonds
(optional)
½ cup wheat germ
½ cup bran
¼ cup vegetable oil
¼ cup honey
1 cup cold water
½ cup raisins, coarsely
chopped prunes, or
coarsely chopped
dried apricots

Combine the oats, coconut, sesame and sunflower seeds, soy grits or flakes, powdered milk, cinnamon, and almonds (if desired) in a large bowl. Add the wheat germ and bran. Mix the oil, honey, and cold water in a smaller bowl. Pour the liquid mixture over the oat mixture. Spread on 2 cookie sheets. Bake until toasted in a preheated 250-degree F. oven, stirring every 15 minutes. Takes about 1 hour. Stir in the raisins or other dried fruit. After the granola cools, store in tight-lid containers. Keep refrigerated or frozen. Makes about 2 quarts.

LOLLIPOP EGGS

This colorful alternative to the kind of lollipops that lead to cavity formation is suggested by Agnes Toms in her book *Natural Foods, Meals and Menus for All Seasons* (Keats, New Canaan, Connecticut).

3 hard-cooked eggs
Pickled beet juice

3 popsicle sticks

Shell the eggs and place them in a bowl or jar of pickled beet juice. Let them pickle several hours or overnight in the refrigerator. Drain. Insert a popsicle stick into the end of each egg. Place in cellophane or a plastic bag for a school lunch box. They are good for more "mature" lunch boxes, too—without the sticks. Makes 3 Lollipop Eggs.

CRUNCHY PEANUT-SESAME SQUARES

The peanut butter, eggs, and soy/wheat flours make this an exceptionally high-protein confection. The butter provides vitamins A, E, and F.

1 *cup homemade or natural (additive-free) peanut butter*
½ *cup butter, softened*
¼ *teaspoon cinnamon*
1 *teaspoon vanilla extract*

¾ *cup honey*
4 *eggs, beaten*
1 *cup minus 2 tablespoons whole wheat pastry flour*
2 *tablespoons soy flour Sesame seeds*

In a bowl, combine the peanut butter and softened butter and beat well. Add the cinnamon, vanilla, honey, and eggs. Beat until fluffy. Combine the whole wheat and soy flours. Add the flours to the peanut butter mixture and beat until smooth.

Spread the mixture (it will be thick) on a greased baking dish 13 x 9 x 2 inches. Cover generously with sesame seeds and bake in a preheated 350-degree F. oven for about 25 minutes—until a toothpick inserted comes out clean. Remove from the oven and cool. Cut into squares (or bars). To make these confections extra festive, spread ⅛ cup carob chips melted with a little butter over all as soon as you remove the baking dish from the oven. Makes 24 two-inch squares.

FRUIT LEATHER

A fun food—tart and chewy, rich in blood-building iron. A chewing gum alternative.

½ *cup dried apricots*
½ *cup raisins*

½ *cup fruit juice— apple, pineapple, or orange*

Combine the apricots and raisins in a jar or bowl. Cover with apple, pineapple, or orange juice, and let soak overnight or longer. The next day, whiz the fruit and juice in a blender till there are no lumps. Line a cookie sheet with parchment paper. Spread the fruit purée in a thin layer over the parchment paper, then set the cookie sheet in a very low oven (the pilot light of a gas oven or the lowest possible setting on an electric oven is enough). It might take 48 hours or more to dry out. When it does, peel off the paper and roll. Also can be frozen and then broken off in chunks. You can make Fruit Leather from any kind of dried fruit or even from apple butter. Makes 1 twelve-inch roll.

BANANA-COCONUT LEATHER

4 to 6 *ripe bananas,*
peeled
3 *tablespoons lemon*
juice

½ *cup unsweetened*
coconut flakes or
chopped walnuts or
pecans

In a blender, combine the bananas with the lemon juice until smooth. Transfer to a bowl and stir in the coconut or nuts. Line 2 large cookie sheets with parchment paper. Divide the mixture between the 2 pans and spread out evenly and very thin. If using a gas oven, you need only the heat of the pilot light to dry it out and form the "leather." It will take 24 to 36 hours. Check it after 24 hours. If it has formed a sheet that can be peeled, gently lift it off and turn it over. Put it back in the oven for a few more hours. There should be no spots that are moist. If using an electric oven, preheat it to 200 degrees F. Leave the cookie sheets in the oven for 5 minutes, then turn off the heat. Check it in a few hours. Turn the oven on to warm for another 5 minutes. Turn oven off and check again in another few hours. In 24 hours, the "leather" should be dry enough to peel. Follow the same procedure as for the Fruit Leather above.

PEANUT BUTTER FUDGE

All the good things rolled into one. This is a "candy" you will be happy to see the children devour: every crumb contributes to health.

⅔ cup homemade or
natural peanut butter
½ cup honey
1 teaspoon blackstrap
molasses
½ cup powdered milk
(spray dried)
3 tablespoons
unsweetened
shredded coconut

¼ cup sesame or
sunflower seeds
or ground nuts
½ cup wheat germ
Unsweetened
shredded coconut
or seeds or nuts
(optional)

In a bowl, combine the peanut butter, honey, and molasses. Add the rest of the ingredients. Spread the mixture in a 9 x 9-inch baking dish and refrigerate. Cut into squares. To make into balls, pinch off pieces the size of filberts and roll each in extra coconut, seeds, or nuts. Refrigerate or freeze. Makes 30 balls or 30 one-inch squares.

RYE-FLAVORED SOFT PRETZELS

Commercial pretzels are usually made from white flour treated with lye, and coated with salt. These soft pretzels, however, are a nosh with nutrients, and they're very easy to make.

1 tablespoon active
dry yeast
1¼ cups lukewarm
water
1 tablespoon honey
2 cups whole wheat
bread flour
1½ cups rye flour

1 teaspoon salt
½ cup soy or whole
wheat bread flour
1 egg
1 tablespoon cold
water
Sesame or caraway
seeds

In a warm bowl, dissolve the yeast in the lukewarm water. Add the honey and set aside for 5 minutes.

Combine the 2 cups of whole wheat bread flour with the 1½ cups of rye flour and the salt. Stir in the yeast mixture.

Turn out this dough onto a lightly floured board and knead with the ½ cup soy or whole wheat flour until smooth. To make pretzel sticks, divide the dough into 48 pieces and roll each into a 5-inch rope, about ½ inch in diameter. To make pretzel shapes or letters of the alphabet, divide into 24 pieces, roll each into a 10-inch rope, and shape as desired.

Place the pretzels on parchment-lined or lightly greased baking sheets. (Use a mixture of ½ teaspoon vegetable oil and ½ teaspoon liquid lecithin to grease the sheets if you're not using parchment paper.) Make an egg wash by beating the egg with the tablespoon of cold water. Brush each pretzel with egg wash. Sprinkle with sesame or caraway seeds.

Let rise in a warm place, uncovered, for 20 minutes. Preheat the oven to 400 degrees F. and bake for 18 to 20 minutes. Makes 48 pretzel sticks or 24 shaped pretzels.

CHEESE-FLAVORED SOFT PRETZELS

You'll be happy to serve these wholesome tasty pretzels to your children, grandchildren, or guests. The wheat germ contributes 48 grams of protein plus B-complex vitamins, vitamin E, and iron. The cheese contributes a delightful flavor and lots of calcium, which helps to balance the high phosphorus content of the wheat germ. The sesame seeds contribute even more calcium.

2 *tablespoons butter*	1 *cup wheat germ*
¾ *cup water*	1 *to 1½ cups whole*
1 *teaspoon honey*	*wheat bread flour*
1 *tablespoon active*	1 *egg*
dry yeast	1 *tablespoon cold*
2 *cups grated Cheddar*	*water*
cheese	*Sesame seeds*

In a saucepan, combine the butter, ¾ cup of water, and honey. Heat to 110 degrees F. Add the yeast and stir until dissolved.

In a large bowl, combine the cheese, wheat germ, and yeast mixture. Mix well. Add just enough flour to make a soft dough that leaves the sides of the bowl. Turn out onto a lightly floured surface. Knead for about 5 minutes, until the dough is elastic. Divide into 30 pieces. Roll each piece into a rope about 10 inches long. Twist each rope into a pretzel shape or form the letters of the alphabet in English or in Hebrew, or make the letters of your children's names. They'll love that. To make the pretzel shape, first make a horseshoe, then cross the strands and press them into the curves of the horseshoe.

Place the pretzels on parchment-lined or lightly greased baking sheets. Grease with a mixture of ½ teaspoon vegetable oil and ½ teaspoon liquid lecithin. Make an egg wash by beating the egg with the tablespoon of cold water. Brush each pretzel with egg wash. Sprinkle with sesame seeds.

Place in warm place, uncovered, to rise for 20 minutes. Preheat the oven to 375 degrees F. Bake for 15 to 18 minutes, until lightly browned. They are very nice served warm. Makes 30 delicious pretzels. Store in a covered container.

BAKED FRENCH FRIES

All kids love French fries. Since I don't like to deep-fry, I bake them in the oven. A surprisingly nutritious snack.

3 *large scrubbed*   1 *tablespoon vegetable*
  potatoes, unpeeled   *oil*
  (preferably chilled)   *Salt (optional)*

Cut the potatoes like traditional French fries or in circles. Drizzle the oil, then spread out evenly. Salt very lightly, if salt is desired at all. Bake at 450 degrees F. for 20 minutes. Turn over the potatoes and bake for another 20 minutes Serves 6 as a snack.

PINEAPPLE-BANANA POPS

1 *can (8 ounces)*
unsweetend crushed
pineapple
1 *ripe banana, peeled*

1 *cup plain yogurt*
1 *teaspoon vanilla*
extract
2 *teaspoons honey*

Drain the pineapple. Reserve the juice for some other use. Mash the banana into the pineapple. Add the yogurt, vanilla, and honey. Combine well by hand or whiz in a blender at low speed for 1 minute or until well blended. Spoon into 3-ounce paper cups (7 should be adequate) and place in the freezer. When the mixture is semisolid, insert wooden sticks (tongue depressors or popsicle sticks) and return to the freezer. When the children are ready for their treat, just peel off the paper cups and voilà! Makes 7 pops.

FROZEN BANANA BARS

When you have these in the freezer, you've always got a great treat on the ready. Make up a lot of them when you have overripe bananas.

1 *cup pitted chopped*
dates
¾ *cup water*

3 *bananas (more or*
less), peeled
Unsweetened
coconut flakes

Whiz the dates and water in a blender to make date butter. Cut the bananas into 2-inch pieces. Cover each piece on all sides with the date butter, then roll in the coconut. Line them up on a cookie sheet and set in the freezer. When frozen solid, transfer them to a freezer container or plastic bag and take them out as needed just a few minutes before serving. Makes 12 bars.

To make frozen pops, cut the bananas larger and insert popsicle sticks before freezing. Makes 6 pops.

GRANOLA JUMBLES

These nifty little jumbles, so easy to prepare, provide the nutritional power of granola plus added protein, essential fatty acids, and the B vitamins. And they have the irresistible appeal of peanut butter.

⅓ *cup honey*
1 *teaspoon arrowroot*
  starch
1 *cup granola*

⅓ *cup homemade or*
  natural peanut butter
½ *teaspoon vanilla*
  extract

Heat the honey with the arrowroot and granola in a saucepan till well combined. Add the peanut butter and vanilla. Mix well. Drop by the teaspoonful onto wax or parchment paper. Refrigerate or freeze to harden. Makes about 32 Granola Jumbles.

COOKIE JAR HERMITS

That old-time favorite made nutritious and protein-rich.

1¾ *cups sifted whole*
  wheat pastry flour
¼ *cup sifted soy flour*
½ *teaspoon salt*
½ *teaspoon baking*
  soda
½ *teaspoon grated*
  nutmeg
½ *teaspoon cinnamon*
¼ *teaspoon ground*
  cloves

½ *cup butter, softened*
½ *cup honey or*
  blackstrap molasses
  (half of each is nice)
1 *egg, beaten*
¼ *cup plain yogurt or*
  sour cream
½ *cup wheat germ*
1 *cup raisins*
½ *cup coarsely*
  chopped walnuts

Combine the sifted flours with the rest of the dry ingredients. In a medium-sized bowl, cream the butter with the honey and/or molasses until fluffy. Beat in the egg. Add the dry ingredients, a third at a time, alternately with the yogurt or sour cream. Stir in the wheat germ, raisins, and nuts.

Drop by rounded teaspoonfuls, about 2 inches apart, on greased cookie sheets. Preheat the oven to 350 degrees F. and bake for about 10 minutes. Makes 24 large cookies.

"Dynamite" Muffins

Made with my special "Dynamite Mix." Very nice to have around for an energy boost that's low on the calorie side, and for marvelous taste. Make a double batch. Keep a supply in the freezer.

"Dynamite" Mix:

1 *cup noninstant powdered milk*
1 *cup soy flour*
1 *cup wheat germ*
1 *cup bran*
¼ *cup nutritional yeast*

Combine all ingredients in a jar and shake well. Store in the refrigerator or freezer. Use 1 cup of this mix in place of 1 cup of flour in any baked goods you want to give the "dynamite" treatment.

Muffins:

1 *cup "dynamite mix"*
1 *cup whole wheat pastry flour*
2 *teaspoons baking powder*
½ *cup raisins*
½ *cup sunflower seeds*
2 *eggs*
1 *cup plain yogurt or buttermilk (or ¾ cup yogurt and ¼ cup sour cream)*
¼ *cup blackstrap molasses*

Mix the first 3 ingredients in a bowl. Add the raisins and seeds. In another bowl, combine the eggs, yogurt or buttermilk, and molasses. Combine the wet and dry ingredients and spoon into a 12-muffin tin greased with a mixture of ½ teaspoon liquid lecithin and ½ teaspoon vegetable oil. Bake for 20 minutes in a preheated 350-degree F. oven. Makes 12 muffins.

PINEAPPLE-COCONUT MUFFINS

Moist pineapple and crunchy coconut give a Polynesian flavor to these high-protein raised-dough muffins. Pineapple contains bromelin, an enzyme which aids digestion.

1 can (20 ounces) unsweetened pineapple chunks
1 tablespoon dry yeast
3 cups minus 3 tablespoons whole wheat pastry flour
3 tablespoons soy flour
½ cup wheat germ
1 teaspoon ground ginger
½ teaspoon cinnamon
2 tablespoons vegetable oil
1 egg
½ cup unsweetened shredded coconut

Drain the pineapple and reserve the juice. In a saucepan, heat the juice to lukewarm. Dissolve the yeast in the juice. In a large bowl, combine all the dry ingredients except the coconut. To this, add the oil, egg, and yeast mixture, beating to blend. Stir in the pineapple chunks and coconut. Cover the bowl and set in a warm place, to rise, for 1 hour or until doubled in bulk. Grease 12 muffin cups with a mixture of 1 teaspoon oil and 1 teaspoon liquid lecithin. Spoon the muffin dough into the muffin cups; let rise again for 30 minutes. Bake in a preheated 350-degree F. oven for 40 to 45 minutes. Makes 12 beautiful muffins.

TEETHING BISCUITS

Let the baby gather nutrients as he or she chomps.

1 egg yolk, beaten
2 tablespoons blackstrap molasses
2 tablespoons vegetable oil
1 teaspoon vanilla extract
¾ cup whole wheat pastry flour
1 tablespoon soy flour
1 tablespoon wheat germ
1 tablespoon noninstant powdered milk

Blend the egg yolk, molasses, oil, and vanilla. Combine the dry ingredients and add to the wet mixture to make the dough. Roll the dough out very thin. Place the dough on an ungreased cookie sheet. Cut it into rectangles no bigger than a baby's finger. Preheat the oven to 350 degrees F. and bake for 12 to 15 minutes. Cool on a wire rack. Store in a covered container. Makes about 36.

14

Beverages for "L'Chaim!"

I well remember the putdown I got from one of our youngsters when he said to me at the dinner table one night, "Mom, why can't we be like other people and have soda?"

I figured I'd better tell it like it is. "You can't have soda," I told him, "because I love you."

He did not return the compliment.

"Very funny," he said. "How come Jeff has soda all the time? Doesn't his mother love him?"

"Well," I parried. "Maybe Jeff's mother doesn't know that soda has lots of sugar, artificial color and flavor, absolutely no vitamins, minerals, or protein, takes up so much room in your tummy, you can't eat the foods that build muscles; it makes you overweight and undernourished. Besides it makes nasty holes in your teeth."

Do you think he was proud of my knowledge? *Anechtegen torg!* Not on your life! He took a big swig of his apple juice and said, "You known sumpn? Somtimes I wish my mother didn't know so darn much!"

You who are reading this book are among those who know so darn much that you're concerned. You know that most of the "drinks" in the marketplace are oversweetened, overprocessed, loaded with additives of dubious safety, and low in the nutrients essential to health and vitality.

What's a mother to do who has a gut-level urge to see the glow of health on the faces of her loved ones?

She goes creative with her blender and dishes up some beverages that are nutritious as well as thirst-quenching and good-tasting.

BREAKFAST BEVERAGE

The wheat sprouts lend a subtle sweetness and good supplies of vitamins C, B, and E to this molasses-flavored breakfast beverage.

¾ cup water or juice
3 tablespoons sprouted wheat, or wheat grains that have been soaked in water overnight

1 teaspoon blackstrap molasses (honey may be substituted)
1 teaspoon nutritional yeast
1 teaspoon powdered milk (spray dried)

Put everything in a blender and whiz. Drink *gezunte hait*. Makes 1 drink.

VARIATION: If you have a busy schedule and cannot eat a substantial breakfast, add 1 egg to this beverage. Increase the quantity of nutritional yeast as you become accustomed to it. Add ½ of a banana for a nice change of pace.

HIGH-PROTEIN BEVERAGE MIX

Always on hand for when you need a quick meal in a glass. This beverage mix is loaded with health-building, morale-boosting nutrients.

½ cup raw sesame
seeds
½ cup sunflower seeds
½ cup almonds
½ cup oat groats or oat
flakes

½ cup carob powder
½ cup wheat germ
1 cup powdered milk
(spray dried)
1½ cups soy powder

Grind the seeds, nuts, and oat groats or flakes very fine. Add the other ingredients and mix throughly. Store in glass jars in the refrigerator or freezer. Makes 5½ cups of dry mix.

To prepare a beverage using the mix, pour 1 cup of the mix into the blender jar. Add 1 banana, 1 teaspoon of blackstrap molasses, and 2 teaspoons of nutritional yeast. Add 1 cup of ice water and whiz. This makes enough for 2.

FRUIT AND NUT SMOOTHIE

A fruit and seed blend devised by Dr. Mike Lerner, of Lexington, Kentucky, especially for youngsters with cavity problems. This is preventive dentistry in action: all the elements essential to tooth structure are included.

½ cup sunflower seeds
1 tablespoon bone
meal powder or
2 tablespoons
powdered milk
(spray dried)
1 tablespoon brewer's
yeast

1 cup unsweetened
orange, pineapple,
or apple juice
1 banana, peeled
1 apple, cut into
chunks
1 tablespoon honey
1 tablespoon plain
yogurt

First, grind the seeds. Place in a blender jar, add the rest of the ingredients, and whiz till smooth. Makes 2 cups. Very young children enjoy this drink, too.

HIGH VITAMIN C PUNCH
Refreshing on a hot summer's day.

2 *cups orange juice*
2 *cups grapefruit juice*
2 *tablespoons lemon*
juice
2 *tablespoons honey*

2 *tablespoons*
powdered milk
(spray dried)
1 *egg yolk (optional)*

Blend all ingredients. Serve in a frosty glass, perhaps with a wedge of lemon or lime as garnish. Makes 1 quart.

MULLED APPLE JUICE

This hot, spicy drink warms your spirits when the winds are howling.

1 *quart apple juice or*
apple cider

4 *sticks cinnamon*
16 *whole cloves*

Place all the ingredients in a large saucepan. Simmer for 7 minutes. Strain into hot cups and sip with pleasure. Makes 1 quart.

NUTTY MILKSHAKE

Especially valuable for those who can't tolerate milk.

⅓ *cup chopped raw*
cashew nuts
1 *cup water or fruit*
juice of your choice
2 *ripe bananas, peeled*

2 *teaspoons to 2*
tablespoons
nutritional yeast
(quantity depending
upon the amount
you can tolerate)
½ *teaspoon vanilla*
extract

Put the nuts and water or fruit juice in a blender for 2 minutes at low speed and whiz to make "nut milk." Add the rest of the ingredients and blend for 1 more minute at low speed. Serve immediately. Enough for 1 or 2.

TRINIDAD SHAKE

We flipped for this shake when we dined at Brownie's Natural Foods Restaurant, in New York. That night we met Danny Kaye there, and I don't know which was more exciting.

1 *cup unsweetened pineapple juice*
2 *eggs*
½ *cup unsweetened crushed pineapple*
⅔ *cup milk (skim or whole)*
2 *tablespoons tahina (sesame butter)*
1 *teaspoon unsulphured molasses*

1 *teaspoon date sugar or honey*
2 *tablespoons soy powder*
2 *tablespoons powdered milk (spray dried)*
2 *tablespoons sesame meal (ground seeds)*
½ *teaspoon vanilla extract*

Whiz all ingredients in a blender for 1 minute. Serves 4. Puts stars in your eyes.

MOUNTAIN COLADA

This is a great Brownie beverage that you can easily make at home. It is adapted from *Cooking Creatively With Natural Foods* (Hawthorn, New York, 1972).

1⅓ cups unsweetened
     pineapple juice
1½ cups carrot juice or 1
     cup grated carrot
⅔ cup orange juice
⅔ cup canned
     unsweetened
     pineapple chunks
½ cup banana slices

½ cup raisins
2 tablespoons honey
⅓ cup toasted
     unsweetened
     shredded coconut
2 tablespoons lecithin
     granules
2 tablespoons soy
     powder

Whiz all ingredients in a blender for 2 minutes. Serves 4. Thin it down with Perrier and it's an elegant party drink.

HOT ALMOND-CAROB DRINK

Almonds are high in protein, linoleic acid (a very important unsaturated fatty acid), iron, calcium, phosphorus, potassium, and the B vitamins. When these nutrients are combined with the fine nutritional values of carob and milk, you get a drink that will satisfy your body's need for vitamins and minerals. For more beverages featuring carob, see Chapter Twelve, Carob Instead of Chocolate.

4 tablespoons carob
     syrup (½ cup carob
     powder plus ½ cup
     water)
1 quart milk
¼ cup honey
3 tablespoons ground
     almonds

1 teaspoon cinnamon
1 teaspoon vanilla
     extract
Whipped cream
     (optional)
Cinnamon (optional)

First, make the carob syrup. In a small saucepan, mix ½ cup of carob powder with ½ cup of water. Bring to a boil over very low heat, stirring constantly. Cook for 5 to 8 minutes or until the syrup is completely smooth. Cool and store, covered, in the refrigerator. You will have ¾ cup of carob syrup. (It's great for milkshakes as well as for this recipe.)

To make the Hot Almond-Carob Drink, combine the milk, honey, ground almonds, carob syrup, cinnamon, and vanilla in a saucepan. Cook over low heat, stirring constantly until the mixture is steaming hot. Beat until frothy. Pour into mugs. Terrific garnished with a dollop of whipped cream and dusted with cinnamon. Makes 1 quart.

MINT-CAROB DRINK

A mint-flavored milkshake that can be frozen into iron-rich popsicles.

1 *cup milk*
1 *banana, peeled*
2 *tablespoons powdered milk (spray dried)*
2 *tablespoons carob powder*

1 *tablespoon honey or blackstrap molasses*
⅛ *teaspoon mint extract*
A few mint leaves

Blend everything but the mint leaves in a blender at high speed for 1 minute. Pour into a tall glass and garnish with the mint leaves. Makes 10 ounces.

SOY MILK

Many people, especially Jews, lack the enzyme needed to digest dairy products. They suffer from colitis, asthma, allergies, and digestive difficulties until they learn of this peculiar sensitivity.

For them, soy milk is a real boon. It can be used in all recipes that call for cow's milk.

Soy milk, being pareve, is also a boon to the kosher housewife. It is nice to be able to serve "milk" at any meal without violating the laws of kashrut.

There are several ways to make soy milk. The least expensive is to use soybeans rather than powder. This milk also has the best flavor.

1 *cup soybeans*	4 *cups water,*
2 *quarts water for*	*approximately*
soaking	

Wash and drain the beans. Allow them to soak in 2 quarts of water overnight. Drain the soaked beans and discard the soak water (feed it to your plants.) Using approximately 4 cups of water, purée the beans in a blender for about 3 minutes.

Strain the ground beans through several layers of cheesecloth into a large kettle. Wring as much liquid from the mash as possible. Do not discard the mash. There are many ways to use it: add it to granola before toasting; mix it into soups, stews, casseroles, etc.; use it as a casserole topping; add it to chopped meat dishes.

The liquid you have strained from the beans is the soy milk. Boil it for at least 15 minutes in order to destroy the trypsin inhibitor, an antinutritional factor present in the raw beans, and also to reduce the beany flavor. Serve the milk hot or cold and flavor it to suit your own taste. Makes 4 cups.

Add a little honey, vanilla, an egg, and a grating of nutmeg and you have a delicious eggnog. Whip it up in a blender with a banana, nutritional yeast, a little molasses, and some tahina or sesame seeds and you have a wonderful milkshake. Soy and sesame are a terrific partnership. Their protein patterns are complementary. Sesame also provides lots of calcium, a mineral which is low in soy milk (47.5 milligrams per 1-cup serving compared with 291 milligrams per 1-cup serving of whole dairy milk).

HOMEMADE SOY MILK FROM SOY POWDER

You can also make soy milk using soy powder, available at natural food stores. This method is much quicker than making the milk from soybeans, though it is a little more expensive. Nonetheless, it is still not so costly as cow's milk.

1 *cup soy powder*   3 *cups water*

Combine the powder and water in a large saucepan and whisk well until dissolved. Bring to a boil over high heat, stirring constantly. Reduce the heat to low and simmer for 3 minutes. Serve hot or cold. Makes 3 cups.

GOGOL MOGOL

This is not a dish you would ordinarily serve at the dinner table unless someone has laryngitis, a sore throat, a cough, or just the blahs from a cold. It's been handed down in our family for generations. Our grandchildren, Jodi and Lisa, ask for a Gogol Mogol as soon as they bounce into the kitchen, even when they are in perfect health. For one Gogol Mogol you will need:

1 *egg yolk*   ½ *teaspoon vanilla*
1 *teaspoon honey*   *extract*
1 *teaspoon fresh*
  lemon juice

In a bowl, beat the yolk with a fork; stir in the rest of the ingredients. That's all there is to it. They lick the platter clean and ask for another. So what could be bad? Serves 1.

15

Don't Buy It—
Make It Yourself

Avoid harmful additives and save a bundle. Make your own mayonnaise, salad dressings, yogurt, cheese, low-calorie butter, nut butters, barbecue sauce, catsup, even baking powder.

Of course it will take more time than the store-bought varieties. But, when you stop to think about it, what is time for? I can't think of a better use for your time than providing health-building food for yourself and your loved ones. The rewards are many.

First of all, there is an elemental joy in making from scratch the foods that sustain your family.

Second, you know exactly what is in that food. You know there are no chemical additives hidden in the fine print or not mentioned at all because those chemicals come under the rule of Standard of Identity. That means that because it is permitted, it need not be stated on the label.

Third, you save a bundle on many items when you make them yourself.

Take salad dressings for instance.

It takes five minutes to make a salad dressing yourself without the propylene glycol, alginate, and edta you get in most commercial varieties. That's less time than it takes to find it in the supermarket and wait in line to check out.

Mayonnaise

With the help of a blender, mayonnaise is surprisingly simple to make and is chemical-free.When you make mayonnaise yourself, the cost is about half as much as the store-bought kind, and when you use yogurt to cut the mayonnaise content in half, you also cut calories practically in half.

> 1 *egg*
> ¼ *cup cider vinegar or lemon juice or ⅛ cup of each*
> 1 *teaspoon honey (optional)*
> ½ *teaspoon dry mustard*
>
> *Dash of cayenne pepper*
> *Pinch of sea salt or kelp*
> 1 *cup vegetable oil*

Combine all ingredients except the oil in a blender and whiz till well combined. Gradually add the oil in a slow continuous stream until it is all blended. Store in a covered glass jar in the refrigerator. Try to use it within 2 weeks; homemade mayonnaise does not have the keeping qualities of the commercial kind. Makes 1¼ cups.

Thousand Island Dressing

Now that you know how to make mayonnaise, use some of it to make this very popular zesty dressing. The egg gives it extra protein.

> 1 *cup homemade mayonnaise*
> 2 *tablespoons chili sauce*
> 1 *tablespoon sugar-free sweet pickle relish (optional—available at health food stores)*
>
> 1 *tablespoon chopped green pepper*
> 1 *hard-cooked egg, mashed*

Combine all ingredients. Serve over a mixed vegetable salad or as a dip with a platter of raw vegetables. Makes 1½ cups.

RUSSIAN DRESSING

1 *cup homemade mayonnaise*
¼ *cup chili sauce*
1 *tablespoon prepared horseradish (red or white)*

1 *tablespoon finely chopped celery (optional)*
1 *tablespoon chopped green pepper*

Combine all ingredients and the dressing is ready to use. As a variation add a chopped hard-cooked egg to this dressing, or serve it over a salad that contains slices of hard-cooked eggs. Makes 1¼ cups.

HERB DRESSING

1 *clove garlic*
⅓ *cup wine vinegar or lemon juice*
⅔ *cup cold pressed oil (I like to use a blend of sunflower and sesame, but any good oil can be used.)*

½ *teaspoon lecithin granules*
¼ *teaspoon each of basil, oregano, thyme, dill, dry mustard, kelp, and paprika*

Crush the garlic into a container. Add the rest of the ingredients. Cover the container and shake well. Makes 1 cup. Excellent with a tossed green salad.

LOW-CALORIE
SESAME-YOGURT DRESSING

Superb for the salads you serve with dairy meals, this dressing is low in calories. And while the yogurt makes this preparation a boon to your digestive system, the sesame seeds provide plenty of calcium and crunch.

1 *clove garlic*
⅔ *cup plain yogurt*
⅓ *cup homemade mayonnaise*
2 *tablespoons lemon juice*

2 *teaspoons sesame seeds*
1 *tablespoon light cream*

Put the garlic through a press. Then mix it well with the rest of the ingredients. Makes about 1 cup of lovely dressing for 2 quarts of mixed greens combined with a sliced Spanish onion, a cup of toasted croutons, and some cubes of your favorite natural cheese. Serve with a good whole grain bread and you have a nice supper for a summer's evening.

BUTTERMILK DRESSING

1 *cup lowfat buttermilk*
1 *teaspoon frozen apple juice concentrate*
1 *teaspoon lemon juice*

1 *teaspoon onion flakes*
1 *teaspoon dill weed*
White pepper
Ground allspice

Mix all ingredients except the pepper and allspice. Add the pepper and ground allspice to taste. Chill. Makes 1 cup.

CREAM CHEESE-YOGURT SALAD DRESSING OR DIP

Good any night of the year. Especially good on the salad you serve when you break the fast on Yom Kippur night. The yogurt will speed up the digestive process that has been slowed down by abstinence.

3 *ounces cream cheese, softened*
¾ *cup plain yogurt*
¼ *cup homemade mayonnaise*
1 *tablespoon lemon juice*

3 *tablespoons honey, or to taste (Start with 1 tablespoon. If your tastebuds have been educated, that will be plenty sweet for you.)*

Cream the cream cheese with the yogurt. Add the mayonnaise and mix well. Add the lemon juice, then the honey; stir. Use this as a dressing or dip, for vegetables or fruit. Makes 1¼ cups.

PAREVE "CHEESE" DIP

2 *cups rolled oats*
3 *tablespoons sunflower seeds*
1 *teaspoon celery seeds*
1 *teaspoon sesame seeds*

1 *teaspoon caraway seeds*
2 *teaspoons dill seeds*
Water
1 *teaspoon Tamari soy sauce*

Combine all the dry ingredients in a wide-mouth jar. Add water to cover and the soy sauce. Cover with cheesecloth or a screened lid and set in a warm place to allow fermentation. In 2 or 3 days it will be pleasantly fermented and will taste a little like blue cheese. Makes about 2½ cups.

Low-Calorie Tartar Sauce

This sauce gives tuna fish and cole slaw a pleasant zippy quality. In fact, it is excellent on all fish and vegetables.

1 *cup plain yogurt*
¼ *cup homemade mayonnaise*
¼ *cup pickle relish*
1 *teaspoon prepared mustard*

Combine all ingredients. Mix well. Makes 1½ cups. Store in the refrigerator.

Tomato Catsup

Avoid the sugar and chemicals in commercial catsup. Make your own and you won't have to worry about the "catsup slurpers." This catsup has a lusty, pungent flavor that tickles your tongue in all the right places.

6 *large plum tomatoes*
2 *tablespoons soy, sesame, safflower, or olive oil*
1 *tablespoon honey*
1 *tablespoon lemon juice*
1 *teaspoon grated onion*
1 *teaspoon Tamari soy sauce*
Pinch of dried basil and oregano

Whiz the tomatoes in a blender until puréed—about 1 minute. Add the rest of the ingredients and whiz again until smooth. Makes about 1 cup. Keep refrigerated and use within a week. If it's not used up as catsup, you can use it as spaghetti sauce.

BARBECUE SAUCE

A tangy barbecue sauce that has the supernutritional benefits of uncooked food. You simply whiz everything in the blender and presto, it's ready.

1 *cup tomato purée*
1 *large tomato, fresh or canned*
2 *tablespoons vegetable oil*
¼ *cup apple cider vinegar*
⅛ *teaspoon cayenne pepper*
2 *tablespoons honey, or to taste*
1 *medium-sized onion, sliced*
½ *green pepper*

Place all ingredients in a blender. Whiz at medium speed until smooth—about 1 minute. Keep refrigerated. Use as a basting sauce for broiled or roasted meats or for chicken.

HOMEMADE TAHINA-NUT BUTTERS

You'll enjoy the fresh wholesome flavor. The tahina enhances the protein value.

PEANUT BUTTER:

2 *cups peanuts*
2 *tablespoons tahina (sesame butter)*
½ *teaspoon cinnamon*
2 *tablespoons peanut oil, approximately*

Put the peanuts in a blender jar. (For chunky peanut butter, reserve some peanuts for chopping.) Whiz the peanuts until they are finely ground. Remove from the blender to a bowl and add the tahina, cinnamon, and only enough oil to make a spreadable consistency. (For chunky peanut butter, chop the reserved peanuts and add.)

NOTE: Peanuts are a legume. Sesame is a seed. The combination is protein-rich. Peanuts are subject to aflatoxin infestation, a disease-causing mold. Of course, not all peanuts are affected, but just for insurance I always use a little cinnamon with peanut butter. The oil in cinnamon has been shown to be highly effective against the fungi of aflatoxin. (*New Scientist,* December 14, 1978.) Besides, the cinnamon enhances the flavor.

OTHER NUT BUTTERS: Cashew, almond, walnut, Brazil nut, and pecan butters are all made the same way, but they usually don't need additional oil. A little tahina added to them enhances the flavor and nutritional value.

DAIRY MILK YOGURT

How to make it at home.

1 *quart whole milk, preferably raw (unpasteurized)*
2 *tablespoons noninstant powdered milk (spray dried)*

1 *package dry Bulgarian yogurt culture or 3 tablespoons commercial plain yogurt*

Heat the milk to the boiling point. Then let it cool down to 115 degrees F. A candy or cheesemaking thermometer is very helpful.

When the milk has reached this temperature, put ½ cup of it in the blender; add the powdered milk and the yogurt culture. Whiz just to blend. Combine with the rest of the milk and mix. Pour the mixture into 4 half-pint glasses that have been freshly washed with hot water. If using a yogurt maker, use the containers that come with it; switch it on and in 5 to 8 hours, you will have yogurt. Refrigerate it when it is firm.

If you don't have a yogurt maker, set the glasses in an electric frying pan at 110 to 115 degrees F. Or, if you have a gas oven with a pilot light, put the glasses on a tray and set the tray on the bottom of the oven. Takes 8 to 12 hours this way. Or, you may place the containers in a deep pan, add water at 118 degrees F. up to the level of the milk, and cover. After 1½ hours again heat the water bath to 118 degrees F. and let the milk incubate until a firm curd is formed. This will take from 3 to 4 hours. Makes 1 quart.

Some Notes About Yogurt:

● You can also make yogurt in a thermos bottle. Just pour the inoculated milk in a thermos that has been freshly washed with hot water; cover and let it sit overnight.

● Be sure to reserve some yogurt from an unused container to make your next batch. It's a good idea to keep 1 container or several 3-tablespoon portions in the freezer to make sure you don't run out of culture.

● I like to use the dry *Bulgarian* culture for my starter because it contains the *Acidophilus* strain along with the *Bulgaricus* and *Thermophilis*. Most commercial yogurts provide the latter two, but not the *Acidophilus*, which is indigenous to the human intestine, where it implants itself and thrives, thus providing continuous benefits to your intestinal tract.

● In Israel it is common medical practice to prescribe yogurt, or *laban*, for anyone who is taking an antibiotic. The antibiotic tends to wipe out the colonies of colon bacteria which keep one's digestive system chugging along in good order. The yogurt feeds the "good guys" in the human intestine, helping them to thrive, while the antibiotic does its job on the "bad guys." Thus, the body is spared some of the intestinal upsets that usually follow in the wake of a course of antibiotic therapy.

● Many women who are subject to yeasty vaginal infection, especially after a course of antibiotic therapy, find that yogurt is their best medicine. But it must be yogurt with *Acidophilus*. This Bulgarian culture, which provides *Acidophilus*, is available at most natural food stores or from the International Yogurt Company, 628 Doheny Drive, Los Angeles, California 90069. This company can also supply cultures for making buttermilk, sour cream, and kefir—another very good fermented milk.

● Many people who cannot tolerate milk *can* eat yogurt.

BERRY YOGURT
Strawberry, raspberry, blueberry.

To make berry yogurt, mash fresh or thawed frozen berries and add to yogurt, about half and half. Sweeten with a little honey if desired.

SOY YOGURT

This yogurt is recommended for those who cannot tolerate dairy products. It is higher in protein than dairy yogurt, but also higher in calories. It has a slightly beany flavor that takes getting used to.

2 *cups soy powder*
4 *cups water, boiled and cooled to lukewarm*
3 *tablespoons honey*
3 *tablespoons lecithin granules*
3 *tablespoons soy oil*
1 *package yogurt starter*

Mix the soy powder with the lukewarm water and cook slowly over steam or in a double boiler for 3 minutes. Cool to 110 degrees F. Add the honey, lecithin, oil, and yogurt starter and whiz in a blender in 3 batches. Pour into clean glass jars or glasses. Cover and process the same as Dairy Milk Yogurt above. Makes 1½ quarts.

YOGURT CREAM CHEESE

This spread has a pleasing tang and is low in calories. The older the yogurt you use (within reason), the more tang this cheese will have.

Place 1 pint of plain yogurt in a colander lined with 3 layers of cheesecloth, or in a cheese bag, and let it drain into a bowl overnight. In the morning, you'll have 6 ounces of wonderful yogurt cream cheese. The liquid you'll find in the bowl is whey, which can be used in potato soup or as the liquid in making vegetarian stuffed cabbage. It is very nutritious. (In the Old Country, the ladies would wash their faces and their hair with whey. Whether they knew it or not, they were restoring the acid balance.) The cream cheese itself can be eaten plain but is also delicious with chives, green onions, caraway seeds, chopped nuts, and chopped olives.

HOMEMADE FROZEN YOGURT

Here is a frozen yogurt without the "junk" found in commercial varieties. This delight can be made with or without an ice cream machine, although an ice cream machine will yield a creamier product.

1 *quart plain or vanilla yogurt*
Fresh fruit—½ to 1 pint strawberries, blueberries, raspberries, peaches, or bananas
½ *cup honey (taste for sweetness—you may need only ¼ cup if the fruit is sweet)*

1 *teaspoon liquid lecithin or kosher gelatin (keeps the mixture from getting icy)*

Whiz all ingredients together in a blender. Pour into the ice cream machine to freeze. Or, if you don't have access to an ice cream machine, pour the mixture into a freezer tray and freeze until the edges harden. Then spoon the mixture into a bowl and beat with an electric mixture until light and fluffy. Refrigerate or freeze for later use. Makes 1¼ quarts.

COTTAGE CHEESE

2 quarts skim milk,
 preferably raw
 (unpasteurized)
2 tablespoons sour
 cream

¼ cup cultured
 buttermilk
½ teaspoon sea salt
 (optional)
½ cup light cream
 (optional)

In a saucepan, heat the milk until it is a little hotter than room temperature—no more than 80 degrees F. Add the sour cream and buttermilk. Cover and let stand at room temperature until the milk solidifies (that is, the milk coagulates to form curd). This might take anywhere from 12 to 24 hours; it takes longer in cold weather. Using a knife, now break the curd into chunks.

Put the saucepan into a larger pot containing 3 inches of hot water. Heat until the curd reaches 100 degrees F. and maintain that temperature for about 20 minutes, stirring occasionally.

Line a colander with several layers of cheesecloth. Place the lined colander inside a large bowl. Pour the curd into the cheesecloth and let it drain for 4 to 6 hours. Turn the curd out into a bowl and break it up into smaller pieces. Stir in the ½ teaspoon of sea salt (if desired). For a creamy cottage cheese, stir in the ½ cup light cream. If you want a low-calorie cheese, omit the cream.

VARIATION: In Israel they add 1 tablespoon of caraway seeds to the cheese, push it into a bag made of unbleached muslin, and press it between 2 boards with a weight—such as a jar of beans—placed on the top board. This makes a delicious farmer cheese.

MOCK SOUR CREAM

¼ cup skim milk
1 cup cottage cheese
 (99 percent fat free)

2 tablespoons parsley
 flakes or onion
 flakes

Combine all ingredients in a blender. Mix at chopping speed, then switch to high speed and liquefy. Makes 1 cup.

Low-Calorie Butter Spread

The good spread at half the price—and half the calories. You'll get a lot more spread out of your butter, and it's delicious. Do not use this butter spread for frying or baking.

1 *cup milk*
1 *tablespoon kosher*
gelatin

½ *pound sweet butter*

In a saucepan, warm the milk to 120 degrees F. Add the gelatin to the milk to soften. In a bowl, place the butter; beat with an electric mixer. Add the milk-gelatin mixture; stir thoroughly until the mixture is creamy. Makes 2 cups—your butter will actually double in volume. You can also make this butter in your blender, and it's quick as a wink.

Polyunsaturated Butter

If you hesitate to use butter because of the saturated fat content, use this creamy concoction. The oil tips the scales in favor of polyunsaturates. The lecithin provides a natural emulsifier that keeps cholesterol in circulation instead of in clots.

½ *pound sweet butter*
1 *cup vegetable oil*

1 *tablespoon lecithin*
granules

Cut the butter into slices. Blend with the oil and lecithin granules in a blender or with an electric mixer. Divide into several covered serving dishes. Keep 1 in the refrigerator for immediate use; store the others in the freezer for later use. Use as a spread, for sautéeing, or for baking. Makes approximately 1 pound of butter.

Baking Powder

Most commercial baking powders contain alum, which can be irritating to sensitive stomachs. They also contain sodium bicarbonate, which increases the sodium burden. You can make your own baking powder without aluminum and without sodium. Use potassium bicarbonate, which is available at pharmacies.

¼ cup potassium   ½ cup cream of tartar
  bicarbonate   ½ cup arrowroot starch

Combine these ingredients well and store in a jar. It keeps well: the arrowroot repels moisture. Makes 1¼ cups of baking powder.

NOTE: To make baking powder for immediate use, combine ¼ teaspoon bicarbonate of soda with ½ teaspoon cream of tartar. This is the equivalent of 1 teaspoon baking powder.

WATERMELON RIND CUBES

Reserve the watermelon rind after you have eaten the red part. Trim off all the pink meat and the hard outer rind. Dice into cubes. Spread on a parchment-lined cookie sheet and freeze.

When frozen, remove the cubes from the cookie sheet and store in plastic bags or freezer containers. Use as needed as a substitute for water chestnuts.

Appendix

Table of Equivalent Amounts

60 drops = 1 teaspoon
a pinch = ⅓ to ½ teaspoon
a speck = less than ⅛ teaspoon
3 teaspoons = 1 tablespoon
2 tablespoons = ⅛ cup
4 tablespoons = ¼ cup
8 tablespoons = ½ cup
12 tablespoons = ¾ cup
16 tablespoons = 1 cup
1 fluid ounce = 2 tablespoons
½ pint = 1 cup
1 pint = 2 cups
2 pints = 1 quart
4 quarts = 1 gallon
1 gill = ½ cup
4 gills = 1 pint
16 ounces = 1 pound
16 fluid ounces = 2 cups
4 cups flour = 1 pound
2 cups ground meat = 1 pound
5 large eggs = 1 cup

8 egg whites = 1 cup
16 eggs yolks = 1 cup
1 square butter = 1 tablespoon
2 cups butter = 1 pound
1 pound fresh peas shelled = 1 cup
1 cup uncooked rice = 2 cups cooked
1 cup uncooked macaroni = 2 cups cooked
1 cup uncooked noodles = 1¼ cups cooked
1 large lemon = ½ cup juice
1 medium orange = ½ cup juice
2 cups dates = 1 pound
3 cups dried apricots = 1 pound
2½ cups prunes = 1 pound
2½ cups raisins = 1 pound
1½ pounds apples = 1 quart
3 large bananas = 1 pound
1 cup shortening = ½ pound
1 cup nut meats = 5 ounces
1 pound potatoes = 4 medium-sized potatoes
1 pound tomatoes = 3 medium-sized tomatoes
#303 can = 2 cups
#2 can = 2½ cups
#2½ can = 3½ cups
#10 can = 13 cups

Conversion Tables

LIQUID MEASURES

American (Standard Cup)	Metric Equivalent
1 cup = ½ pint = 8 fl. oz.	2.37 dl.
1 Tbs. = ½ fl. oz.	1.5 cl.
1 tsp. = ⅙ fl. oz.	0.5 cl.
1 pint = 16 fl. oz.	4.73 dl.
1 quart = 2 pints = 32 fl. oz.	9.46 dl.

British (Standard Cup)	Metric Equivalent
1 cup = ½ pint = 10 fl. oz.	2.84 dl.
1 Tbs. = 0.55 fl. oz.	1.7 cl.
1 tsp. = ½ fl. oz.	0.6 cl.
1 pint = 20 fl. oz.	5.7 dl.
1 quart = 2 pints = 40 fl. oz.	1.1 liter

1 cup = 16 tablespoons
1 tablespoon = 3 teaspoons
1.1 quart = 1 liter = 10 deciliters = 100 centiliters

SOLID MEASURES

American/British	Metric Equivalent
1 lb. = 16 oz.	= 453 grams
2.2 lbs.	= 1000 grams = 1 kilogram
1 oz.	= 28 grams
3½ oz.	= 100 grams

OVEN TEMPERATURES

Degrees Fahrenheit	Degrees Centigrade	
240-280	115-135	Very slow
280-320	135-160	Slow
320-340	160-170	Warm
340-370	170-185	Moderate
370-400	185-205	Fairly hot
400-450	205-230	Hot
450-500	230-260	Very hot

Glossary

alte bubbe   Old grandmother.

a gut'n Shabbos   Good sabbath. The greeting exchanged on the Sabbath.

anechtegen tog   Go find yesterday—it will never happen!

balebusta   An excellent and praiseworthy homemaker, very efficient. She can mastermind a party for 24 kids without getting a headache.

baylick   White meat of the chicken.

billig vie borscht   Dirt cheap; literally, cheap as borscht.

bissel   A little bit.

bletl, bletlach   Singular and plural of the pancakes in which filling is wrapped for blintzes. Also known as crepes.

blintzes   Crêpes filled with cheese, potatoes, blueberries, etc.

bobke   Coffee cake made from yeast dough.

boeksur   Carob.

bris   Circumcision ceremony.

brust   Breast of beef.

bubbe(s)   Grandmother(s).

bulkalach   Little rolls.

challah   Sabbath twist—a rich bread made with eggs.

charoses   A Passover dish representing bricks made without straw, a task forced upon Israelites when they were slaves in Egypt.

chazerai Junk food.

cholent A Sabbath preparation that cooks from before sunset on Friday and is ready to be eaten and enjoyed for Saturday lunch.

chutzpah Nerve to the nth degree; guts.

es gezunte hait Eat in good health.

eshet chayil A woman of valor, one whose deeds are praiseworthy, in the home and in the community.

feeselach Feet.

fleishig, fleishedig (also spelled **fleishik, fleishedik**) Pertaining to meat foods; also the dishes, pots, pans, utensils, and silverware used with meat meals.

forshpice Appetizer.

freilach Happy.

gedempte flaish Stewed meat.

geshmache Very tasty, like Mama used to make.

ge'shrai! A loud scream, a piercing cry, a terrific outlet for pent-up frustration.

gevalt! A cry of amazement, horror or dismay, frustration. "Gevalt! How am I going to get the house ready for Pesach!"

gezunte hait Good health. *See* es gezunte hait.

glatt kosher Extremely kosher.

gorgel Neck of the chicken; good in soup and in fricassee.

grieben, grieven Chicken cracklings, crisp and tasty.

gut yomtov Happy holiday—a greeting.

Haftorah A reading from the Prophets, chanted usually by Bar Mitzvah boys and Bat Mitzvah girls.

halachic According to the law.

halke Grated potato dumplings.

hamantaschen A pastry eaten on Purim, tricornered in shape.

hamotzi The prayer said when breaking bread, thanking God who brings forth wheat from the ground.

hechsher A symbol denoting that a food is kosher.

heint is Purim Today is the holiday of Purim.

hipsher bissel An extremely large quantity.

hock-messer Chopping knife, used with a wooden bowl.

holopches Stuffed cabbage.

hora A very lively Israeli dance.

hutzpah   *See* chutzpah.

is nisht gefellah   It's not so terrible, it could be worse.

kai and shpai   Literally, "chew and spit."

karnatzlach   Hamburgers shaped to resemble frankfurters.

kasha varnishkas   Buckwheat groats with bow ties (pasta).

kashrut, kashruth   The laws and practices derived from the dietary laws set forth in the Book of Leviticus.

keylitch   A very large challah used on special occasions.

kibitzer   One who teases, humors, joshes, or gives unwanted advice.

kichlach   Very light, airy cookies.

kinder   Children.

kishke   Stuffed derma, usually made from beef casings.

knaidlach (pl), **knaidle** (sing)   Dumplings, usually made from matzo meal and eggs and served in soup.

knish   A crisp strudel dough encasing one of a variety of fillings. Usually served hot.

kosher   Pertaining to the Jewish dietary laws.

kreplach   Various foods wrapped in dough—something like wonton.

kugels   Puddings.

laban   A kind of yogurt.

latkes   Delicious pancakes.

l'chaim!   To life!—a toast.

Litvak   A native of Lithuania.

lukshen kugel   Noodle pudding.

mamaligge   Cornmeal mush.

mandelbrodt   A crisp cookie.

mandlin   Almonds.

mazel tov!   Literally "good luck," but usually used to express "Congratulations" or "Thank God!"

mench, mensch   A decent person, someone of consequence.

merin   Carrots.

meshigina   One who acts mad, crazy, or loony.

meshuga   Mad, crazy, loony.

milchedig, milchig (also spelled **milchedik, milchik**)   Pertaining to dairy foods, dishes, or utensils.

miltz   Spleen—an organ meat, rich in iron.

mishigasim Crazy or foolish deeds.

mitzvah A good deed; a kind, considerate act.

mitzvot(h) Plural of mitzvah.

nisht gefellah! Not so terrible!

nosh A snack between meals, a bite.

nosherai Plural of nosh.

noshing Act of indulging in a snack.

oi vei! Literally, "oh woe!" An expletive used to express a whole range of emotions from dismay to delight.

Oneg Shabbat Joy of the Sabbath; a sociable tea in honor of the Sabbath.

pareve Neither milchig nor fleishig, but neutral. Pareve foods include fruit, vegetables, fish, eggs, oil, etc. *See* milchedig *and* fleishig.

Pesach Passover, the Festival of Freedom, observed for eight days, during which time no bread is eaten and other specific dietary laws are observed.

Pesachdik Suitable for use on Pesach.

pirogen Turnovers, served with soup or meat.

piroshki A small version of pirogen.

pletzels Flat rolls, usually topped with onions.

pulkes Chicken legs.

pultabulchas Cinnamon buns.

Rosh Hashanah The Jewish New Year.

rozhinkes Raisins.

rozhinkes mit mandlen Raisins with almonds.

rugelah A delightful rolled-dough pastry filled with nuts and raisins.

schlemiel A clumsy person who spills the soup, drops the eggs, and trips over his own feet.

schmaltz Chicken fat.

schochet One who slaughters animals ritually.

Shabbos The Sabbath.

shepp naches Derive joy (*see* shepping naches).

shepping naches Deriving joy and pride, usually from children and especially from grandchildren.

shpilkes Literally, "pins and needles." One who has *shpilkes* is uneasy, raring to go, and can't sit still. Hyperactive kids have *shpilkes*.

shtait geshribben   It is so written, authoritative.

shtetl   A small town; a village.

strudel   A pastry dough rolled around a filling.

Siddur   Prayerbook.

simchas   Joyous occasions.

takke   Really? Is that so?

Talmud   A massive compendium of commentaries interpreting every nuance of the teachings of the Torah (the first five books of the Bible).

tam   A special flavor.

tsimmes   A side dish usually of carrots, prunes, and sweet potatoes; also, stewed fruit.

tsouris   Trouble, suffering, sickness.

tsitzel   A heavy rye bread with a thick crust, the bottom coated with cornmeal. Also known as corn bread.

verenikes   Similar to pirogen or kreplach.

yeshiva   Jewish school of learning.

yeshivot(h)   Plural of yeshiva.

yontiff   Holiday.

zemmel   A crusty roll, soft on the inside.

zits flaish   Literally, "flesh to sit on." One who has no *zits flaish* is one who can't sit still, has ants in the pants, is hyperactive.

zoll zein mit glick   "May you have good luck; may your new venture meet with success."

Index